THE 1930
CENSUS

THE 1930 CENSUS

A Reference and Research Guide

Edited by Thomas Jay Kemp

HeritageQuest® from ProQuest
North Salt Lake, Utah
2003

HeritageQuest® products from ProQuest
PO Box 540670, North Salt Lake, Utah 84054-0670

Printed in the United States of America

06 05 04 03   5 4 3 2

ISBN 1-59178-012-8

To William M. Steuart, Director of the Bureau of the Census,
the 100,000 enumerators, and the 124 million people
living across the United States of America
and her territories who made the 1930 Census possible.

Contents

Introduction

In 1929, when planning was well underway for the 1930 Census it was heralded that it would be the "most detailed census" ever compiled.[i] President Herbert Hoover issued a proclamation calling upon "every person to answer all questions on the census schedules...promptly, completely and accurately."[ii] William M. Steuart, Director of the Census said, "The 1930 Census is going to be, we hope and believe, the most nearly perfect tabulation of population, business and other basic facts ever taken in the history of this world."[iii] And best of all, it would be accomplished in one month.

The 1930 Census did begin on April 1, 1930, but it would take the more than 100,000 enumerators until August 6th, when the last township, in Clearfield County, Pennsylvania reported its returns.[iv] For William J. Little of San Bernardino, California, serving as an enumerator almost cost him his life. He set out to record the 198 persons living in the desert valley, which covered about 5,000 square miles. "...Little left here (San Bernardino) on a 1,000 mile journey over the scantily populated valley. While twenty-five miles from Darwin, a desert outpost in the Panamint Mountains, his car broke down. He attempted to walk back to safety over the baking sands, but ten miles from the town he collapsed from thirst and exhaustion. Tantalizing mirages danced before his eyes and the stories of desert deaths crowded his mind. After he had given up hope of rescue he was found by a prospector and taken in an automobile to Darwin."[v]

Not every census taker's experience was so difficult. In Athens, Georgia the enumerator visited a family just after a baby boy had been born. The family was so pleased to have the child and the family recorded that they named the baby "Census Tooken."[vi]

OTHER NATIONAL CENSUSES TAKEN IN 1930

Austria	Census of Agriculture	Denmark	Census of Population
	Census of Industry		Census of Agriculture
Belgium	Census of Population		Census of Housing
	Census of Buildings and Housing	Estonia	Census of Agriculture 1929/30
	Census of Industry & Commerce	Finland	Census of Population
Czechoslovakia	Census of Population		Census of Agriculture 1929/30
	Census of Agriculture		Census of Housing
	Census of Housing	Greece	Census of Industry & Commerce
	Census of Industry		
	Census of Localities	Hungary	Census of Population
		Iceland	Census of Population

Italy	Census of Agriculture	Norway	Census of Population
Latvia	Census of Agriculture 1929/30	Portugal	Census of Population
		Rumania	Census of Population Census of Industry & Commerce
Liechtenstein	Census of Population		
Lithuania	Census of Agriculture		
Luxemburg	Census of Population Census of Housing	Spain	Census of Population
		Sweden	Census of Population
Netherlands	Census of Population & Occupations Census of Agriculture Census of Industry	Switzerland	Census of Population

The 1930 Census was the last to ask who could read or write and the first to ask, "Does your household have a radio?" It also was the last census in which everyone was asked the same set of questions. In 1940, a statistical sample of households received a "long form" with a set of questions in addition to those that were asked of all households.[vii]

The 1930 Census, the nation's Fifteenth Decennial Census was actually multiple census enumerations taken from 1926 to 1933. In addition to the Census of Population and the Census of Merchant Seamen taken in 1930, there were the Census of Religious Bodies (1926-1928); Census of Agriculture (1930); Census of Manufactures (1929, 1930); Census of Mines & Quarries (1929); and the Census of Distribution (1930).

ACCESSING THE 1930 CENSUS

Researchers can search the 1930 Census on microfilm, digital CD-ROM and online. The National Archives, ProQuest's HeritageQuestOnline, Genealogy.com, Ancestry, Inc. and others provide copies of the census to individuals and/or to libraries.

National Archives

In addition to the D.C. location, the National Archives has made complete sets of the 1930 Census available for viewing on microfilm at each of its 13 Regional Research Centers, in the following areas (it is not available at the Presidential Libraries):

Alaska	Anchorage - NARA. Pacific Alaska Region
California	Laguna Niguel - NARA. Pacific Region
	San Bruno - NARA. Pacific Region (San Francisco)
Colorado	Denver - NARA. Rocky Mountain Region
D.C.	National Archives Building
Georgia	Atlanta - NARA. Southeast Region
Illinois	Chicago - NARA. Great Lakes Region
Massachusetts	Pittsfield - NARA. Northeast Region
	Waltham - NARA. Northeast Region (Boston)
Missouri	Kansas City - NARA. Central Plains Region

New York	New York City - NARA. Northeast Region
Pennsylvania	Center City Philadelphia - NARA. Mid Atlantic Region (Philadelphia)
Texas	Fort Worth - NARA. Southwest Region
Washington	Seattle - NARA. Pacific Alaska Region

Other Sources

Commercial firms such as ProQuest, Genealogy.Com and Ancestry.com. also provide access to the 1930 Census.

ProQuest's HeritageQuest Online <www.heritagequestonline.com> provides libraries and individuals with ready access to the entire range of Federal Census records with enhanced digital images of every page of the census from 1790 through 1930. Individuals can view these records from home via online access from their local library. No additional plug-ins are required. HeritageQuest has prepared new indexes to these records making it easy to instantly locate and view the correct page of a census needed. HeritageQuest indexes are recognized for their high accuracy and completeness. ProQuest is the world's largest producer/vendor of microfilm and sells film copies of the census in both silver halide and diazo formats. They were the first to completely digitize and enhance the entire U.S. Census and make it available on CD-ROM.

Genealogy.com has also been a leader in providing online and CD-ROM access to indexed digital census records. They sell "auto-renewing" online subscriptions to the U.S. Census records and indexes as well as CD-ROM versions of the same content. They provide access to the 1900 Census and will be adding the rest of the census years this year. These subscriptions may be viewed directly from an individual's home and no additional plug-ins are required.

Ancestry.com has mounted the images and indexes to the U.S. Census as well. Currently Ancestry provides online access to the images and indexes for the 1790-1850 Census; a partial index to the 1860 and 1920 Census and images only for the 1870-1910 Census. They have begun to add images and indexing for the 1930 Census as well. Subscriptions are available to individuals or to libraries through GaleAncestryPlus <www.gale.ancestry.com>. Individual subscriptions may be viewed from home, but library subscriptions may only be viewed from the subscribing library's in-library computers. Libraries and individuals need to download the free MrSID plug-in viewer, version 1.3, to be able to view the census images.

The 1930 Census: A Reference and Research Guide

The 1930 Census: A Reference and Research Guide provides researchers with a comprehensive overview of the information gathered in the census and what records survive and are available for examination. Included are background material on the census, the instructions for enumerators, a table of military installations and veterans' facilities, and a set of the maps prepared for the 1930 Census to show the boundaries of the 96 largest metropolitan areas across the country.

Endnotes

[i] "Most Detailed Census Requires but a Month," *New York Times,* 10 Nov 1929, Section XX, 4.

[ii] "Hoover Urges all to Aid Census Work," *New York Times,* 23 November 1929, 17.

[iii] "Most Detailed Census...."

[iv] "Last Town Reports in National Census. Returns from Little Pennsylvania Community Slightly Alters Country's Total," *New York Times,* 7 August 1930, 23.

[v] "Death Valley Nearly Conquers Census Taker, Saved by Miner after Collapse in Desert," *New York Times,* 20 April 1930, 21.

[vi] "(Family Names) Child 'Census Tooken,'" *New York Times,* 19 April 1930, 7.

[vii] "National Archives Opens 1930 Census to the Public," Press Release, US Department of Commerce, CB02-CN.62, 28 March 2002.

About the Authors

Several authors have contributed to *The 1930 Census: A Reference and Research Guide* including Thomas Jay Kemp, Jake Gehring, Merrill E. Gillette, and Leland K. Meitzler.

Thomas Jay Kemp, is the editor of the *Local History & Genealogy Librarian* and Chair of the American Library Association's Genealogy Committee. He has served as Chair of the Council of National Library & Information Associations; President of the American Society of Indexers and on the Board of Directors of the Federation of Genealogical Societies. He is a life member of the Association for the Bibliography of History, the New York Genealogical & Biographical Society, the New England Archivists and the New Hampshire Library Association. He is the author of more than two-dozen books and databases, including the recently released *American Census Handbook* and the *International Vital Records Handbook* (4th ed.). His numerous articles regularly appear in national and state library, archival and genealogical journals.

Jake Gehring is a graduate of Brigham Young University's genealogy/family history program, former editor of *Genealogical Computing,* and frequent lecturer and author. He has been involved with publishing the digital versions of the federal census and its various indexes for several years at HeritageQuest and Ancestry.com. His experiences with digital imagery, advanced search techniques, data entry accuracy, optical character recognition, and census records themselves provide a valuable guide to the problems and promise of research in the information age.

Merrill E. Gillette, AG, was born in Utah and has lived in California, Colorado, Denmark, and Germany. He has been involved in genealogy since his teens, with research interests that span from Denmark and Sweden to Utah. While serving as a volunteer at the Family History Library (FHL), in Salt Lake City he received his accreditation as a genealogist. He has worked for a number of years in the United States and Canada reference area each summer as a part-time reference consultant for the FHL. While working at the FHL he also worked on several VIP research projects. He has worked with a number of private clients as well in such diverse research areas as Sweden, Denmark, England, Germany and many areas in the United States. Since 1998 he's been a researcher at Heritage Quest (now ProQuest Information and Learning™) and is an assistant editor and advertising coordinator with *Heritage Quest Magazine.*

Leland K. Meitzler has been professionally involved in genealogy for over 20 years. He founded *Heritage Quest Magazine* in 1985 and has worked as Managing and Executive Editor with that publication ever since. An active genealogist, Leland has given over 2,000 lectures on genealogical topics. He has traveled over 100,000 miles researching his family and continues to actively pursue his ancestral roots.

Appeal of the 1930 Census

1

IMPORTANCE TO THE GENEALOGIST

One of the leading research pursuits in the United States and across the world is that of genealogy. Genealogists understand that censuses are a unique tool to be used in their research, although they were not created with the genealogist in mind. They know that the census is the most easily available, universal resource for information regarding family relationships and location for American family history. They also recognize that while the census data is not considered a primary source, the census is a primary source for the location of the family at the moment the enumerator visited. The census contains a vast amount of clues that are available to the genealogist, based on the individual's response to the enumerator's questions. The dramatic advances in technology have made access to the 1930 Census easier and quicker. Genealogists and family historians have the opportunity to find the names of their parents, grandparents and other family members.

The census is the most easily available, universal resource for American family history.

THE 1930 UNITED STATES CENSUS

The Fifteenth Decennial Census was taken just five months following the stock market collapse of 1929. In this period of growing distrust of the government, due in part to a perceived lack of oversight of the stock market and of the banking industry, men and women were being sent into the homes of the citizens. Here they would ask the questions that prompted the results of the 1930 Census.

WHAT CAN WE LEARN FROM THE CENSUS?

The first item of the census header sheet informs the researcher that the individual lived in a specific town/city, within a particular county (or independent city), and in the state or territory. Already the possibilities for research opportunities and subjects open up to the researcher. These include searches of the following types of records and many others:

Land Ownership
Civil and Criminal Court
Probates
Vital Records
Churches
Cemeteries
Newspapers
Military Draft

In the 1930 Census, the street is given, providing the opportunity for the researcher to possibly find where his/her father and mother lived as parents or perhaps as children. With this knowledge the researcher can better understand the life and times of his parents and grandparents. When the grandfather states that he had to walk uphill to school the researcher may find why that statement makes sense.

Some genealogists will find themselves listed in the 1930 Census as children and such a listing may trigger memories long forgotten. The names of the parents or guardians are also present along with ages and relationships. Perhaps a maiden aunt lived with her brother and his expanding family, but today her name and even existence is unknown to the family. The census with the relationship column may help uncover additional branches of the family tree. Maybe a researcher remembers that the grandparents lived nearby and with the help of the 1930 Census finally understands the relationship of one neighborhood to another.

The 1850 to 1930 Census Named Every Individual

Beginning with the 1850 Census every individual within a family unit has been listed by given name and surname. Sometimes the given name is different than the given name used in other documents and sources, adding to the store of knowledge concerning a family member. It is possible to trace a family unit backward and forward in time using the censuses. Frequently we find that married couples have lived in the same neighborhood prior to marriage, and with a little work sometimes the maiden name of a woman may be discerned. Unknown cousins may potentially be located by use of the census, combined with family knowledge obtained in interviews or research.

See the Appendix for *Instructions to Enumerators,* Section 120 for the definition of a "family unit"

What did Grandpa pay in rent and did he own a radio?

The enumerators of the 1930 Census were asked to obtain the value of the home in which the respondents lived or if they were renters, to state the monthly rent. Home ownership indicated a degree of prosperity and would indicate that land records may need to be searched. Another question concerned whether there was a radio in the home. Maybe that's why every Friday evening the grandparents would visit, because they could not afford such a luxury. The radio was beginning to gain a very vital place in the homes of America. It would soon be one of the principle methods used by Franklin Delano Roosevelt to lift the spirits of the American people, who would begin to wonder if the depression would ever end.

Sometimes the questions became a little personal and sparked some controversy. The creators of the 1930 Census wanted to know how many children respondents had, their occupations and if they were citizens. What was the person's age at their last birthday? By using their age and the known "census day" a person's birth may be calculated to within a year. Was the individual married? If the answer was affirmative it was followed by a question concerning the age of the respondent at the first marriage. If either the bride or groom were underage, one would want to determine if parental permission had been provided when the application was made for a marriage license.

A standard question in previous censuses was repeated in this census concerning an individual's education. Had the respondent attended school or college since September 1, 1929? This was immediately followed by the question about the individual's ability to read and write.

The enumerators would then ask where the individual was born and the respondent would usually answer by naming the state or country. The same question is asked regarding his or her parents.

The New Deal Network: An Educational Guide to the Great Depression may be found at www.newdeal.feri.org

Personal information was asked for by the enumerator.

These are clues as to where additional searches need to be concentrated. Another clue to the place of earlier residence is contained in the response to the question regarding the native tongue of a person.

Individuals were asked to provide their year of immigration into the United States. The response to the question suggests that perhaps searches need to be conducted in the Ship Passenger Lists or similar records. Was the respondent a naturalized citizen? A positive answer provides to the researcher the information that he or she will need to search the various naturalization records.

The year of your ancestor's immigration may be found in the 1930 Census.

Where did Grandpa work and what did he do?

With the stock market crash less than six months in the past, the next questions have some importance to the researcher of today. The first in this group concerned the type of occupation that provided the income for the individual. Was he or she in a trade, profession, or other type of work? What type of industry did the individual find in which to use their trade or profession? These questions may help you locate and identify that person if they were forced to move to another location. Statistically you could determine which types of employers were forced to close before the census date.

The next set of questions relate to actual employment of the individual by asking if the person had worked the day before (last regular working day). A positive response indicates to the researcher that at least by April 1, 1930 that person had not lost their employment. A negative response would indicate that perhaps the events of October 1929 had already impacted the respondent. The enumerator was requested to then complete an additional form for the unemployed and to enter the number from the unemployment form. Unfortunately the Unemployment Schedules were destroyed following the extraction of statistical data.

The individual veteran's status is listed in the census.

There were some Civil War Veterans who were still living in 1930 as well as veterans from other wars down to and including WWI. They were asked to tell which war or expedition they had participated in. Not only does the researcher learn that the person was a veteran but also which military records and possibly pension records to search for additional information.

If the family was living on a farm then the enumerator was required to complete an additional form and to provide the line number from that form on the census page. Most Agricultural Schedules were also destroyed following the compilation of the statistical information, with the exception of Outlying Territorial schedules.

Finding the names of family members is always a thrill but what a greater thrill it would be to find the name of a parent, grandparent or sibling in this census while they are still living and available to answer questions. The 1930 Census is the last census to ask the same questions of every individual listed; beginning with the 1940 Census some of the respondents were asked questions from a "long" form while others were asked to respond to the questions listed on a "short" version.

Civil War Veteran, Captain Montgomery G. Cooper.

2 Structure and Content of the 1930 Census

The population schedules for the 1930 U.S. Federal Census are identified by the National Archives and Records Administration (NARA) as record group 29, microfilm series T626.[i] The schedules are grouped alphabetically by state (as well as the District of Columbia). Territories such as Alaska, Hawaii, Puerto Rico, and the Virgin Islands appear after the states. Counties and similar subdivisions are grouped and filmed alphabetically within each state or territory (see table 1).

The collection consists of 2,667 rolls of microfilm numbered 1 through 2,668 (roll number 1602, slated for Queens, New York, was skipped in the filming process[ii]).

A full size reproduction of a blank census form is in the Appendix.

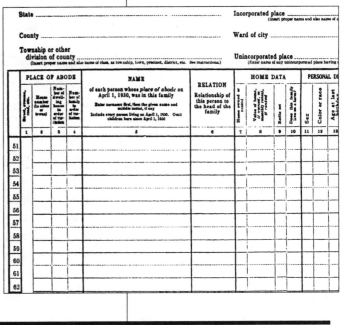

Table 1: 1930 Census States and Territories

State or Terr.	Film Range	State or Terr.	Film Range
Alabama	1-54	New Mexico	1392-1400
Arizona	55-63	New York	1401-1670
Arkansas	64-99	North Carolina	1671-1730
California	100-228	North Dakota	1731-1745
Colorado	229-252	Ohio	1746-1891
Connecticut	253-285	Oklahoma	1892-1938
Delaware	286-291	Oregon	1939-1958
District of Columbia	292-305	Pennsylvania	1959-2167
Florida	306-335	Rhode Island	2168-2183
Georgia	336-394	South Carolina	2184-2216
Idaho	395-404	South Dakota	2217-2232
Illinois	405-573	Tennessee	2233-2286
Indiana	574-639	Texas	2287-2413
Iowa	640-691	Utah	2414-2425
Kansas	692-730	Vermont	2426-2432
Kentucky	731-781	Virginia	2433-2483
Louisiana	782-826	Washington	2484-2525
Maine	827-842	West Virginia	2526-2559
Maryland	843-882	Wisconsin	2560-2620
Massachusetts	883-971	Wyoming	2621-2625
Michigan	972-1077	Alaska Territory	2626-2628
Minnesota	1078-1136	American Samoa and Guam	2629
Mississippi	1137-1173	Consular Services	2630
Missouri	1174-1251	Hawaii	2631-2637
Montana	1252-1264	Panama Canal and Consular Services	2638
Nebraska	1265-1295	Puerto Rico	2639-2667
Nevada	1296-1297	Virgin Islands	2668
New Hampshire	1298-1307		
New Jersey	1308-1391		

The images on microfilm provided by NARA were produced from the same schedules enumerators used as they made their rounds. The handwriting and notations are theirs, though in some cases government staff later examined and corrected/completed entries. This microfilm now represents the earliest known copy of the population schedules as the originals were destroyed in 1956.

The population schedules used by enumerators were 23" by 16" pre-printed forms. The obverse side of the page (marked "A") contained a header section listing the locality in question. The remainder of the page was reserved for the actual enumeration. Column headings run horizontally across the page just beneath the header followed by lines numbered from 1 to 50. The opposite side (marked "B") contains lines numbered 51 through 100 (see fold-out blank form in the Appendix).

GENERAL INSTRUCTIONS TO ENUMERATORS IN 1930

Enumerators were instructed to personally visit every family and farm within their territory.[iii] Individuals and families were to be recorded according to their "place of abode," which was generally understood to be where they slept. All members of the family were to be listed (except those who had moved out and were permanently located elsewhere). Students, for example, were to be enumerated at home, even if currently at school, as their position and abode as a student was understood to be temporary.

Also enumerated with the family were any members who were ill and residing temporarily in hospitals and the like. Any servants or employees sleeping on the premises were also to be enumerated with the family, as were any permanent boarders or lodgers in the home. Information about people not personally present during the enumerator's visit was to be gathered based on input from other family members, friends, or neighbors.

The census taker was given specific instructions about who not to include in his/her enumeration of the local residents, including:

- Persons visiting with the family
- Transient boarders or lodgers[iv]
- Persons from abroad temporarily visiting the U.S.
- Students boarding with the family
- Persons who take meals with the family but who sleep elsewhere
- Servants or laborers who sleep elsewhere
- A family member who is now a long-time resident of an asylum, prison, etc.

Despite the specific instructions given above regarding whom to include or exclude in the population schedules, an enumerator was allowed certain leeway in making exceptions—the operative question being whether it was likely that an individual present would be represented by proxy at another location.

It was assumed that soldiers and sailors were to be recorded as if their current post of duty was their place of abode. This included cadets at Annapolis and West Point but not attendees at other military academies. If unsure as to where exactly someone in the military was enumerated in 1930, examine the listing of military enumerations by state and county as reported by NARA in the Appendix .

The government-issued instructions to the enumerators regarding how to fill out the population schedules is located in the Appendix.

Regarding the crews of U.S. merchant marine vessels in 1930, census takers were instructed to enumerate the crews of such vessels (with the exception of officers, who were included in the population schedules from homes ashore if they had such). This enumeration of vessels was made on a separate *Crews of Vessels* schedule and has been released by NARA as microfilm publication M1932. The three rolls of microfilm in this series are organized by homeport. More information about these and other non-population schedules for 1930 can be found in Chapter 3, "1930 Special Schedules."

Citizens Abroad

For those persons living in a foreign country in 1930, enumeration likely did not take place abroad. This depended mostly on the occupation of the citizen in question and whether they had a place they called home in the U.S. Those temporarily in a foreign country on business or traveling would be enumerated from their homes in the United States based on information provided by family. Even those who were intending a lengthy stay abroad were to be enumerated at home in the U.S. as long as they were intending to return at some point.

Consular Service Schedule "Foreign Service" sample.

On the other hand, federal civilian employees (like customs officials or diplomats) stationed abroad were treated by enumerators as residing at their current post.[v] These were enumerated in the normal population schedules on two films cataloged as "consular service."[vi] U.S. military and naval personnel stationed abroad or at sea were also enumerated separately, presumably by post or by ship as with the 1910 and 1920 censuses. However, these military and naval schedules have not been released with the rest of the 1930 Census nor cataloged by NARA and are presumed destroyed.

All enumeration was to be completed within 30 days of "census day," which was the 1st of April, 1930 (in Alaska enumeration occurred six months earlier due to cold-weather concerns). All information entered on the population schedules was to relate to census day. Thus a child born later in the month would not be enumerated as he or she had not yet been born as of April 1.

Information Recorded in the Header Section

The upper section of the population schedule is referred to as the header. It contains information that applies to all the individuals enumerated below. To the left of the header researchers will find blanks for state and county, which serve as the major geographic subdivisions of the census. Use of the other location fields in the header vary widely depending on the area of the country being enumerated. Large cities are commonly parceled into wards, precincts, administrative districts, or some other urban subdivision.

Occasionally an "institution" will be enumerated separately from the city or town in which it is situated. Examples of institutions include hospitals, jails, almshouses, military installations, orphanages, soldiers' homes, schools and academies, etc. It is important to remember that in cases such as schools and hospitals, the schedule will only list permanent residents such as staff and administration.

The right side of the header contains the signature of the enumerator, the date of enumeration (which may indicate the day the page was begun and is often updated in the left margin running down the page), and the enumeration district (ED) number. Enumeration districts and supervisors' districts were created to serve an administrative need and were given to enumerators as a predetermined set of boundaries before the census began. However, since EDs are quite regular in their structure and refer to small sections of the population, they are often used in finding aids and indexes created for the census.[vii]

The far right of the header contains page information. The "A" and "B" sides of the form were pre-printed and sheet numbers were written by the enumerator within each ED. Additional pagina-

Enumeration District No. ....*1–8*....

Supervisor's District No. ....**7**....

The two-part ED number is a unique code that represents first the county and then the district. Often one district was assigned to one enumerator for that census.

The enumerator filled in the Sheet Number with consecutive numbers.

tions in this area of the header are quite common and are usually created to number an entire county or counties in one run. The "A" sides of pages in 1930 contain a stamped page number for this purpose, which was applied after the enumeration was complete.

There were occasional problems with these later paginations. A new page may have the same stamp as the previous one, resulting from either a mistake in the stamping or from the page itself being microfilmed or scanned twice. There may be gaps in stamped page numbers as well. Researchers should always examine the pages around the one containing the information they seek to get a feel for the context and format of the enumeration and to identify and work around any such anomalies.

Information Recorded in the Body

Place of Abode

The first section of the body relates to location of the family. The name of the street on which they live (if any) is written sideways down the page. There may be several streets on a given census page, in which case an enumerator was asked to mark when streets change using a heavy line across columns 1 and 2 (see illustration). The actual house number was written in column 2 (though these did not exist in most smaller towns and rural areas), followed by a "dwelling number," and the "family number." The enumerator incremented these last two numbers whenever he/she encountered a new dwelling or a new family, respectively.[viii]

Name

The name fields follow next on the census form. Heads of the household were to be enumerated first within a family group, then wife (if any) and any children. Any other relations, servants, boarders, etc. were written last. Enumerators were generally instructed to write surname followed by given name and middle initial. Given names were to be written in full—a given name was to be abbreviated or reduced to initials only if that was how the individual was called.[ix]

Relation

Each member of the household was related to the head in some fashion. This relationship was indicated in column 6. Enumerators were given specific examples such as *wife, father, mother, son, daughter, grandson, daughter-in-law, uncle, aunt*, etc. Terms like *officer, inmate, patient, prisoner*, were used for institutions.[x] The "home-maker" in the family (the one responsible for the care of the

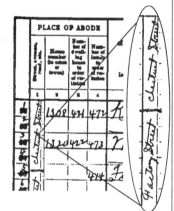

When the households on several streets were enumerated on one census page the Enumerator would write the name of the street sideways in Column 1 of the sheet.

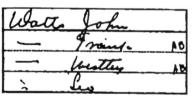

Not all were present when the enumerator came calling. In such cases enumerators were asked to mark names of absent family members with an "AB" after their names in the schedules. Notice here John Watts with his sons Frank, Westley, and Leo. Frank and Westley have been marked absent.

home and family) had the letter "H" added to the relationship, so "Wife" may have become "Wife—H."[xi]

Home Data

Each family within a dwelling was asked whether they owned or rented their home. Ownership could only be claimed by one family within a dwelling. Depending on the answer either the estimated value of the home or the amount of monthly rent was indicated in the next column.[xii]

According to 1930 Census statistics, over 40 percent of the nation's households owned a radio set. This was marked by enumerators with an "R" in column 9. At this time in the nation's history, commercial radio was exploding—over 500 broadcasting stations were in operation, the major media networks (or their predecessors) had been created, and the federal government was struggling with how best to administer and deal with not only this media, but with television as well, which had already made at least an experimental debut in the early 1930s.[xiii]

The final question in the "Home Data" section of the census asks whether the family lives on a farm, which in this cases refers to *where one lived* as opposed to *how one made one's living*. A family may have lived on a functioning farm but not been farmers, in which case the response would still have been "yes." After enumeration, census coding clerks marked an "X" for each family member in this column for farm dwellers and "V" for those not living on the farm. These extra marks were made to assist the data entry of this column for statistical purposes. In urban areas this question is sometimes not asked at all in 1930.

Personal Description

The next section of the population schedules lists personal information about each member of the family starting with their sex. If left blank by the enumerator then the column was to be filled out by the coding clerk based on either the relationship to the head of the household or the given name.[xiv]

The color or race column was to be filled out by code (see illustration, right) or by writing out the individual's race or color if it did not match the supplied examples. Situations of mixed blood were treated as follows: A person of mixed White and Negro blood was to be returned as Negro, no matter how small the percentage...; someone part Indian and part Negro was also to be listed as Negro unless the Indian blood predominated and the person was generally accepted as an Indian in the community. A person of mixed White and Indian blood was to be returned as an Indian, except

Excerpts of the race column options. The enumerator used the codes provided at the bottom of the census sheet.

where the percentage of Indian blood was very small or where he or she was regarded as White in that community…. Any mixture of White and some other race was to be reported according to the race of the parent who was not White; mixtures of colored races were to be listed according to the father's race, except Negro-Indian as previously mentioned.[xv]

The next columns list age at last birthday (with children under 5 years of age also showing "fractional ages," meaning some number of years and then months out of twelve listed as a fraction), marital status (the term "widowed" here refers to either a man or a woman), and age at first marriage. As mentioned above, any ages in the census refer to one's age on census day, April 1, 1930.

Education

Column 16 is marked "yes" for anyone who has attended school (including night school), college, or any other educational institution within the last seven months. The column asking whether an individual can read or write was to be filled out for anyone over ten years of age. The question does not necessarily refer to English—any language, both read and written by the individual, will qualify as a "yes" answer.[xvi]

Place of Birth

The next three columns in the census list the individual's place of birth and the birthplace of his/her parents. Enumerators again were specifically instructed not to abbreviate these fields, though this did sometimes occur (i.e., "Irish F.S." for "Irish Free State" or "ChSlavia" for "Czechoslovakia").

Enumerators were to list specific U.S. states or territories, though the term "U.S." is frequently used in the parents' columns if it was not known exactly where they were born in the U.S.[xvii] If an individual was born outside the U.S., the country of birth was listed. These foreign birthplaces were to be recorded according to current country boundaries (i.e., Poland in 1930, instead of Prussia in 1868). In cases where neither the enumerator nor the individual were sure in what modern country a birthplace was located, a province or city could be listed (see excerpt from a Chicago enumeration at left). Census coding clerks would correspond these entries to the proper modern-day countries from tables at their disposal.[xviii]

If the individual being enumerated was listed in the race column as Indian, the parents' birthplace fields were used for a different purpose, namely to show full or mixed blood in column 19 and the

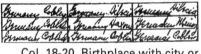

Col. 18-20. Birthplace with city or region for those born outside the U.S.

Col. 18-21. Birthplace fields for those of the Indian race. See the Appendix, "Instructions to Enumerators," Section 174a.

name of the tribe in column 20 (see Navajo example, left). A listing of Indian tribes with their geographic range and some historical description is provided in the Appendix.

Mother Tongue

The enumerator was asked to indicate the mother tongue of any individual not born in the United States. The remaining fields in this section were filled in by coding clerks after enumeration and are based on the responses provided in the birthplace and mother tongue columns. These codes contain no information not already provided on the population schedule and were created for convenience in making statistical tabulations after the census taking was complete.

Citizenship, etc.

Questions relating to immigration and citizenship were asked of anyone not born in the U.S. or one of its territories. Column 22 asks the year of immigration (or the first year of immigration if there have been any back-and-forth trips) to the U.S. The next column asks individuals to specify their naturalization status as one of the following three cases:

a) *Naturalized.* This response was given if the individual has taken out second or final naturalization papers, or has become naturalized by the naturalization of parents while a minor, or by the naturalization of a husband prior to 1922.
b) *First Papers.* Given if the individual was not naturalized but had taken out "first papers."
c) *Alien.* Given to all individuals not meeting the first two cases.

The abbreviations for these answers are given at the bottom of the census form and examples of each (including an "unknown" entry supplied by a coding clerk) are shown to the right. The final column in this section relating to the ability to speak English is again only asked of individuals ten years of age and older.

Alien

Naturalized

First Papers

Unknown

Excerpts from the Naturalization column.

Occupation and Industry

Enumerators were instructed to fill out the occupation column for every person on the population schedules. The entry was to be listed as "none" if the individual was not currently gainfully employed (one who earns money or a money equivalent, or one who assists in the production of marketable goods).[xix] Individuals who worked part time in gainful employ were listed under their respective occupations as long as they worked at least one day per week. Those who have an occupation but who were temporarily unemployed were listed by the occupation they would have if employed. Those with multiple occupations were asked to provide the one that provided the most income. The following column then lists further clarification provided by the individual as to the industry or business in which the person works.

The code field in the occupation section is again compiled by coding clerks after enumeration in order to assist in statistical tabulation for further demographic/sociological study and does not contain or represent any information not already found on the population schedule. The class of worker column is filled out in this section as follows:

a) *Employer.* One who employs helpers (other than domestic servants) in transacting his own business (i.e., not a superintendent, manager, foreman, etc.).

b) *Wage or Salary Worker.* Any person working for wages or salary, at piece rates, on commission, and is subject to the control and direction of an employer.

c) *Working on Own Account.* Not an employer but an independent worker such as a farmer or proprietor of a small business with no employees.

d) *Unpaid Family Worker.* A wife, son, or daughter or other relative of the head of household who works regularly but without wages or salary in the family business (i.e., farm, shop, etc.).

Employment

Enumerators asked those under gainful employ whether they were at work on their previous working day (whether actually the day before enumeration or on the last logical day when a worker should have been working). Reasons for answering negatively would have included sickness, accidents, lay-offs or terminations, strikes, closure of business, etc. Anyone answering negatively was also enumerated on an Unemployment Schedule. For more information on 1930 Unemployment Schedules, see Chapter 3.

Veterans

Those having served in the Army, Navy, or Marine Corps who were mobilized for any war or expedition or who were in the service[xx] during a time of war would indicate his service and the war or expedition in question (see examples at left).

Civil War

Coast Guard

Indian Wars

Merchant Vessel

Mexican Expedition

Nicaragua

Panama

Philipine

Spanish-American War

World War

Boxer Rebellion, Mexican War, World War

Philipine, World War, Spanish-American War, Mexican Expedition

Farm Schedule

This column indicates an entry in the Farm Schedule (with a reference number) for this household. Such schedules have only survived for U.S. territories (Alaska, Hawaii, Puerto Rico, Virgin Islands, etc.) and not for the states. See Chapter 3 for more information.

Endnotes

[i] Soundex and Miracode Indexes for the 1930 Census have been given series numbers on a state-by-state basis. See Chapter 5, "Finding Ancestors Using Soundex Code and Miracode."

[ii] This skipped roll results from an inadvertent gap in film numbering and does not represent missing microfilm. See *U.S. National Archives and Records Administration. 1930 Federal Population Census: Catalog of National Archives Microfilm* (Washington, D.C.: National Archives Trust Fund Board, 2002), p. 51, footnote.

[iii] Bureau of the Census, *Instructions to Enumerators: Population and Agriculture* (Washington D.C.: GPO, 1930), 2.

[iv] As regards transient individuals or boarders, it is generally assumed that such persons have a permanent home, either at the locale in question (in which case they are classified as permanent boarders or lodgers and enumerated with the family) or at some other place (meaning that such persons are temporary boarders or lodgers and should be enumerated at their "usual places of abode"). Instructions also dealt with a possible third case: that an individual called no place home and are members of a "floating population." These were to be enumerated where they happened to be stopping at the time of the census.

[v] Karen M. Mills, "Americans Overseas in U.S. Censuses," [Census Bureau Technical Paper 62] (Washington, D.C.: U.S. GPO, 1993), 2, 26.

[vi] The enumerations of those in "consular service" are contained on rolls 2630 and 2638 of the 1930 population schedules. These rolls are not currently cataloged in the online NARA *Microfilm Locator* like U.S. states and territories but they are organized alphabetically by city.

[vii] The enumeration district number in 1930 has two components separated by a hyphen. The first number is a county code and is the same for all EDs in a particular county. The second number is the district itself. The addition of the county code in 1930 creates a unique run of codes for an entire state rather than EDs that start with the number 1 for each county and could be confused with one another if the county information were somehow lost.

[viii] It is common for the dwelling numbers and family numbers not to match for a given family as enumerators are likely to find dwellings in which more than one family reside. An apartment house, for example, is counted as one dwelling but would contain many families.

ix Despite the instruction to write given names in full, abbreviations may exist. Refer to Richard H. Saldana, ed., *A Practical Guide to the "Misteaks" Made in Census Indexes* (Bountiful, UT: HeritageQuest, 1987). or Kip Sperry, *Abbreviations and Acronyms: A Guide for Family Historians* (Orem, UT: Ancestry, 2000).

x Though the relationship examples in the enumerator instructions were relatively few, over a hundred were in common usage in the U.S. census. See William Dollarhide, *The Census Book: A Genealogist's Guide to Federal Census Facts, Schedules and Indexes* (North Salt Lake, UT: HeritageQuest, 2000), 72-74 for a listing.

xi Census, *Instructions to Enumerators*, 23.

xii Ibid, 24-25.

xiii Donna Halper, "The History of Radio," www.old-time.com/halper/index.html [April 2002].

xiv Bureau of the Census, *Fifteenth Census: Coding Instructions for the Population Schedule.* (Washington, D.C.: GPO, 1930), 4.

xv Leland K. Meitzler and Merrill E. Gillette, A.G., "Enumerating the Population in 1930," *Heritage Quest Magazine*, March/April 2002, (98) 13.

xvi Census, *Instructions to Enumerators*, 28.

xvii The term "U.S." in a birthplace field indicates that an individual was born in the U.S., but the exact state is not known. An entry of "Un" or "Unknown" in a birthplace field indicates that the individual was born outside the U.S., and the exact location is again unknown.

xviii Census, *Coding Instructions*, 9-10, 17-41.

xix Women doing housework or children doing chores or doing odd jobs do not qualify per 1930 Census definitions as "gainful workers" unless (a) housework was performed for wages, in which cases entries like "housekeeper," "servant," or some such would be entered; or (b) children or women doing regular work other than chores (these would be entered as "farm laborers." Individuals who worked part time in gainful employ were listed under their respective occupations as long as they worked at least one day per week. See *Instructions to Enumerators*, 32.

xx Anyone in the service during 1917 and 1921 would be identified as a World War veteran. The same is true for Spanish-American War service from 1898 and 1902 and the Civil War from 1861 to 1866. The Mexican Expedition refers to actions in 1914 and 1916 and not to the Mexican War of 1846–1848. See *Instructions to Enumerators*, 41.

3

1930 Special Census Schedules

The Census of Population was not the only census taken in 1930. As before, other schedules were taken to assist the government in accounting for a variety of statistical information. The Fifteenth Census involved a number of separate censuses and reports. These included:

Census of Agriculture (1930)

Census of Crews of Vessels
(Merchant Seamen) (1930)

Census of Distribution (1930)

Census of Manufactures (1929, 1930)

Census of Mines and Quarries (1929)

Census of Religious Bodies (1926-1928)

Census of Unemployment (1930, 1931)

The special Census of Horticulture was begun in 1930 and is included with the section on the Census of Agriculture. *Some of these were destroyed* after the statistical information was captured, *while others are still extant today.*

In addition to these schedules, the Bureau used two new supplemental schedules—the Absent Family Schedule and the Nonresident Family Schedule—to amend the Census of Population. The Census Bureau also continued the practice of taking special population censuses of various cities and counties in between the decennial census years, called Special Municipal Schedules.

ABSENT-FAMILY SCHEDULE
AND NON-RESIDENT FAMILY SCHEDULE

The Bureau began to account for absent and non-resident families as of the 1930 Census. Families were enumerated as though they were present at their customary place of residence even if they were living outside of the country or had moved to other parts of the United States.

"One of the greatest difficulties of the Census of Population is that of enumerating people at their residence or 'usual place of abode.' An Absent-Family Schedule was provided for the enumeration of families *temporarily away* from their usual place of residence at the time of the census, the idea being that this schedule would either be filled out by such families prior to their departure if they were leaving shortly before April 1, or if they had already gone and their temporary address was known, [it] would be mailed to them to be filled out and returned by mail to the local supervisor."[i]

In the case of citizens *living overseas* at the time of the census, enumerators were instructed to include them on the Census of Population Schedule as if they were present at their customary place of residence. The instructions stated: "It does not matter how long the absence abroad is continued, provided the person intends to return to the United States."[ii]

The Non-Resident Family Schedule was devised as a counterpart to the Absent-Family Schedule, and it "…was to be used where families were found temporarily residing in a locality but *claiming permanent residence elsewhere*. These schedules were sent directly to Washington, where they were allocated to the city or other locality which the family claimed as its place of residence."[iii]

More than 10,000 Non-Resident Family Schedules were completed and submitted to the Census Bureau in Washington, D.C. These schedules enumerated about 22,000 individuals. This was "…the first time in the history of the census that this plan for transferring nonresidents to their usual place of residence has been applied [to the Decennial Census]. It is of interest to note that about 45 percent of the non-resident schedules were received from two states—California and Florida."[iv]

CENSUS OF AGRICULTURE

By 1930, the Census of Agriculture had been taken for 90 years, beginning with a few questions on one schedule in 1840, and had developed into a variety of schedules containing many questions. It was shifted to off-years with a farm schedule taken in 1925.

Sixteen supplemental schedules were used to return the information in the 1930 agricultural census:

the **General Farm Schedule**,

two schedules on **Irrigation**,

one schedule on **Drainage**,

two supplemental schedules for **Special Fruits and Nuts**,

two schedules for **Incidental Agricultural Production and Livestock, Poultry, and Bees** not on farms or ranges,

two special schedules for **Sheep,** for use in thirteen western States,

and six schedules on **Horticulture**.[v]

OUTLYING TERRITORIES –
CENSUS OF AGRICULTURE SCHEDULES

All of the original schedules of the Census of Agriculture were destroyed, *except for the outlying Territories of Alaska, Guam, Hawaii, Puerto Rico, American Samoa and the U.S. Virgin Islands.* Like the Census of Population the enumeration date was April 1, 1930, and statistical information on crops was for the year 1929. One exception to the census date was Alaska, where "…because of the unusual climatic conditions … the date of enumeration … was fixed as of October 1, 1929 and the agricultural census covered the farming operations for the 12 months ending on that date."[vi] No provision had been made for the Philippine Islands to be counted in the 1930 Census. The last census taken there had been the census completed by the Philippine government as of December 31, 1918.[vii] And there was no agricultural census taken for the Panama Canal Zone.[viii]

In contrast with the mainland, only two agricultural schedules were used in the outlying Territories. "The schedules for Guam and [American] Samoa called for statistics on *(1)* cultivated crops and *(2)* livestock. A General Farm Schedule and a schedule for livestock

There were 712,500 reindeer on farms or ranges and in enclosures in Alaska in 1930. This is up from 92,933 in 1920. In contrast there were 59,278 people there in 1930 up from 55,036 in 1920.

In Alaska... "Vast tracts of land, still under Government ownership, are available to homesteaders." *Census of Agriculture. Outlying Territories – Alaska,* page 28.

not on farms and ranges were used in collecting the agricultural statistics for Alaska, Hawaii, Puerto Rico and the [U.S.] Virgin Islands. The general schedule for farms and ranges contained inquiries covering all the different subjects of the farm census, including farm acreage, farm values, farm debt, farm expenses, and crops harvested. Livestock on farms and livestock products were also reported on the general schedule."[ix]

"The statistics for Guam and [American] Samoa are very limited, due to the limited number of [enumerations] for these places; the data for Alaska and the [U.S.] Virgin Islands are in more detail than those given for Guam and [American] Samoa; while the statistics for Hawaii and Puerto Rico are presented in almost as much detail as those for [the] continental United States...." There were 52,965 farms documented in Puerto Rico, 500 in Alaska, 5,955 in Hawaii, 329 in the [U.S.] Virgin Islands, 2,104 in Guam, and 815 in American Samoa.[x]

Alaska. In 1930, Alaska had no organized county jurisdictions, but the Territory had been divided into four judicial *divisions* in 1909, the equivalents of counties. "About 65,000 square miles of land in Alaska are suitable for agriculture. A large part of this land is located in the Matanuska Valley in south central Alaska and in the Tanana Valley farther north. Areas in southeastern Alaska, southwestern Alaska, and on the Alaska and Kenai Peninsulas are also suitable for farming. The artic region, however, is unfavorable to crop production except in a few isolated places where hardy vegetables grow well on southern slopes."[xi] The official returns for Alaska showed a population of 59,278, with 500 farms, only one farm was reported for the Second Division (the most northerly part of Alaska), and this schedule was included with the returns for the Fourth Division.

American Samoa. American Samoa came under U.S. control on February 19, 1900. The civil divisions were: Manua District, Eastern Tutuila District, Western Tutuila District; and Swains Island—annexed to American Samoa in 1925. The districts were made up of 12 counties. The total population in 1930 was 10,055, and of the 815 farms enumerated, almost all were family operated.

The official census report noted that to properly understand any of the census returns for American Samoa, you had to understand the family unit. At the head of each social group—called an *aiga* or family—is a *matai*, which may be freely translated as "master." The *matai* rules his *aiga* and directs its economic and political activities. "A Samoan family may consist of the *matai* and his wife and children, his other relatives, adopted children, and servants. These families vary greatly in size. As many as 50 persons may be members of a Samoan family. In rare instances a *matai* may be the only surviving member of his family. Each normal Samoan family is a self-sustaining economic group, the members of which, including the matai, contribute the products of their labor to the family fund."[xii]

Of the 2,855 Samoan workers, 2,012 were working in agriculture, which included 131 counted as matais and 530 others as farm owners or tenants. They produced field crops, fruits, nuts, and livestock, with principal products being coconuts, breadfruit, bananas, and taro. "The coconut is the most important product of the soil of Samoa. A law requires each taxpayer to plant at least 30 [coconuts] a year, if he has the land." The report added that, "No sheep are raised as the natives will not eat mutton."[xiii]

Guam. Guam was ceded to the United States by Spain December 10, 1898. The 1930 Census enumeration is divided into eight municipalities (like county divisions), created by a decree of the Governor on March 21, 1930. These eight municipalities: Agana, Agat, Asan, Inarajan, Merizo, Piti, Sumay, and Yona; plus Naval reservations, which included personnel on U.S. ships stationed in Guam, totaled to a population of 18,509.[xiv] There were 2,104 farms enumerated in Guam, where the definition of a farm had changed from previous enumerations. The official report noted, "Agriculture is the chief industry of Guam.... A 'farm' for census purposes, is all the land which is directly farmed by one person, either by his own labor alone or with the assistance of members of his household or hired employees." The report added, "In addition to their small farms, nearly all of the natives of Guam have town houses, adjacent to many of which are gardens where are grown vegetables as well as tropical fruits. The natives live in these town houses and go to and from their farms on foot or in carts, thus wasting much time."[xv]

Hawaii. The Territory of Hawaii included nine inhabited islands, divided into four counties designated as: Hawaii, Honolulu, Kauai, and Maui. The population was counted by its six Representative Districts, formed in 1925:

    Dist. 1, Hawaii County–Hilo area

    Dist. 2, Hawaii County–Kona area

    Dist. 3, Maui County–included the islands of Maui, Kahoolawe, Lanai, and Molokai

    Dist. 4, 5, Honolulu County–Oahu, and Midway Islands

    Dist. 6, Kauai County–islands of Kauai, and Niihau

The population of Hawaii soared from 89,990 in 1890 to 368,336 in 1930. A majority (65.3 percent) were born in Japan or of Japanese ancestry, and of the 5,955 farms in Hawaii in 1930, 4,191 of them

In Samoa, "A law requires each taxpayer to plant at least 30 [coconuts] a year, if he has the land." *1930. Outlying Territories. Census of Agriculture – American Samoa,* page 310.

were owned and operated by Japanese Americans; 510 by native Hawaiians; 633 by Caucasians; 335 by Chinese Americans; 172 by Filipino Americans; 111 by Korean Americans; two by African Americans and one of unknown origin.

There were no farms reported on Midway Islands (Eastern Island and Sand Island), which were enumerated as part of Honolulu County's District 5; though 36 people were enumerated as living there in the Census of Population.

It should be noted that per the instructions to enumerators "…on a plantation the land operated by each cropper or tenant was reported as a separate farm, and the land operated by the owner or manager by means of wage hands likewise was reported as a separate farm."[xvi]

Puerto Rico. Of Puerto Rico's 1,543,913 population, 249,845 were involved in farm work. There were a total of 52,965 farms enumerated in its 77 municipalities. The islands of Culebra and Vieques were each treated as separate municipalities. Catano is the only new municipality organized since the 1920 census– from Bayamon. Enumerated with Catano is the barrio of Palmas. Puerto Rico's production of fruits, nuts, and coffee was down for the harvest of 1929, due to the cyclone that swept the island the previous year (September 1928).[xvii]

Samples of the Puerto Rico Census of Agriculture and a map of Puerto Rico from *Census of Agriculture. Outlying Territories – Puerto Rico,* page 121.

U.S. Virgin Islands. St. Croix, St. John and St. Thomas, the three principal islands of the former Dutch West Indies were purchased from Denmark on March 31, 1917. The three main divisions in 1930, for purposes of enumeration, corresponded with these three largest islands. With a total population of 22,012, there were 329 farms enumerated in the Census of Agriculture. Of these, 270 farms were operated by their owners, or by tenant farmers, and 2,944 total worked in agriculture. The 1930 count of the Virgin Islands' population showed an overall decrease from 26,051 in the special census of 1917. The islands' highest population recorded was 43,178, in its first census taken in 1835.[xviii]

General Farm Schedule

Planning for the General Farm Schedule began on 29 June 1928. "A tentative … schedule was prepared and copies were sent to officials of the Department of Agriculture, state agricultural colleges and others known to be especially interested."[xix] This generated more than 2,000 additional proposed questions for the census. In the end there were a few new questions added to the General Farm Schedule making a total of 353 questions.[xx]

Enumerators went to farms across the country to gather this information and in rural areas without a USDA county agent the forms were mailed directly to the farmers, based on names and addresses from the 1925 farm schedule. In addition more than 4.5 million copies of the schedules were distributed through members of Congress so that farmers would be familiar with the types of questions asked. In all 10,512,410 copies of the Agriculture Census schedules were distributed.[xxi] Census Bureau Director, William M. Steuart, underscored in his report that this huge schedule was just "too complicated." He noted, "…the Bureau must depend upon an army of inexperienced enumerators, hastily organized and instructed, the term of service being limited in most cases to one month. Under these conditions the farm schedule should be limited to such questions as the average farmer can answer readily."[xxii]

Irrigation and Drainage Report

These reports give the statistical details of irrigated lands, drainage basins, sources of water supplies, character of water rights, and the date of the beginning of such companies.[xxiii] The statistical data has been published, *but the original schedules have been destroyed.*

Special Fruits and Nuts

There were two supplemental schedules prepared for this report. One schedule, with 128 questions, was used in Arizona, California, Idaho, and Oregon; and the other, with 102 questions, was used in Alabama, Florida, Mississippi, and Texas. The statistical data has been published, *but the original schedules have been destroyed.*

Livestock and Crops Not on Farms or Ranges

This supplemental schedule was added to the Census of Agriculture in 1900 and was expanded in 1930 to include questions on "poultry, bees; crops of all kinds...for sale on places ... not classified as farms, if the amount sold amounted to $50 but less than $250 in value."[xxiv] The issue of what constitutes a farm has been an issue for decades. The definition used in 1930, and earlier censuses is: "...a tract of land of three acres or more on which agricultural products are produced, or a tract of less than three acres which produces agricultural products to the value of $250 or more."[xxv] The statistical data has been published, *but the original schedules have been destroyed.*

Census Of Horticulture

Although the Bureau of the Census had planned the Census of Agriculture long before April 1, 1930 not everyone was pleased with the questions that were asked. The General Farm Schedule had asked only two questions about horticulture and at the request of the leading trade associations this special census was organized and implemented. This special census had six parts, (I) Flowers, Plants & Vegetables Grown under Glass, and Flowers Grown in the Open; (II) Nurseries; (III) Bulb Farms; (IV) Flower and Vegetable Seed Production; (V) Mushrooms and (VI) Blueberries (including Huckleberries).[xxvi]

A conference was held April 15, 1930 at the Census Bureau, which included representatives of fourteen trade organizations.[xxvii] along with representatives of the U.S. Department of Agriculture and the U.S. Tariff Commission to discuss their options. Since the enumeration of the Census of Agriculture, which was mandated to be completed in thirty days, was already well underway it was decided that this census should be carried out and that it could best be conducted by mail. A mailing list was generated from the 1920 Census of Agriculture, trade associations and other lists. Although the first mailing was not sent until August 13, 1930 to 93,000 growers, the information was to be accurate as April 1st of that year. Given the last minute nature of this census it was difficult for the Census Bureau to obtain a comprehensive canvas of this industry while at the same time carrying out their responsibilities with the rest of the Fifteenth Census. Repeated follow-up mailings were required.[xxviii]

CENSUS OF CREWS OF VESSELS
(MERCHANT SEAMEN)

The Bureau of the Census made a diligent effort to document merchant seamen. The enumeration began before April 1, but was to record their "place of abode" as of April 1. The questions included: Name; Sex; Color or Race; Age at Last Birthday; Single, Married Widowed or Divorced; Whether Able to Read or Write; Place of Birth; Naturalized Alien; Whether Able to Speak English; Occupation; Veteran; If so, What War; Address of Wife or Next of Kin.

The *S.S. Lewis Lukenbach.* The ship was fitted as an Army Hospital ship in WWII.

This last question, the "Address of Wife or Next of Kin" is a goldmine for genealogists. The responses range from specific addresses to the names of town and countries. The enumerators were asked to write a code in the right hand margin to describe which category the "next of kin" was. The three categories were, wife (*W*), parent (*P*) or other relative (*R*). Please see the sample page from the enumeration of the *S.S. Lewis Luckenbach.*[xxix]

The enumerators were instructed to include everyone on the ship except for "…officers who have regular or fixed places of abode ashore."[xxx] The enumerations were counted with the town that was the ship's home port; but the series of schedules have been microfilmed separately, arranged by state on three rolls of microfilm.[xxxi]

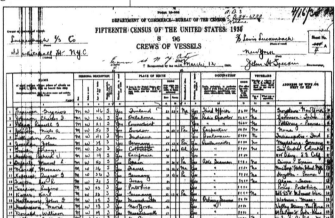

Page from Census of Crews of Vessels for the *S.S. Lewis Luckenbach,* completed March 12th.

The crews of U.S. Navy ships were enumerated on the regular Census of Population schedules and are included with the registration for the town where the ship was home ported. For example, the crew of the Navy's *U.S.S. Cassin* was enumerated at New London, New London County, Connecticut in ED 6-77. *No original schedules have been found for U.S. Naval personnel, based on ships home ported overseas.*

The *U.S.S. Cassin* was commissioned August 9, 1913 and was transferred to the Coast Guard and redesignated CG-1 on June 7, 1924.[xxxii] On June 1, 1930 it was transferred to Division 3, Destroyer Force as the flagship. It had a compliment of six officers and 82 men. The ship was decommissioned from the Coast Guard and returned to the Navy in 1933 and then removed from the U.S. Navy list and scrapped on August 22, 1934.

CENSUS OF DISTRIBUTION

The Census of Distribution was first taken in 1930, "…in response to the demand for comprehensive information concerning the distribution or marketing of commodities. It originated as the direct result of the National Distribution Conference, held under the auspices of the Chamber of Commerce of the United States in 1925. Preparatory to this initiation of [this census] a so-called experimental census was conducted in Baltimore, Atlanta, Chicago, Denver, Fargo, Kansas City (Missouri and Kansas), Providence, San Francisco, Seattle, Springfield (Illinois), and Syracuse.…"[xxxiii] *None of the original schedules for this census or for the experimental census survived.*

CENSUS OF MANUFACTURES

"Since 1810 the Census of Manufactures has provided the only comprehensive measure of the industrial growth and expansion of the United States. Its reports summarize quantities and values of manufactured products; products; employment; earnings; raw materials consumption; expenditures for plant and equipment and other data."[xxxiv]

"The Census of Manufactures taken in 1930 covered industrial activities during 1929, as reported by all manufacturing and printing and publishing establishments whose output during the year was valued at $5,000 or more. Each establishment was assigned, according to the character of its product or class of products of chief value to … one of the 327 industries … in the census classification. As a rule the term 'establishment' refers to a single plant or factory. In some cases however, it represents two or more plants operated under a common ownership and located in the same city, or in the same county but in different cities or unincorporated places having fewer than 10,000 inhabitants, which operated under a common ownership or for which one set of books of account was kept."[xxxv] While extensive statistical data has been published *none of the original schedules or special reports used to enumerate the 1930 Census of Manufactures survived.*

CENSUS OF MINES AND QUARRIES

The Census of Mines and Quarries for 1929 covered all aspects of the mining industry including coal , metal, and placer gold mines, quarries, open pit operations, concentration mills, washers, crushers etc.[xxxvi] With this census the Department of Commerce began to also collect information on the sand and gravel industry.[xxxvii] The statistical data has been published *but the original schedules (Form 100-MQ and the short form 100-X) have been destroyed.*

CENSUS OF RELIGIOUS BODIES

The 1926 Census of Religious Bodies, which was part of the Fifteenth Decennial Census, gathered information about the finances, membership, and leadership of the religious groups in the continental United States. More than one million schedules were distributed to individual congregations, ministers, and to the central offices of the various denominations. *The original returns are available to researchers.* The summaries of these returns have been published in tables and reports [xxxviii] as was the information for the Census of Religious Bodies for 1906 and 1916.

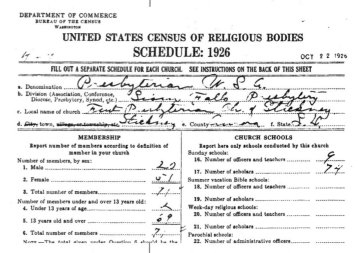

Completed return from the Presbyterian Church, USA from Stickney, SD.

"A much less comprehensive Census of Religious Bodies, with fewer inquiries, was taken in conjunction with the decennial enumeration of population in 1890.... No statistics are available for 1880, for while church and Sunday school statistics were collected at that census, the tabulations were never compiled. A few inquiries were made regarding churches by denominations at the censuses of 1850, 1860, and 1870...."[xxxix]

The last Census of Religious Bodies was taken in 1946. An appropriation of $146,000 was sufficient for the "preparatory work ... the designing and mailing of questionnaires. An additional sum of $463,000 for the succeeding fiscal year was requested by the Bureau for processing and tabulating the results, but this was denied by the Congress. As a result, the replies received, representing about two-thirds of the estimated total, were not tabulated and no report was published."[xl] It was estimated that if a Census of Religious Bodies were to be conducted in 1956 it would cost $1,250,000 and plans for it were dropped.

In 1966 during the planning for the Eighteenth Decennial Census, 1970, there was discussion of asking a question on religion as part of the Census of Population. This would then generate a direct count of the members of the various faiths instead of having the denominations themselves determine these statistics. A. Ross Eckler, Director of the Census Bureau testified before the House Subcommittee on Census and Statistics, "Most citizens probably would not object to answering a question about religion if it were included in the 1970 census without prior publicity ... but a number of groups are strongly opposed to it ... and it has become an emotional issue.... Among those who favor including the question ... are business interests, religious statisticians and Roman Catholic and Protestant groups. Those most strongly opposed are Jewish, Southern Baptist and Christian Scientist groups."[xli]

In the 1926 census the Bureau found that there were 213 separate religious denominations in America. This was an increase of twelve new denominations from the 1916 census.

Detailed Tables

The returns of this census were compiled into detailed statistics about each denomination that are of value to genealogists and local historians.

In the accompanying example of the Presbyterian Church, U.S.A. in Stickney, SD we learn that the First Presbyterian Church of Stickney had 71 members, a church building, and a parsonage; that the pastor, Rev. F. C. Gleason, served two congregations and that he had attended Wabash College and McCormick Theological Seminary. If we check the Religious Bodies, 1926 report for Detailed Table 32, "Members in Selected Denominations by Counties: 1926," for Aurora County, SD[xlii] only 229 members of the Presbyterian Church, U.S.A. are in the entire county. Perhaps this was the sum of both of Gleason's congregations.

The report also presents, in Table 31, the statistical details of all denominations for every city with a population of 25,000 or more inhabitants. A search of the table for Lorain, Ohio would show that there were 45 different congregations in Lorain including six Methodist churches; 16 Roman Catholic parishes; four Baptist churches, etc. With this knowledge, a genealogist can see how many different churches might need to be contacted to consult records for this time period.

CENSUS OF UNEMPLOYMENT

When the 1930 Census began it was intended that the Census of Population would generate the statistical data about the nation's unemployment. With the rapid collapse of the U.S. economy it was determined to make an additional separate Special Unemployment Census of eighteen cities and three boroughs of New York City "to be taken over a two week period to begin in January 1931.[xliii] The data from both the 1930 Census of Population and this Special Census of Unemployment, January 1931 were reported jointly.[xliv]

The eighteen cities selected were: Birmingham, Boston, Buffalo, Chicago, Cleveland, Dayton, Denver, Detroit, Duluth, Houston, Los Angeles, Minneapolis, New Orleans, Philadelphia, Pittsburgh, St. Louis, San Francisco, Seattle; and the three boroughs: the Bronx, Brooklyn, and Manhattan.

"Each enumerator was supplied with a family record book which was used by the supervisors as a check against the completeness of the enumeration. The enumerator was required to make an entry for every call made in his district, whether any unemployed persons were found or not."[l] This record included the name of the head of household, number of persons in the household (including boarders), address, and related data. *Unfortunately these family record books and the original schedules were not preserved.*

CONSULAR SCHEDULES

The Consular Schedules are arranged separately from the rest of the Census of Population. These schedules contain the enumeration of U.S. State Department Foreign Service personnel based in other countries. The returns include officials, their families, and, in a number of cases, military and other civilians living overseas.

The Absent Family Schedule was to be used to record families living overseas who had no connection to the Foreign Service.

As of 1930 there were 137,645 personnel[xlvi] in the U.S. Army. Those living abroad totaled over 24,000 and were stationed in:

Hawaii	15,155
Philippines	4,690
Puerto Rico	1,098
China	1,008
Alaska	315
Nicaragua	280
France	37
Other Posts	1,506

U.S. Army personnel based in the United States, Alaska, Hawaii and Puerto Rico living on military bases were enumerated as part of distinct enumeration districts and recorded with their respective state or territorial returns. Those living in civilian housing were enumerated with the local resident population.

Beginning with the Special Municipal Schedule for Okmulgee County, Alabama, taken on August 15, 1918, it was Census Bureau policy to enumerate military personnel based *overseas* in the Census of Population for their home communities, *as if they were living at home.*

The Consular Schedules generally only include those military personnel who were serving with the Foreign Service as designated Military Attachés and their immediate staff. However, the returns for Japan include two pages of U.S. Army personnel. Given that there were more than 100,000 enumerators creating the Fifteenth Census it is inevitable that there were variations in the enumeration.

A Census of Population was taken in the Panama Canal Zone as part of the Fifteenth Decennial Census. The enumeration reported a total population of 39,469 including 10,470 Army and 1,315 Naval personnel[xlvii] *but these schedules apparently did not survive.*

SPECIAL MUNICIPAL SCHEDULES

There were a number of Special Municipal Schedules, Census of Population that were taken between the decennial censuses. The very first one taken was for Tulsa, Oklahoma, in 1915. The cost of these censuses was paid by the localities that requested them. The original schedules of the fifteen censuses prepared after the 1930 Census have been preserved and will be released as their creation date reaches its 72nd anniversary.

The Census Bureau took its first Special Municipal Census in Tulsa, OK in 1915.

Special Municipal Schedules taken after the 1930 Census were prepared at the request of local officials, and fill 167 volumes.[xlviii] Following is a list of the localities enumerated:[xlix]

Hickory, NC.	1932
Monticello, IN.	1933[l]
North Vernon, IN	
Petersburg, IN	
Rensselaer, IN	
Johnsonburg, PA	
Alexander City, AL	1935[li]
Clanton, AL	
Crestwood, IL	1936
Rock Falls, IL	
Sterling, IL	
Lincolnwood, IL	1938
Markham, IL	
Riverside, IL	
Poplar Bluff, MO	

Special Municipal Schedules taken after the Thirteenth Census, 1910 include:

Tulsa, OK – April 15, 1915: "This enumeration marks a departure in the work of the Census Bureau in that it is the first time a census was ever taken of a municipality, separately from the state in which it was located, between census years."[lii] U.S. Senator Owen requested this census. The Bureau of the Census assigned Eugene F. Hartley to direct the work of the local enumerators. He arrived in Tulsa on April 9, 1915, and began the census on April 16. It was completed in six working days.[liii]

Hamtramck, MI – June 25, 1915: The Hamtramck Village Council requested this census. Eugene F. Hartley and a stenographer were assigned by the Bureau of the Census to direct the work of the local enumerators. They arrived in Hamtramck on June 23, 1915, began the census on June 25, and it was completed in four working days.[liv]

St. Clair Heights, MI – November 18, 1915: The St. Clair Village Council requested this census. The Bureau of the Census assigned Emmons K. Ellsworth to direct the work of the six local enumerators. The census was begun November 18, 1915, and was completed on November 20.[lv]

Okmulgee County, AL – August 15, 1918: The County Board of Commissioners requested this census. William C. Hunt and several assistants were assigned by the Bureau of the Census to direct the work of fifty-eight local enumerators. They arrived in Okmulgee City on August 10, 1918, began the census on August 19, and completed the census several weeks later. It is interesting to note that "as an aid to completeness" they added the information for 1,762 men from the records of the local draft board so that "...the county might be credited with all the population to which it was entitled...."[lvi]

Ottawa County, OK – December 16, 1918: The Board of County Commissioners requested this census. The Bureau of the Census assigned Richard B. Leach and three assistants to direct the work of the local enumerators. They arrived in Miami on December 15, 1918, began the census on December 16, and completed the census on January 11, 1919. In this case they also added enumerations for 402 men who were away in the military based on the records of the local draft board.[lvii]

Tulsa County, OK – January 15, 1919: The Board of County Commissioners requested this census. The Bureau of the Census assigned Richard B. Leach and three staff members to direct the work of the eighty-one local enumerators. They arrived in Tulsa on January 12, 1919, began the census on January 15 and completed it February 12, 1919. The enumerators "were given special instructions" to inquire about and add the names of those away serving in the military. It is interesting to note, "In the city of Tulsa, the house numbers ... recorded on the enumerator's schedules were checked

In the city of Tulsa, the house numbers recorded on the enumerator's schedules were checked against the house numbers reported in the new city directory, just off the press on January 27, 1919.

against the house numbers reported in the new city directory, just off the press on January 27, 1919.... The few houses that had been omitted were added to the schedules, together with the names of the persons residing in them.... By this system it is believed a very close count of the population was secured."[lviii]

Special Municipal Censuses taken after the Fourteenth Census, 1920 include:

High Point, NC – March 26, 1923: High Point Mayor, John D. Hedrick, requested this census. The Bureau of the Census assigned two staff members to direct the work of the eighteen local enumerators. They arrived in High Point on March 19, 1923, began the census on March 26, and completed the census by March 31.[lix]

Greensboro, NC – April 16, 1923: Greensboro Mayor, Claude Kiser, requested this census. Samuel D. Rhoads and George B. Weitzle were assigned by the Bureau of the Census to direct the work of thirty-two local enumerators. They arrived in Greensboro on April 8, 1923, began the census on April 16, and completed the census on April 23.[lx]

Endnotes

[i] Bureau of the Census, *Eighteenth Annual Report of the Secretary of Commerce, 1930* (Washington, D.C.: GPO, 1930), 77.

[ii] Bureau of the Census, *Instructions to Enumerators, Population and Agriculture* (Washington, D.C.: GPO, 1930), sec. 78:14.

[iii] Census, *Eighteenth Annual Report*, 77.

[iv] Ibid.

[v] Ibid., 78.

[vi] Bureau of the Census, *Fifteenth Census of the United States, 1930: Outlying Territories and Possessions. Number and Distribution of Inhabitants, Composition and Characteristics of the Population, Occupations, Unemployment and Agriculture* (Washington, D.C.: GPO, 1932), iii.

[vii] Census, *1930: Outlying Territories*, 1.

[viii] Ibid., 2.

[ix] Ibid.

[x] Ibid.

[xi] Ibid., "Alaska," 27-28.

[xii] Ibid., "American Samoa," 310.

[xiii] Ibid., 313-16.

[xiv] Ibid., "Guam," 289-90.

[xv] Ibid., 299.

[xvi] Ibid., "Hawaii," 42, 105-08.

xvii Ibid., "Puerto Rico," 123-24, 193, 206-08.

xviii Ibid., "Virgin Islands," 259-60, 275-278.

xix Census, *Eighteenth Annual Report*, 78.

xx Ibid., 79.

xxi Census, *Eighteenth Annual Report*, 73. This compares with the distribution of 2,673,399 copies of the Population schedules; 599,038 Unemployment schedules; 489,930 Incidental Livestock not on Farms; 922,429 Special Fruits & Nuts schedule; 390,138 Irrigation; 284,273 Supplemental Blind & Deaf Mute; and 355,550 Supplemental Indian Population schedules.

xxii Ibid., 79.

xxiii Bureau of the Census, *The 1930 Census: Description of the Bound Reports and Final Figures* (Washington, D.C.: GPO, 1931), 11.

xxiv Census, *Eighteenth Annual Report*, 79-80.

xxv Ibid., 80. In later censuses this was changed to "ten acres or more from which $50 or more of agricultural products were sold." See also: "When Is a Farm not a Farm?" *New York Times*, 20 February 1977, 6.

xxvi Ibid., 81.

xxvii These included: American Association of Nurserymen; American Horticultural Legion of Honor; American Horticultural Society; Florists' Exchange & Horticultural Trade World; Florists' Publishing Company; Florists' Telegraph Delivery Association; New York & New Jersey Association of Plant Growers; New York Florists' Club; Seed World; Society of American Florists & Ornamental Horticulturists; Southern Nurserymen's Association; Tennessee Nurserymen's Association; Washington Florists' Club and the Wholesale Cut Flowers Protective Association.

xxviii There were 61,000 second requests; 35,000 third requests; 26,000 fourth requests and 20,000 fifth & final requests sent. See: Bureau of the Census, *Fifteenth Census of the United States, 1930*, "Horticulture. Statistics for the United States and for States, 1929 and 1930" (Washington, D.C.: GPO, 1932), 5.

xxix The S.S. *Lewis Luckenbach* was built May 8, 1919 by Bethlehem Shipping in Quincy, Massachusetts. It was the largest hospital ship in the world at 10,000 tons and 527 feet long, the 22nd Army Hospital Ship (May 1944-May 1945). The *Luchenbach* cost over $7 million and was sold for scrap in 1957. It was named for J. Lewis Luckenbach (1883-1951), Chairman of the Board of the American Bureau of Shipping and owner of the "world's fourth largest fleet," more than 3,500 ships. For his obituary, see: *New York Times*. July 5, 1951, 25.

xxx *1930 Federal Population Census. Catalog of National Archives Microfilm.* (Washington, D.C.: National Archives Trust Fund Board, 2002), ix.

xxxi NARA Microfilm Publication M1932, rolls 1-3.

xxxii For information on its work in stopping bootleggers see: "Two Destroyers Here, Dry Fleet's Vanguard." *New York Times*. August 30, 1924, 3.

xxxiii Bureau of the Census, *1930 Census: Description of the Bound Reports and Final Figures* (Washington, D.C.: GPO), 18.

[xxxiv] U.S. Department of Commerce, *Appraisal of Census Programs. Report of the Intensive Review Committee to the Secretary of Commerce.* (Washington, D.C.: GPO, 1954), 37.

[xxxv] Census, *1930 Bound Reports*, 13.

[xxxvi] Bureau of the Census, *Census of Distribution, Manufactures and Mines and Quarries, 1929. Instructions for Preparing Distribution, Manufactures and Mines and Quarries Reports. Cities Having 10,000 or More Inhabitants*, (Washington, D.C.: GPO, 1930), 43-55; and, Bureau of the Census, *Census of Distribution, Manufactures and Mines and Quarries, 1929. Instructions for Preparing Distribution, Manufactures and Mines and Quarries Reports. Small Cities and Rural Regions.* (Washington, D.C.: GPO, 1930), 6-7.

[xxxvii] Census, *1930 Bound Reports*, 16.

[xxxviii] Bureau of the Census, *Religious Bodies: 1926* (Washington, D.C.: GPO, 1930), 2 vols.

[xxxix] Ibid., 3.

[xl] Commerce, *Appraisal of Census Programs*, 55.

[xli] "Census Religion Query Doubtful, Bureau Chief Tells House Panel." *New York Times*, August 24, 1966, 37.

[xlii] Census, *Religious Bodies: 1926*, vol. 1:673.

[xliii] "Unemployment Census." *Wall Street Journal*, 13 December 1930.

[xliv] Bureau of the Census, *Fifteenth Census of the United States, 1930*, "Unemployment" (Washington, D.C.: GPO, 1932).

[xlv] Ibid., vol. 2:609.

[xlvi] U.S. War Department, "Report of the Secretary of War to the President, 1930" (Washington, D.C.: GPO, 1930), 310.

[xlvii] Bureau of the Census, *Annual Report of the Governor of the Panama Canal, 1930* (Washington, D.C.: GPO, 1930), 79-80.

[xlviii] *Records of the Bureau of the Census. Preliminary Inventory 161* (Washington, D.C.: National Archives and Records Service, 1964), 110.

[xlix] *Guide to Federal Records in the National Archives of the United States.* (Washington, D.C.: NARA, 1995), vol. 1, Rec. Grp. 29.8.3.

[l] Bureau of the Census, *Twenty-Second Annual Report of the Secretary of Commerce, 1934* (Washington, D.C.: GPO, 1934), 23. Note that the report only mentions four enumerations. "Special censuses were taken during September and October 1933...for four places in Indiana..."

[li] Bureau of the Census, *Twenty-Third Annual Report of the Secretary of Commerce, 1935* (Washington, D.C.: GPO, 1935), 28.

[lii] Bureau of the Census, *Special Census of the Population of Tulsa, OK, April 15, 1915*, "Summary Report" (Washington, D.C.: GPO, 1915), 10.

[liii] Ibid., 9.

[liv] Bureau of the Census, *Special Census of the Population of Hamtramck, MI, June 25, 1915*, "Summary Report" (Washington, D.C.: GPO, 1915), 9-11.

[lv] Bureau of the Census, *Special Census of the Population of St. Clair Heights, MI. November 18, 1915. Summary Report.* (Washington, D.C.: GPO, 1916), 2.

[liv] Bureau of the Census, *Special Census of the Population of Okmulgee County, OK, August 15, 1918,* "Summary Report" (Washington, D.C.: GPO, 1919), 6-7.

[lvii] Bureau of the Census, *Special Census of the Population of Ottawa County, OK. December 16, 1918. Summary Report.* (Washington, D.C.: GPO, 1919), 7-8.

[lviii] Bureau of the Census, *Special Census of the Population of Tulsa County, OK. January 15, 1919. Summary Report.* (Washington, D.C.: GPO, 1919), 8-9.

[lix] Bureau of the Census, *Special Census of the Population of High Point, NC. March 26, 1923. Summary Report.* (Washington, D.C.: GPO, 1923), 3.

[lx] Bureau of the Census, *Special Census of the Population of Greensboro, NC. April 16, 1923. Summary Report.* (Washington, D.C.: GPO, 1923), 3.

4 Census Bureau Vital Statistics Reports

The Census Bureau issues special reports that are of value to genealogists. These were pulled from the Census of Population Schedules and include statistical reports on: Birth, Marriage, and Divorce, as well as Mortality Statistics developed from the Mortality Schedules of the census enumerations from 1850 to 1900.

VITAL STATISTICS

The Census Bureau has been compiling vital statistics data since the 1850 census. This changed with the establishment of the Census Bureau in 1902. The collection of birth and death statistics was also authorized by the act that established the Bureau of the Census. It stipulated that "...the statistics should be obtained only from the registration records..."[i] of the states. The two earliest studies of marriage and divorce statistics were conducted by the Department of Labor and covered the years 1867 to 1886.[ii] "The statistics were largely collected by ... special agents and experts of the Department, but in some of the more sparsely settled or distant counties the collection was by local authorities, who made their returns by mail."[iii]

The second study was conducted by the Census Bureau and covered the years 1887 to 1906.[iv] The Department requested and received funding to conduct the next study for the years 1907 to 1916, but because of World War I the next report was for only the year 1916. This canvass was done almost completely by mail and was considered so successful that the Bureau made plans to continue gathering this information only by mail. The next was for the year 1922 and it has been annual thereafter. In 1926 a report on Annulments was added.[v]

BIRTH STATISTICS

When the Bureau began issuing it's *Annual Report of Birth Statistics*[vi] in 1915 only about one third of the states had reached the required level of 90 percent completeness for birth registration in their state. A Registration Area was organized that included Connecticut, Maine, Massachusetts, Michigan, Minnesota, New Hampshire, New York, Pennsylvania, Rhode Island, Vermont, and the District of Columbia. When South Dakota came on board in 1930 every state was included except Texas. The Territories of Hawaii and the U.S. Virgin Islands were also included.

MARRIAGE, DIVORCE AND ANNULMENT STATISTICS

There was a form for requesting divorce information from the Census Bureau, first used in 1923, it was amended to its current arrangement in 1925.

Marriage and Divorce statistics have been published annually since 1922, and annulments since 1926. By 1930 marriage, divorce, and annulment data was being received from every state. Only 14 counties did not send in complete registrations.[vii] The Bureau developed a set of forms for requesting this information from each State Board of Health, the local courts, etc.

While the recitation of vital statistics may not seem directly useful to some genealogists the analysis and reports of the Bureau can provide important clues for family historians.

In 1930 "...no divorces were granted in ... South Carolina, [which repealed its divorce laws in 1878] ... or in 84 [other] counties..." across the country. *Ninth Annual Report on Marriage and Divorce, 1930*, pages 12, 84.

The Bureau reported in 1930, "The very high marriage rates for a state or county are sometimes due to the fact that the marriages reported include the marriages of non-residents who come there to be married, either because of the relatively lenient marriage laws or because of a desire to avoid publicity."[viii] "...the most notable variations in the marriage rates are due largely to the differences in state marriage laws."[ix]

This type of legal influence on where a couple decided to marry has long been referred to as a "Gretna Green" wedding. In 1754 England enacted a law requiring parental permission before anyone under twenty-one was allowed to marry. That same law did not apply to neighboring Scotland where the law permitted anyone sixteen years or older to marry without parental permission. The small town of Gretna Green was the first town on the main road leading from England to Scotland and immediately the marriage rate there soared. To this day the town of Gretna encourages couples to come there to be married.

California and its effect on AZ and NV

California imposed a three-day waiting period for marriages as of July 29, 1927. The result on two border counties was that the marriage rate in Yuma County, AZ about eleven-fold from 1926 to 1930; for Washoe County, NV it increased more than seven-fold in the same period. In contrast the marriage rate in Orange County, CA fell by almost half. If you can't find a marriage in California, maybe they went to Arizona or Nevada to marry.

Delaware and its effect on MD

Delaware requires a one-day waiting period after obtaining a marriage license, while Maryland has no waiting period. The bordering Cecil County, Maryland has a marriage rate that is eight times greater than the state of Maryland, and 27 times greater than the state of Delaware.

North Carolina and its effect on SC

On July 1, 1929 North Carolina changed the legal age for marriage and increased the marriage rates in nearby Dillon and York Counties in South Carolina.

Ohio and Pennsylvania's effect on WV

"Brooke County, WV lies in the northern 'panhandle' of the State between Ohio and Pennsylvania; and because the marriage-license laws of West Virginia are less stringent than those of Ohio and Pennsylvania a large portion of the marriages in Brooke County were of couples from these two adjoining states."

Tennessee and its effect on AR, GA and KY

Tennessee changed its marriage laws to require a five-day waiting period before obtaining a marriage license effective July 1, 1929. The Bureau's analysis concludes that this had an effect on Crittenden County, AR; Dade and Walker Counties, GA and Fulton and Simpson County, KY.[x]

For more information See Gretna Green, Scotland's Official Web Site: www.gretnaonline.net/ HistoricGretnaGretnaGreen.asp

Texas and its effect on AR, LA, NM and OK

On June 13, 1929 Texas imposed a three-day waiting period and began to require a physician's examination. The effect was that the number of marriages reported, "...for practically every border county of Texas steadily decreased." At the same time the border counties of Miller County, AR; Calcasieu Parish, LA; Curry, and Lea Counties, NM; Bryan, Choctaw, Cotton, Harmon, and Love Counties, OK, all dramatically increased.[xi]

Examples from Other Cities, Counties and States

Couples Went From	To Get Married In
Crittenden County, AR	Memphis, TN
Orange County, CA	Los Angeles, CA
All Counties, CO	Denver, CO
Baker County, FL	Jacksonville, FL
Dade & Walker County, GA	Chattanooga, TN
Lake County, IL	Chicago, IL or to Milwaukee, WI
Monroe County, IL	St. Louis, MO
Clark County, IN	Louisville, KY
Hancock County, IN	Indianapolis, IN
Mills County, IA	Omaha, NE
Jonson County, KS	Kansas City, MO
Campbell County, KY	Cincinnati, OH
St. Bernard Parish, LA	New Orleans, LA
Cecil & Kent Counties, MD	Wilmington, DE
Howard County, MD	Baltimore, MD
Clay County, MO	Kansas City, MO
St. Charles County, MO	St. Louis, MO
Dakota County, NE	Sioux City, IA
Sarpy County, NE	Omaha, NE
Camden County, NC	Norfolk, VA or Portsmouth, VA
North Dakota	Moorehead, Clay County, MN
Wood County, OH	Toledo, OH
Oregon	Clarke County and Skamania County, WA
Pennsylvania	Garrett County, MD
Union County, SD	Sioux City, IA
Comal County, TX	San Antonio, TX
Kendall County, TX	San Antonio, TX
Rockwell County, TX	Dallas, TX
Davis County, UT	Salt Lake City, UT
Alexandria, VA	Washington, DC
Clarke County, WA	Portland, OR
Skamania County, WA	Portland, OR

Couples Went From	To Get Married In
West Virginia	Garrett County, MD
Wisconsin	Waukegan, Lake County, IL or Winona County, MN

Divorce and Annulments

In the 1930s an annulment was sometimes more socially acceptable than divorce. South Carolina, which by law did not permit divorce, granted 13 annulments in 1930. California and New York each led the states in the number of annulments granted. There were 4,370 divorces in the U.S. in 1930. Half of them were granted in two states, California with 1,476 and New York 1,030.[xii]

"...figures still show a persistent increase in the divorce rate since 1887." Ninth Annual Report on Marriage and Divorce, 1930, page 14.

MORTALITY STATISTICS

By 1931 the Bureau regularly received copies of the original death and stillbirth certificates from the entire country, except for parts of the state of Texas. In "...1931 the state of South Dakota met the requirement of 90 percent complete registration and was admitted to the registration area of the United States for deaths. There are now 47 States, the District of Columbia, the Territory of Hawaii, the Virgin Islands and eight cities in the nonregistration State of Texas."[xiii] The cities in Texas that were in compliance and submitted information were Beaumont, Dallas, El Paso, Fort Worth, Galveston, Houston, San Antonio and Waco. The Bureau received copies of over 1.3 million death certificates for 1930. The accompanying map[xiv] is particularly useful to genealogists as it shows the year that each state had reached the level of registering at least 90 percent of all deaths. This is a good indication to researchers why the certificates they are seeking are not on file.

Mortality schedules had been taken in every census from 1850 to 1900. The Registration Area for Deaths was established in 1880 and included Massachusetts, New Jersey and the District of Columbia. Added in 1890 were Connecticut, Delaware, New Hampshire, New York, Rhode Island and Vermont. By 1900 Indiana, Maine and Michigan were added, but Delaware was dropped. Delaware was readmitted in 1919.[xv] With the transition to obtaining this information directly from the states the Bureau began issuing statistical data, the *Annual Report of Mortality Statistics.*

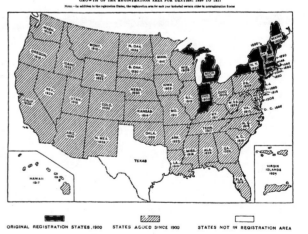

Map: Growth of the Registration Area for Births, Deaths, 1880 to 1931.

Endnotes

[i] Bureau of the Census, *Birth Statistics for the Registration Area of the United States, 1915: First Annual Report* (Washington, DC: GPO, 1917), 9.

[ii] U.S. Department of Labor, *A Report on Marriage and Divorce in the United States, 1867 to 1886.* (Washington, DC: GPO, 1987).

[iii] Bureau of the Census, *Marriage and Divorce*, 1922 (Washington, DC: GPO, 1925), 1.

[iv] Bureau of the Census, *Marriage and Divorce,* 1887-1906 (Washington, DC: GPO, 1908).

[v] Census, *Marriage and Divorce,* 1930, 1.

[vi] Bureau of the Census, *First Annual Report. Birth Statistics for the Registration Area of the United States, 1915* (Washington, DC: GPO, 1917), 5, 9.

[vii] Census, *Marriage and Divorce,* 1930, 1.

[viii] Ibid., 8.

[ix] Ibid. 10.

[x] Ibid.

[xi] Ibid.

[xii] Census, *Marriage and Divorce,* 1930, 44.

[xiii] U.S. Department of Commerce, *Nineteenth Annual Report of the Secretary of Commerce, 1931* (Washington, DC: GPO, 1931), 70.

[xiv] U.S. Department of Commerce. *Mortality Statistics, 1931: Thirty-Second Annual Report* (Washington, DC: GPO, 1935), 2.

[xv] Ibid., 3.

5 Finding Ancestors Using Soundex Code and Miracode

SOUNDEX CODES

The use of the United States Censuses would be vastly different and far more difficult without the use of indexes. These usually consist of alphabetical and Soundex type indexes, which generally index the names of the heads of household rather than every name. This chapter will briefly discuss Soundex indexing and some of the special rules that govern the creation and subsequent use of the index.

Beginning in the 1930s, as part of the *Works Progress Administration* (WPA), the government put individuals to work indexing the 1880, 1900, 1910, 1920 and 1930 U.S. Federal Censuses. The Soundex method of indexing was used to quickly index and group names. The resulting information, handwritten index cards or computer databases, was then filed by a four-character *Soundex Code*—made up of a combination of the first letter of the surname followed by three coded numbers (resulting in codes that could range from *A000* through *Z666*). Finally, the cards and data entries were filed alphabetically by the spelling of the given name of the head of household.

Example of a handwritten Soundex Code index card.

Soundex questions and rules:

1) Where does the first letter of the code come from?

Rule: *The first character in the Soundex Code is always the first letter of a surname, never a number.*

This is perhaps the easiest question to answer. For example, the name of *Fogle* would produce the letter *F*. The name *Andrews* would produce the letter *A*.

2) Where do the numbers come from?

Rule: *Use the Soundex-code chart to determine the number signifying each consonant.*

The numbers are derived from a chart listing six numbers, *1-6*, each with one or more consonants represented by the number.

The Soundex Coding Guide.

Soundex Coding Guide

Letter	Number
B, F, P, V	1
C, G, J, K, Q, S, X, Z	2
D, T	3
L	4
M, N	5
R	6

Letters that are not coded—
Vowels: A, E, I, O, U;
Silent Letters: H, W, Y.

3) The letters *H, W* and *Y* are not listed on the coding chart. Why?

Rule: *The letters H, W and Y are not numerically coded but may be used as the alphabetical character in the code.*

H, W and *Y* are nearly silent when spoken in English. The surname of *Harold* will yield a beginning letter *H* (H643). But, the *h* in the surname *North* will not be numerically coded (N630).

Use vowels only as an alphabetical character in the first position.

4) What about the vowels?

Rule: *Vowels are used only as an alphabetical character in the code.*
Example: *Anderson* (A532) or *Erlich* (E642).

The code consists of only one alphabetical character and three numbers.

5) How many characters in each Soundex Code?

Rule: *The code consists of only one alphabetical character and three numbers.*

The consonants in the surname *Fogle* to be coded are *g* and *l*. The *g* is represented by the number *2*, and *l* by the number *4*. So far the code for *Fogle* is *F24_* but another number is needed in order to have three numbers following the letter. With no more consonants to code, we add the number *0*, making the code for *Fogle, F240.*

6) Why are there 0's in some Soundex Codes if 0's are not listed on the chart?

Zeros are used to complete a code.

Rule *When all consonants are coded, fillers of 0 are added to complete a code of one letter and three numbers.* (Note: The fillers are zeros, not the letter *o*.)

Using this rule the surname of *Lee* would yield a code of *L000*, the surname of *Ohai* would code as *O000* (read as Letter O, zero, zero, zero) because there are no consonants available to be coded.

7) Some surnames have double letters. How are these coded?

Rule: *Double letters are coded as if they were a single letter.*

Gillette has two combinations of double letters, which would be coded as if it were spelled *Gilete*. The *l* is represented by *4*, and *t* by *3*, with a filler *0* added, for a code of *G430*. The surname *Terry* is coded as if it were spelled *Tery*. The *r* is represented by *6* and two fillers of *0* added for a code of *T600*.

8) In some names not all of the consonants are coded. Why?

There is a special coding rule for coding two or more consecutive consonants.

Rule: *Two or more consonants of the same numeric value, which are side-by-side in a surname will be coded as if only one consonant were present.*

An example would be the surname of *Jackson*; the *c, k,* and *s* are all represented by *2*. The *c* would be coded as *2*, the *k* and *s* would be ignored, *n* is represented by *5*, and a filler *0* is added. *Jackson* would then be coded as *J250*.

9) I have an ancestral surname that has more than three consonants that can be coded. What do I do about the extra consonants beyond the three needed for the code?

Rule: *Only the first three consonants that can be coded are needed. The additional consonants are not coded.*

Using the surname *Brighton* as an example the coding would be: *B*, with r represented by *6*, and *g* by *2*, and *t* by *3*, for a code of *B623*. The *n* would not be used.

10) Is there a rule for when the beginning letter is followed by a consonant sharing the same numeric value as that letter?

Rule: *A consonant side by side with a leading letter of the same numeric value is not coded.*

The leading letter and a following consonant such as in the name *Skelton* would be coded *S, k* has the same numeric value as the *S* and is not coded, *l* is represented by *4, t* by *3,* and *n* by *5,* for a code of *S435.*

Prefixes are usually coded as part of the name.

11) An ancestor has a surname that begins with a prefix. How are prefixes coded?

Rule: *Prefixes should be coded as part of the name but were sometimes disregarded by indexers.*

Some of the more common prefixes for surnames are *Van, Von, Con, De, Di, La,* and *Le* (with many others less well known). It would be well to code the surname with and without the prefix. This sounds like maybe doesn't it? Example: *Van Gogh* should be coded as follows: *V, n* is represented by *5, g* by *2,* the second *g* (which is separated by a vowel) is coded as *2,* for a code of *V522. Gogh* would be coded as *G,* the second *g* represented by *2* and then two *0's* as fillers, for a code of *G200.*

12) What about the use of *Mc, Mac,* and *O'* as part of the surname? Are these considered prefixes?

Rule: *Mc, Mac,* and *O'* are not considered as prefixes.

Generally the *Mc, Mac,* and *O'* are considered as part of a complete name. Example: *McArthur* would be coded as follows, *M, c* would be represented by *2, r* by *6, t* by *3,* for *M263* (the ending *r* is not coded).

Are there any exceptions to the Soundex rules?

There are exceptions to Soundex Rules.

Of course there are exceptions, and some of the more important are listed below. Others may be found by obtaining a free pamphlet from the National Archives concerning the Soundex entitled, *"Using the Census Soundex,"* by sending an e-mail request to: inquire@nara.gov. Ask for *Government Information Leaflet #55 (GIL 55)* and be certain to include your name, and postal address.

Titles such as President, General, Mr., Mrs., Doctor

Rule Exception: *Titles are ignored.*

Example: President *Eisenhower* would be coded as *E256* and the title of *President* is ignored.

Individuals belonging to religious orders

Individuals in religious orders are coded by their honorific.

Rule Exception: *Names of individuals belonging to religious orders, using the formal address of Sister, Mother, Brother, or Father should be coded by Sister, Mother, Brother, and sometimes Father.*

Females and males belonging to religious orders usually took a single given name such as Maria or Josephine, for females, and John or Mathew, for males, and then used the honorific of Sister, Mother, or Brother. The indexer/coders addressed this problem by coding the honorific address of *Sister, Mother, or Brother.* Example: *Sister Maria* would be coded as *S236, Mother Josephine* would be *M360,* and *Brother John* would code as *B636.*

Males with the honorific address of Father would normally be indexed by the surname. However, infrequently only the given name will be given and then the indexers coded the honorific title of *Father* as *F360.*

Sometimes the honorific addresses used for females and males were abbreviated as *Sr., Br., M., F.,* or *Fr.* These will be found under the soundex codes as *S600* for *Sr., B600* for *Br., M000* for *M., F000* for *F.,* and *F600* for *Fr.*

Native American names

Rule Exception: *If the surname for a Native American is not clearly identifiable the searcher must check the coding for the first part of the name and then each possible part of the name if needed.*

Native American names are coded normally if there is an identifiable surname such as: *Running Deer Johnson (J525).* If there is some doubt as to the surname amongst a multi-component name generally the first part of the name listed will be coded. Example: *Shinka-Wa-Samay* should be coded under: *Shinka (S520).*

If the use of the first part of the multi-component name does not produce an identifiable index entry then try coding the other parts of the name and rechecking the index.

Oriental names (excepting Japanese and Thai)

Rule Exception: *The surname for an Oriental (excepting those for Japanese and Thai) is usually the first part of the name.*

Multi-component oriental names were frequently anglicized and the first component of the name was probably coded. Here, as well, the researcher must code and check one or more of the several possibilities. Example: Chin Wo Lee, *Chin (C500),* should be the name that was coded. The name could also appear as *Chinwolee,* which would be coded as *C540.* If there are no viable index entries try the other components of the name.

Oriental names other than Japanese and Thai are usually coded by the first part of the name.

Japanese and Thai names (excepting other oriental names)

Rule Exception: *The last component of Japanese and Thai names will be the surname and should be the name coded. However, if there are no index entries then try the rules for the Oriental names above.*

Consonant separators—these are a little tricky but they are part of the rules.

There are a few tricky consonant separators.

Rule Exception: *When two consonants of equal numerical value are separated by a vowel, each consonant is coded separately.*

An example would be the surname of *Tymczak.* Coded: *T,* followed by *5* representing *m,* then *2* for *c, z* is ignored (see Rule # 8 above), and *2* for the *k,* making a code of *T522.*

Rule exception: *When two consonants of equal numerical value are separated by H or W the consonant to the right of H or W is not coded.*

An example is the name of *Ashcraft* which is coded *A*, with *2* representing *s*, *h* is the separator between *s* and the non-coded *c*, and *6* for *r*, and *1* for *f*, the final code is *A261*. *T* is disregarded.

If you think that these exceptions are difficult, remember that the coder/indexer had to try to remember the rules and the exceptions. So if it doesn't work to code by the rules, try using the exceptions to the rules.

Are there alternative systems to the Soundex?

There is another system that has seen some limited usage during the indexing of some states for the 1930 as well as the 1910 U.S. Federal Censuses, called *Miracode*.

What is the Miracode?

Miracode indexes are similar to Soundex indexes.

The Miracode uses the same coding rules that are used with the Soundex. The main difference between the Miracode and the Soundex is the way the indexed information is presented. The Soundex information is presented on handwritten cards, while the Miracode index is comprised of computer-generated sheets with four to five families listed on each sheet. Eventually, both were microfilmed.

Only a few states were indexed for the 1930 Census.

States indexed for the 1930 U.S. Census

Chart of Indexed states

Alabama	Mississippi
Arkansas	North Carolina
Florida	South Carolina
Georgia	Tennessee
Kentucky (Counties: Bell, Floyd, Harlan, Kenton, Muhlenberg, Perry & Pike)	Virginia
	West Virginia (Counties: Fayette, Harrison, Kanawha, Logan, McDowell, Mercer & Raleigh)
Louisiana	

The indexing for the above listed twelve states are the only known indexes provided by the U.S. Census Bureau or the National Archives. Some states were indexed by the Soundex system and others by the Miracode system.

Miracode Sheet from Georgia 1930 Census.

USING THE SOUNDEX AND MIRACODE INFORMATION TO LOCATE INDIVIDUALS AND FAMILIES IN THE 1930 CENSUS

The indexing instructions for 1930 were different than those used in the 1880 and 1900-1920 census indexing. In 1930, the information provided by the coded indexes is generally comprehensive enough that the data on the card or sheet will allow rapid location of the particular family or individual within the Population Schedules.

How to find the microfilm that has the Soundex Code you're looking for

Refer to a catalog available at the your local library if they have a genealogy section, your local historical or genealogy society, or log onto the co-hosted Web site for NARA and HeritageQuest online catalog at: www2.heritagequest.com/1930census. If using the *1930 Census Microfilm Locator* first select the state of interest and press "Continue." A new screen will appear where you may search by the surname, or Soundex Code if known. Enter the appropriate data and press "Search." If the search was by surname the next screen will have the surname displayed with the matching Soundex Code. Scroll down the screen and a chart with NARA film number(s) will be listed. If the number of entries for a Soundex Code is covered on two or more rolls of microfilm then the ranges of the given names will be displayed (remember the index was arranged by Soundex Code number and then alphabetically by the given name). Select the appropriate roll of microfilm and click on the film series number or roll number, for information about purchasing the film. You may also note the film number and access the films at the National Archives in Washington D.C., or at the regional facility nearest you.

Finding the individual index reference on the Soundex microfilm

Once you have access to the Soundex microfilm, scroll through the records, looking at the alpha-numeric code until you come to the code for your ancestor. If the roll begins with a much smaller soundex code, you may need to turn quickly through the film, stopping to check frequently, until the proper Soundex Code is located.

Then search the individual cards using the alphabetical sequence of *given names* until your ancestor's family is located. Sometimes there are many instances of the same given name, such as: James, John, Mary, William, etc. In these instances the searcher needs to know enough about the family to pick out the correct one from the many.

Find the correct microfilm for a particular Soundex Code by using the *1930 Census Microfilm Locator*.

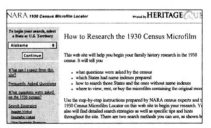

Home page of the *Locator* at: www2.heritagequest.com/1930census

322. Jackson EDs 32-21 to 32-39, 32-
    Jefferson EDs 33-1 to 33-13
    Lake EDs 35-1 to 35-23, 35-24 (
323. Leon EDs 37-1 to 37-28
    Lafayette EDs 34-1 to 34-6
    Lee EDs 36-1 to 36-27
    Levy EDs 38-1 to 38-8

1930 Census Soundex catalog (page 18) showing Lee County, Florida.

1930 Soundex Card for Lee County, Florida.

Population Schedule for Lee County, Florida showing Visitation Number 112 for the widow Florence Camson with two boarders.

Soundex Index card for Fred H. Conekin and Family of Jacksonville, Florida. (NARA Film M2051-17)

1930 Census Population Schedule with William C. Kuhn family as Visitation Number 48, when the family sought was Fred H. Conekin, also as Visitation Number 48.

Glean the numbers and county name

When the correct family or individual is located in the Soundex, make a note of the numbers in the upper right-hand corner of the card. The Volume and ED numbers found in the Sounndex are the two-part ED number used in the Census Schedules and will help you locate the correct census microfilm, and identify the family on the census page.

Vol.: Indicates the bound books in which the census schedules were previously stored. However, it is especially important to note that the Volume number also correlates to the number given to the county. The numbers in the catalog are given as two groups of numbers joined by a dash. An example (left) is: 36-11 with 36 being the code for Lee County in Florida and the 11 is the ED number for a particular location in Lee County. (See illustration from page 18 of the 1930 Census Catalog, Soundex Code films.)

ED: Meaning the Enumeration District. The number assigned to a part of a county (and the enumerator), is a very important number. With this number you can narrow your search to just a few pages, which can be read in minutes.

County: Be sure that you have noted the county name listed on the card or sheet.

Sheet/Visitation: The Soundex cards for the 1930 Census were filled out differently than previous census indexes. The most important difference is the use of the space marked "Sheet" in the upper right-hand corner of the card. This box was used for a page number on Soundex cards in previous census years; however, in the 1930 Soundex it has been used to indicate the "Visitation Number" taken from the Population Schedule, column 4, *Number of family in order of visitation.*

Duplicate Enumeration Districts

If you do not find the family at the expected place on the Population Schedule do the following:

Check to see if the Population Schedule has a County/ED number with the word "Assistant" following the number (see illustration on next page). The number appears in the upper right-hand corner of the sheets. This means that the official enumerator had an assistant and it is possible that he used a different ED number, which may have been changed, upon completion of his or her work, to the ED number of the official enumerator.

Examine all of the Population Schedules for that ED to see if there are duplications of the Visitation Number in the fourth column of the schedules. If so, check for the family name you are seeking at the duplicate number. Be sure to cover the whole district.

I know how to use the Soundex-index cards but the Miracode index numbers are very different. How are these used?

Miracode is made up of computerized sheets rather than individual index cards and the information is in a different format. The same general instructions for finding names in the Soundex indexes apply here. When the correct family or individual is located, note the series of numbers in the upper right-hand corner of the entry. This will be a grouping of three sets of numbers. Example, John Atkins, Mobile Alabaama: 077 0021 0064. *(Note: Copy the entire string of numbers as it is on the entry, and note the name of the county.)*

The first set of numbers (three digits) is a volume number but it is not the number assigned to the county, as it was for the Soundex card in the examples above. The second set consisting of four digits is the ED number. The third set, made up of four digits, is the Visitation Number as assigned by the census enumerator. You'll also need to make note of the county name, usually in the upper left area of the Miracode sheet.

I need to find the census page. How is the correct microfilm found?

Now go back to the *1930 Census Microfilm Locator* and do a "Geographic Search." First, select the state or territory from the pull down menu. Then scroll down to the Geographic Search area of the screen. Enter the ED (including the county number) in the "Search Enumeration Districts" box, and hit "enter." You will then be given the roll number of the film you're looking for.

If you do not have access to the Internet and the *Locator*, return to the catalogs that were first used to find the microfilm numbers for the Soundex. Within the state section (not the Soundex index section) locate the name of the county, or if a large city, the name of the city. Locate the ED number for that section of the city or county and make a note of the microfilm number.

The census microfilms, like the Soundex films discussed earlier, are available through the National Archives. They have also been digitized and enhanced by HeritageQuest and are available on CD-ROM, and the Internet through your public library system.

How do I find the correct entry on the 1930 Census film or CD?

Using the numbers and county name gleaned from the Soundex or Miracode index, scroll through the census film. Locate the two-part ED number in the upper right-hand corner of the page. Remember the first part is the county number and corresponds with the Volume number found in the Soundex (look for the county name in the upper left area of the census page); the second part is the Enumer-

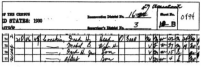

1930 Census Population Schedule with the correct family of Fred H. Conekin family at Visitation Number 48. Note: the word "Assistant" in the far upper right-hand corner.

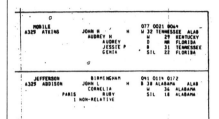

Miracode index sheet for Alabama. The first family listed is for John H. Atkins, with a visitation number of 64. (NARA Film M2049-128)

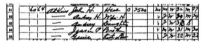

Census Schedule for Mobile County, Alabama showing the family of John H. Atkins, with a Visitation number of 64. (NARA Film T626-40)

Finding the correct entries in the census.

ation District, and corresponds with the ED number in the Soundex. When the correct ED number is located then search for the Visitation number in column four, which is the Sheet number from the Soundex. (Note: The indexed names are the names of the Heads of Household, not every name in the family unit. An exception is the names of those in a household whose surname differs from the Head of Household, or those living in boarding houses and various institutions.)

The Soundex is a system of rules governing the indexing of millions of names of Heads of Household. The rules generally work, but *sometimes* even though everything was done correctly, the family may not be found.

SELECTED BIBLIOGRAPHY

Selected Web Sites

National Archives. *The Soundex Indexing System* www.nara.gov/genealogy/soundex/ soundex.html

www.HeritageQuest.com/1930census

Rootsweb. *Soundex Conversion* www.genealogy.org/soundex.shtml

RootsWeb. *Soundex* www.genealogy.org/census/ intro-6.html

Much of the material for this chapter was taken from *Soundex Codes* by Merrill E. Gillette, AG, *Heritage Quest Magazine* # 98, pages 44 –50

Dollarhide, William. *The Census Book: A Genealogist's Guide to Federal Census Facts, Schedules and Indexes* (Bountiful, Utah: Heritage-Quest, 1999).

Eakle, Arlene, and Johni Cerny. *The Source: A Guidebook of American Genealogy* (Salt Lake City: Ancestry, 1994).

Else, Willis I. *The Complete Soundex Guide* (Apollo, PA: Closson Press, 2002).

Greenwood, Val D. *The Researchers Guide to American Genealogy, 2nd ed.* (Baltimore: Genealogical Publishing Co., 1990).

Hinckley, Kathleen W. *Your Guide to the Federal Census for Genealogists, Researchers and Family Historians* (Cincinnati: Betterway Books, 2002).

Using the Census Soundex. Washington D.C.: National Archives and Records Administration, (#55 Government Information Leaflet).

Steuart, Bradley, ed. *The Soundex Reference Guide* (Bountiful, Utah.: Precision Indexing).

Szucs, Loretto Dennis, and Mathew Wright. *Finding Answers in U.S. Census Records* (Orem, UT: Ancestry Publishing, 2001).

6 Research Finding Aids for Unindexed Areas

Chapter Five addressed the Soundex indexing for the 1930 Census. This indexing covered the states in the South, with only parts of Kentucky and West Virginia. There remains the question of how to find an individual in the rest of the country—urban (big city) or rural (small towns and farms)—without a Soundex. Veteran genealogists know that the locating of an individual in these circumstances often requires the use of city directories, enumeration district descriptions, and maps.

Each county or city was sub-divided into smaller geographical divisions called Enumeration Districts (ED), which were assigned consecutive numbers that started with "1" and ended with however many districts were needed for that county. Descriptions of each district were created by the Census Bureau. EDs varied in size. There was an ED in California that comprised only 198 individuals, but covered over 5,000 square miles. Along with the name of the county, the ED numbers are one of the vital pieces of information needed to locate an individual within the census pages.

CITY DIRECTORIES

City Directories are vital to Urban research in the 1930 Census.

Knowing a person's street address can help you find the enumeration district for urban residents. City directories not only give the street address where a person lived, but also may provide such information as place of employment, length of residence if newly arrived, and relationship of residence to features of the city. City directories were not created by the local governments but rather by commercial enterprises that sometimes competed for the local advertising dollars.

Jacksonville, Florida 1930-31 City Directory, Alphabetical Listing.

One characteristic of large cities is a transient population. Many residents never leave the city, and since they don't own the buildings they live in, they often move from place to place.[i] Remember also that your ancestor may have moved into the city shortly before or after a census was taken. They may have done the same thing just before or after the area was canvassed for the information used in the city directory. Look for "late listings" in the directory. These are often found just before the resident listing.[ii]

STREET DIRECTORIES AND WARD BOUNDARIES

Street directories are a crucial part of any city directory.

Many directories include a separate "street directory" of the streets within the city, which follows the listing of residents. Also, there may be a list with the cross-streets, as well as the numbers on both sides of the street at each intersection. This data can enable you to narrow the location of a particular ward, maybe to within one or two census districts. In this way a city directory can be used as a substitute for a census index.

Equally important are the descriptions of ward boundaries.

"Wards are the jurisdictional unit used in most city records. From draft records, to death registrations, to census, to voter lists, persons were identified by the ward of residence. A few city directories indicated the ward in the street directory. More commonly, you will find a few pages, often near the street directory, with a description of each ward. These descriptions can be difficult to read. You will be most successful if you can find a map of the city and plot out the key wards near the relative's address. The census used ward boundaries as part of their method of dividing up a city. For the censuses taken in 1850 and later, the census office compiled books of enumeration district descriptions, which identify what geographic areas were in which census districts. In cities, these districts are always described as certain portions of existing wards. Knowing in which ward a family lived allows the researcher to review the enumeration district descriptions, to learn where to look for the family. Census indexes also use ward boundaries to identify where an entry is found on the census. By searching the directories before using the census index, and knowing in what ward a family lived, the researcher can choose the most likely index entries. This is especially helpful with common surnames."[iii]

If you happen to live near the National Archives (700 Pennsylvania Avenue NW, Washington, D.C.) or one of its branches, keep in mind that NARA purchased, for use in their facilities, selected microfilmed city directories for the years around 1930.

Also, the Library of Congress holds copies of city directories for over 800 U.S. cities in a collection that continues to grow. A list is avalable at: www.loc.gov/rr/genealogy/bib_guid/telephon.html. All U.S. city and state directories up to and including 1860 are included in a self-service microfiche collection housed in the Microform Reading Room (LJ 107). Dorothea Spear's American Directories Before 1860 (Z5771.S7 LH&G and Z5771.2.S68 1978 MRR Ref Desk) is a guide to this collection. For the years primarily 1861 through 1960, there is a large self-service collection of U.S. city directories on microfilm available in the Microform Reading Room (LJ 139B). For details about the cities included and the years available for those cities, consult U.S. City Directories on Microfilm in the Microform Reading Room, www.loc.gov/rr/microform/uscity.

Another extensive collection of bound and microform city directories is located at the Family History Library in Salt Lake City, Utah. Additionally, many other major libraries have large collections of city, county, and business directories that may be of use to the researcher. Check with your local library for Inter-Library Loan possibilities for access to the directories needed for your research.

Kathleen W. Hinkley, in her book, Your Guide to the Federal Census, points out that addresses can also be found by researching birth certificates, prior years' census records, court records, death certificates, funeral home records, hereditary and lineage applications, land and tax records, letters and postcards, marriage and

---

CAMBRIDGE DIRECTORY, 1930   65

WALL AV
From 515 N 4th east to 509 N 8th
310 Wheeler Earl*
312 Rubicam Geo W*
313 Butler Chas A*
314 Casterline Ivan C
315 Stiffler Henry*
316 Lawrence Chas W
317 Kenworthy Thos H
318 Wendell Oscar
319 Carlisle Adam O
    Grumsley Ogle C
321 Shatto Jas R*
322 vacant
323 Kambouris Geo
325 Straus Jno J*
    4th crosses
400 Shelton August A
402 White Lee H
411 Williams Clinton D*
415 Rose Jas
416 Dollison Miles H
418 Abels Elzie M*
419 Gallagher Irenaeus A*
423 Stewart Pearl C*
424 Berry Thos A*
425 Gildea Margt*
430 Mapel Wm B*
431 Pulley Dwight M*
436 Bennett C C*
    5th crosses
511 McFee Wm B*

714 Vance Alva A*
715 Davidson Elmer E

WALNUT AV
From 1343 Elm
501 Adams Wilfred R
504 Ross Jas W
505 Degenhart Chas*
508 Finley Carl J*

WATER
North from 66 Gomber av
233 McKinney Martin R*
237 Campbell Asa J
301 Moorhead Elmer*
305 Brill Berl
315 Neff Herman*
317 Gaskill Robt A*
318 Kimmey Milton H*
322 vacant
354 Fair Jno T*
356 Abels Harry C*
356-A Bennett Jno H*
    Beatty av crosses
434 Allshouse Margt T*
436 King Terence E*
440 Brooks Wm A
463 Curtis Sylvester
rear Spicer Wm
465 Clark Geo B*
rear Harris Zachariah
467 Lawson Jas H
500 Bonnell Geo W*
501 Sigman Laura M
534 Williams Percy

Cambridge, Ohio 1930 City Directory, Street Directory.

The Library of Congress holds copies of city directories for over 800 U.S. cities. For online availability check out www.loc.gov/rr/microform/uscity/

divorce records, military records, naturalization and passenger arrival records, oral interviews, notations on the backs of photographs, and school records.

ENUMERATION DISTRICTS: DESCRIPTION AND IMPORTANCE

One of the tasks performed prior to the taking of the 1930 Census was the division of cities and counties into smaller geographical units called *Enumeration Districts*. The divisions were actually completed by using the then current maps of the areas and marking the districts in grease pencil or by other means. Some districts covered only a few city blocks and others covered many square miles but they were all sized so that the enumerator could complete the census in a reasonable time.

From the resulting maps the next step was to write a physical description of the district, so that the individual enumerator would understand where he or she was to go in order to perform the assigned duties. These descriptions then became part of the permanent record of the census, and when used with the maps have become marvelous finding aids for genealogists looking for families in non-indexed areas.

The ED number is of prime importance to locating the correct section of the census whether on microfilm or CD. Without the ED number the searcher must search all of a city such as Chicago, which is covered on *80 rolls* of microfilm. Knowing the ED number can reduce the number of microfilms to search. When searching an area that is not indexed, use the address found in the City Directory along with the ED descriptions and maps to determine the correct ED to search.

MORE FINDING AIDS

The 1930 Census Microfilm Locator and it's Geographic Search

This unique Locator Web site will help you begin your search.

The first and easiest finding aid is the *1930 Census Microfilm Locator* discussed in Chapter Five (available at www.HeritageQuest.com/1930Census). This aid not only helps to determine the Soundex Code of a surname but also assists in a Geographical Search to help quickly determine the possible ED number(s) to be searched. This feature is available for the entire United States and its Territories with over 120,000 places listed. The National Archives and HeritageQuest have jointly sponsored this unique Web site to help the researcher find families in the 1930 census. There are step-by-step instructions prepared by NARA census experts and the *1930 Census Microfilm Locator* on the HeritageQuest.com Web site to help you begin your research. You will also find detailed search strategies, as well as specific tips and hints throughout the site.

Enumeration District Maps – M1930

The Bureau of the Census used contemporary maps upon which it overlaid, often just with grease pencil notations, the boundaries and numbers of enumeration districts. The quality and visual clarity of these maps varies considerably.

Index to Selected City Streets and Enumeration Districts, 1930 Census– M1931

National Archives Microfilm Publication M1931, (7 rolls). This series is a reproduction of a 57-volume city streets index used for the 1930 Census. The index cross references street addresses of 50 cities with enumeration districts.

Certain streets are listed as having "no population" however, so it is likely that the final version was made after the completion and tabulation of the census. These volumes are typescript mimeographs on which annotations have been handwritten in red ink.

Fifteenth Census of the United States 1930 – Metropolitan Area Maps

Another fine resource is a volume titled *Fifteenth Census of the United States 1930 - Metropolitan Districts - Population and Area;* published by the U.S. Dept. of Commerce, Bureau of the Census, Washington D.C. 1932. This 253-page soft cover volume is statistical in nature, listing population data for cities with over 50,000 in population. The data given begins with a summary of the population and area of the city, both metropolitan areas and combined surrounding suburbs, with a comparison between 1920 and 1930 figures. Next, the population for each community is listed, not only in total, but by Sex, Color, Nativity, and Age (by category—Under 5, 5 to 14, 15 to 24, and so forth). Each metropolitan area has a map included with it. These maps have been reproduced in this book.[iv] (See the Appendix.)

USING THE FINDING AIDS

Census Locator

Soundex Search

Refer to Chapter Five for a discussion of the Soundex.

Geographic Search

If the state of interest was not indexed using the Soundex, then by clicking on "Continue" on the *Locator* home page after selecting the State, one is led to a page where one can search by county or in some instances by city name. From the drop down menus select the appropriate county or city and press "Continue." The resulting screen will provide the numbers of rolls of microfilm and enumeration districts for the selected locality. Clicking on the small page numbers under the heading for Enumeration Districts or Institutions will provide a list of 40 brief Enumeration District descriptions. For large cities it will help you to use a map to plot the boundaries in relation to the address obtained from the City Directory.

Note that the Enumeration Districts are not always found on the film in numeric order. For this reason alone, doing a Geographic Search on the *Locator* is worthwhile, even if you already know the film number, based on a Soundex search.

Searching For Walter McDonald in Chicago

You are looking for your ancestor, Walter D. McDonald and his wife Laura. You know they lived in Chicago, and by consulting the Chicago City Directory, you found that they lived at 1221 Roscoe Street.

By setting up a search for Chicago, then entering the name "Roscoe" in the *Refine Your City/County Results* portion of the Geographic Search in the *Locator*, you will find that Roscoe St. is located in 32 separate, though nearby, Enumeration Districts. Those 32 EDs are on 6 rolls of film. That may sound like a lot, but keep in mind that the City of Chicago is on 80 rolls of film! Also note that you now have specific EDs to look for on each roll—as well as the street address you found in that City Directory.

On the next page is a screen print of the *Locator* showing the situation described above and some of the EDs that used Roscoe Street as a boundary street. If Roscoe Street had not been a boundary street the *Locator* would not show the street name.

If you look at each census roll in numerical order, you will find Walter McDonald in the 14th ED searched, which is on the fourth roll (ED 16-1680). When focusing on the EDs as you scroll through

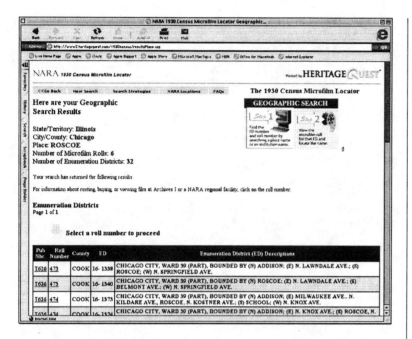

the film, also watch for the street name written sideways in the first column, the House Number in the second column, and of course, the family in the fifth column.

Enumeration District Maps

Researchers can use the above resources, along with contemporary non-census maps, current maps, and other local geographical information, to narrow their search to only a few EDs. Carefully study the ED descriptions for your area from the *Locator*. Then compare these descriptions to known information about the location, such as street names and place names and likely places of residence for the family being searched. Searches conducted via the geographic approach often can refine the search area down to only a portion of a single roll of microfilm.[v] Searchers should be aware that the descriptions of an enumeration district will list the boundary streets but will not list the other street names within the district. Consulting a map will help the searcher to determine in which ED(s) a street is located.

The *Enumeration District Maps* have been microfilmed and are available at some genealogical libraries, at the National Archives Center in Washington D.C., and all 13 regional facilities. The complete set of enumeration district maps are in *Enumeration District Maps for the Fifteenth Census of the United States, 1930*, National Archives Microfilm Publication M1930, (36 rolls).[vi]

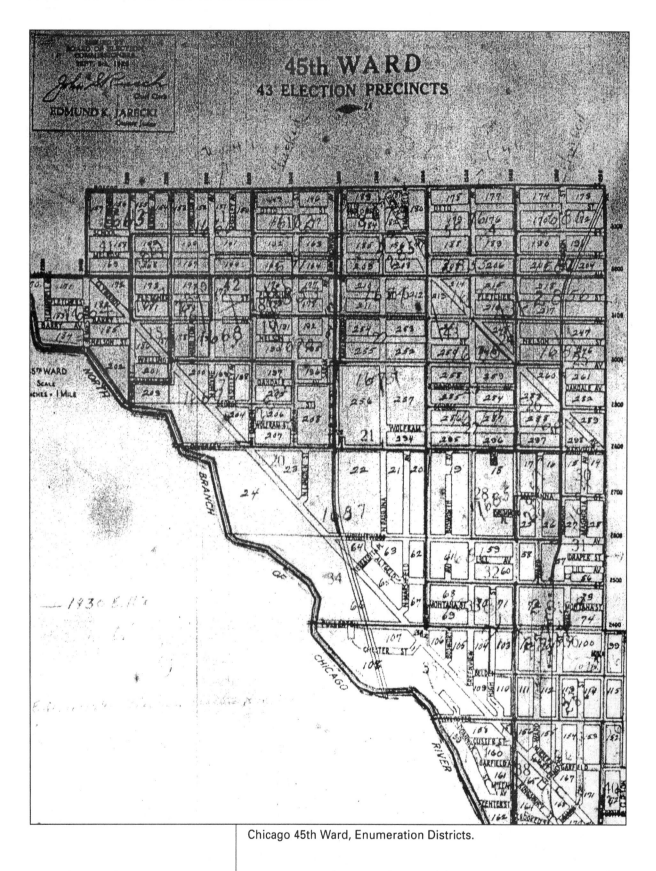

Chicago 45th Ward, Enumeration Districts.

Enumeration District Descriptions of EDs 1678, 1679 and 1680. These EDs may be plotted on the map of The Chicago 45th Ward Enumeration districts by using the block numbers.

Enumeration District Descriptions – T1224

Enumeration district descriptions are found in *Descriptions of Enumeration Districts, 1830-1950,* National Archives Microfilm Publication T1224, (156 rolls). The descriptions are arranged by state, county, city, or township and then by ED number. The 1930 descriptions can be found on rolls 61 through 90. Although they describe the boundaries of a particular enumeration district; they do not indicate all of the streets within that ED, streets within the EDs may be identified by use of a map. The enumeration district descriptions are transcribed and are part of the "Geographic Search" portion of the *Locator.*[vii]

1930 Population Schedule for Chicago showing Walter D. McDonald living on Roscoe Street with his family. See the ED map and descriptions above.

Index to Selected City Streets and Enumeration Districts, 1930 – M1931

Most of the volumes contain all or part of a major U.S. city; a few also contain smaller cities. Except as indicated, each volume includes the following:

1. Title page. This indicates the city (or cities) included and a short table of contents.

2. List of enumeration district (ED) numbers. This indicates the bound census volume in which each ED is found.

3. List of named streets (roads, boulevards, avenues, lanes, etc.) arranged alphabetically. This indicates the EDs in which the street is located, as further described below. Streets with a prefix such as

North, East, South, or West may be listed either under the prefix or under the street name. For example, East Archwood Avenue might be listed as "E. Archwood Ave." or as "Archwood Ave. E."

4. List of numbered streets (roads, boulevards, avenues, lanes, etc.) arranged numerically. This indicates the EDs in which the street is located, as further described below. Prefixes such as North, East, South, or West do not affect the arrangement. Thus, E. 26th and W. 26th will both be found together. There may be a few exceptions to this rule; for example "Six Mile Road" in Detroit is listed with named streets and not with the numbered streets. In Los Angeles, there is a separate list for "Avenue 16" through "Avenue 67," but other numbered avenues (i.e., 16th Ave.) will be found in the list of numbered streets.

5. List of institutions and named apartment buildings. This indicates the ED in which the institution or apartment building will be found.

6. List of unnamed apartment buildings. This indicates the ED in which the apartment building will be found. Only a few of the larger cities have this list.

Corrections. The Bureau made handwritten corrections on these lists, presumably after the census was completed.

Information Provided for Named and Numbered Streets. For named and numbered streets, the two-part ED number is given for ranges of house numbers. If the street was entirely within one ED, the house number range is not given. If odd house numbers were in one enumeration district and even house numbers in another, the word "odd" or "even" follows the range of house numbers. For examples from Detroit, Michigan:

Streets	House Nos.	ED
Aaron	———————-	82-385
Abbott	(400-900)	82-88
	(1000-1200)	82-143
	(1300-1400)	82-142
	(1500-1800) even	82-194
	(1500-1800) odd	82-193
Aberle Ave.	———————-	82-190

If the street had no population, the words "(no pop.)" follow the house number range. Streets with alternative names have a "see" designation, such as "Weston Rd. (See E. Archwood Ave.)"

Special Cases

North Carolina. The Bureau created special finding aids for this state:

Index to 22 Cities over 10,000 Population. These cities are arranged alphabetically in one volume, and listed for each city is: the street name, house number range, and ED number information described above.

Index to Named Places under 10,000 Population. Named places are arranged alphabetically by name, and for each, the following information is given: county in which located, ED number, and adjacent ED numbers (if any). For example:

Place	County	ED	Adjacent
Rominger	Watauga	95-10	95-13; 15
Ronda	Wilkes	97-5	97-6; 16; 8
Rooks	Pender	71-5	71-4
Roosevelt	Henderson	45-5	——-

Index to Townships. Townships are listed alphabetically. The following information is given: county in which located and its enumeration district number(s).

Index to Institutions. Institutions are listed alphabetically by name, and for each the following information is given: county or city in which located and enumeration district.

County Maps. These consist of hand-drawn rough sketches of each county. The enumeration district numbers and their approximate boundaries are shown. These maps were probably drawn to assist Bureau employees in using the four North Carolina indexes described above.

Philadelphia. In 1930, the city of Philadelphia and Philadelphia County shared the same boundaries. The Philadelphia index, however, indicates for many streets the name of the neighborhood in which the street is located, such as: Blue Bell Hill, Bridesburg, Bustleton, Chestnut Hill, Fox Chase, Falls of Schuylkill, Frankford, Germantown, Holmesburg, Manayunk, Olney, Palm West Philadelphia, Roxborough, Somerton, Tacony, and West Philadelphia.

Roll List of M1931

Roll 1. **Arizona:** Phoenix

California: Berkeley; Long Beach; Los Angeles county (6 vols.) includes Los Angeles city and Alhambra, Arcadia, Avalon, Azusa, Bell, Beverly Hills, Burbank, Claremont, Compton, Covina, Culver, Davidson, El Monte, El Segundo, Glendale, Glendora, Hawthorne, Hermosa Beach, Hollywood, Huntington Park, Inglewood, La Verne, Lynwood, Manhattan Beach, Maywood, Monrovia, Montebello, Monterey Park, Pasadena, Pomona,

Redondo Beach, San Fernando, San Gabriel, San Marino, San Pedro, Santa Monica, Sierra Madre, Signal Hill, South Gate, South Pasadena, Temple, Torrance, Tujunga, Verdugo, Vernon, West Covina, Whittier, and Wilmington

    Vol. 1: A – Colon
    Vol. 2: Colonial – Harkins
    Vol. 3: Harkness – Mayfield
    Vol. 4: Mayflower – Romney

Roll 2.   **California** (continued):
Los Angeles County (continued):
    Vol. 5: Romona – Wheeler
    Vol. 6: Wheeler – Z
        1st – 263rd (St., Ave., Rd., Pl., etc.)
        Ave. 16 – Ave. 67
        Institutions and Apartments
        Minor Civil Divisions

San Diego, San Francisco

Colorado: Denver

District of Columbia

Florida: Miami, also includes Miami Beach and South Miami, Tampa

Georgia: Atlanta

Roll 3.   **Illinois:** Chicago
    Vol. 1: Abbott – Nutt
    Vol. 2: Oak – York; 5th – 138th; and Institutions and Apartments
Peoria

Indiana: Fort Wayne, Gary, Indianapolis, South Bend

Kansas: Kansas City, Wichita

Maryland: Baltimore

Roll 4.   **Michigan:** Detroit: also includes Hamtramck and Highland Park, Grand Rapids

Nebraska: Omaha

New Jersey: Elizabeth, Newark, Paterson

New York: Bronx and Manhattan (interfiled)

Brooklyn
Vol. 1: A – Oxford
Vol. 2: Pacific – York; 1st – 108th; and Institutions and Apartments

Roll 5. **New York** (continued):
Queens
Vol. 1: Aberdeen – Zoller; and 1st – 43rd
Vol. 2: 44th – 271st; and Institutions and Apartments
Richmond

North Carolina:
Cities over 10,000 Populations, Vol. 1: Asheville, Charlotte, Concord, Durham, Elizabeth City, Fayetteville, Gastonia, Goldsboro, Greensboro

Roll 6. **North Carolina** (continued):
Cities over 10,000 Population, Vol. 2: High Point, Kinston, Lexington, New Bern, Raleigh, Rocky Mount, Salisbury, Shelby, Statesville, Thomasville, Wilmington, Wilson, Winston-Salem

Named Places Under 10,000 Population, Vol. 1: Aaron – Parker Crossroads

Named Places Under 10,000 Population, Vol. 2:
Parker Ferry – Zorah
Townships: Abbotts – Youngsville
Institutions: A – Z
County Maps: Alamance – Yancey

Ohio: Akron, Canton, Cincinnati

Roll 7. **Ohio** (continued): Cleveland, Dayton, Youngstown

Oklahoma: Oklahoma City, Tulsa

Pennsylvania: Erie

Philadelphia
Vol. 1: A – Myrtlewood
Vol. 1: N – Zerelda; 1st St – 80th St.; 64th Ave, 80th Ave.; 23rd N. 35th N.; and Institutions and Apartments

Reading

Tennessee: Memphis

Texas: San Antonio

Virginia: Richmond[viii]

FIFTEENTH CENSUS OF THE UNITED STATES 1930 – METROPOLITAN DISTRICTS

While not as easy as using an index to find the ED number of a particular location the above methods do work and have been used successfully by many genealogists of varying skill levels. The key is being methodical and very patient as the various parts of the search strategy are completed. Each step must be completed, as short cutting may lead to incorrect information and frustrating delays. Remember, have fun!

Endnotes

[i] National Archives:
1930census.archives.gov/searchStrategiesResources.html

[ii] Library of Congress:
www.loc.gov/rr/genealogy/bib_guid/telephon.html

[iii] National Archives:
www2.heritagequest.com/1930census

[iv] *Fifteenth Census of the United States 1930 - Metropolitan Districts - Population and Area;* U.S. Dept. of Commerce, Bureau of the Census, Washington D.C. 1932

[v] National Archives:
www2.heritagequest.com/1930census

[vi] *Fifteenth Census of the United States 1930 - Metropolitan Districts - Population and Area;* U.S. Dept. of Commerce, Bureau of the Census, Washington D.C. 1932

[vii] *Descriptions of Enumeration Districts, 1830-1950* National Archives Microfilm Publication T1224

[viii] National Archives:
1930census.archives.gov/cityStreets.html#streets

Appendixes

Index of
Military Installations and
Veterans' Facilities

The pages that follow contain a list of many military installations enumerated separately in the 1930 U.S. Federal Census. As mentioned in Chapter 3, enumerators were instructed to record soldiers and sailors as if their current post of duty was their place of abode. This may also be true for individuals in veterans' homes and hospitals if such locations were understood to be their long-term residence.

Use this helpful section to locate roll numbers and enumeration districts for various military locales or to quickly survey a list of bases, posts, army and navy hospitals, soldiers' homes, etc. for a given state or county.

ST	County	E.D.	Roll	Installation/Institution	ST	County	E.D.	Roll	Installation/Institution
AK	1st Judicial Div.	1-43	2626	Soapstone Point Compass Stat.	CT	Fairfield	1-117	256	Fitch's Home For The Soldiers and Soldiers Hosp.
AK	1st Judicial Div.	1-38	2626	Soapstone Point Radio Stat.	CT	New Haven	5-34	275	Sailors Home
AK	1st Judicial Div.	1-18	2626	U.S. Coast Guard Cutter Unalga	CT	New London	6-36	282	Coast Guard Academy
AK	1st Judicial Div.	1-36	2626	U.S. Naval Radio Stat.	CT	New London	6-76	281	U.S. Naval Stat. Submarine Base
AK	2nd Judicial Div.	2-1	2627	U.S. Coast Guard	DC	Wash, DC	1-112	295	Army War College
AK	2nd Judicial Div.	2-1	2627	U.S. Signal Corps	DC	Wash, DC	1-345	302	Naval Air Stat.
AK	3rd Judicial Div.	3-9	2627	U.S. Naval Radio Compass Stat.	DC	Wash, DC	1-24	292	Soldiers, Sailors, and Marines Home
AK	3rd Judicial Div.	3-7	2627	U.S. Naval Radio Stat.	DC	Wash, DC	1-129	295	Temporary Home For Ex-union Soldiers and Sailors
AL	Baldwin	2-21	2	Fort Morgan	DC	Wash, DC	1-347	302	U.S. Naval Magazine
AL	Calhoun	8-6	5	Camp McClellan	DC	Wash, DC	1-168	296	U.S. Naval Observatory
AL	Chilton	11-9	7	Jefferson Manley Faulkner Soldiers Home	DC	Wash, DC	1-91	294	U.S. Navy Hosp.
AL	Macon	44-3	36	U.S. Veterans Hosp. No. 91	DC	Wash, DC	1-126	295	U.S. Navy Yard
AL	Mobile	49-44	41	U.S. Coast Guard	DC	Wash, DC	1-328	301	U.S. Soldier's Home
AL	Mobile	49-46	41	U.S. Coast Guard	DC	Wash, DC	1-185	297	U.S. Veterans Hosp. No. 32
AR	Garland	26-16	75	Army and Navy General Hosp.	DE	New Castle	2-114	287	Fort Delaware
AR	Pulaski	60-77	92	Ft. Roots U.S. Veterans Hosp. No. 78	DE	New Castle	2-115	287	Fort Dupont
AR	Pulaski	60-44	90	U.S. Army Airport	DE	New Castle	2-115	287	U.S. Army Post Hosp.
AZ	Cochise	2-36	55	Camp Harry J. Jones	DE	Sussex	3-41	291	Cape Henlopen U.S. Coast Guard Stat.
AZ	Cochise	2-15	55	U.S. Army Post Hosp.	DE	Sussex	3-33	291	Fenwick Is. U.S. Coast Guard Stat.
AZ	Pima	10-56	62	U.S. Veterans Hosp. No. 51					
AZ	Santa Cruz	12-5	62	Camp Stephen D. Little	DE	Sussex	3-41	291	Indian River Inlet U.S. Coast Guard Stat.
AZ	Santa Cruz	12-5	62	U.S. Army Stat. Hosp.					
AZ	Yavapai	13-27	63	U.S. Veterans' Hosp. No. 50	DE	Sussex	3-39	291	Parramore Beach U.S. Coast Guard Stat.
CA	Alameda	1-224	100	U.S. Coast Guard Vessels					
CA	Alameda	1-262	109	U.S. Veterans Tuberculosis Hosp. No. 102	DE	Sussex	3-41	291	Rehoboth Beach U.S. Coast Guard Stat.
CA	Humboldt	12-25	120	U.S. Coast Guard	DE	Sussex	3-39	291	Sixth District U.S. Coast Guard Office
CA	Imperial	13-18	119	Camp Beacon					
CA	Los Angeles	19-601	156	Fort Macarthur (Lower Reserve)	DE	Sussex	3-30	291	U.S. Coast Guard Stat.
CA	Los Angeles	19-597	156	Fort Macarthur (Military Post)	FL	Brevard	5-2	307	Chester Shoal U.S. Coast Guard Stat.
CA	Los Angeles	19-596	156	Fort Macarthur (Upper Reserve)	FL	Broward	6-9	307	U.S. Coast Guard Base
CA	Los Angeles	19-1049	131	U.S. Veterans Hosp. No. 104	FL	Columbia	12-15	308	U.S. Veterans Hosp.
CA	Marin	21-42	177	Fort Baker and Post Hosp.	FL	Dade	13-73	311	U.S. Coast Guard Stat.
CA	Marin	21-43	177	Fort Barry and Post Hosp.	FL	Duval	16-38	313	Confederate Soldiers Home
CA	Marin	21-45	177	Fort McDowell and Post Hosp.	FL	Escambia	17-3	315	U.S. Army Res., Including Ft. Barrancas, Ft. McRae, Ft. Pickens, and U.S. Army Post Hosp.
CA	Mendocino	23-3	177	U.S. Coast Guard Stat.					
CA	Napa	28-22	180	Veterans Home of California					
CA	San Diego	37-50	191	Army and Navy Academy					
CA	San Diego	37-219	193	Fort Rosecrans and Post Hosp.	FL	Escambia	17-4	315	U.S. Naval Air Stat.
CA	San Diego	37-221	193	Naval Fuel Depot	FL	Escambia	17-4	315	U.S. Navy Hosp.
CA	San Diego	37-221	193	Naval Radio Stat.	FL	Escambia	17-51	315	U.S. Navy Res.
CA	San Diego	37-56	191	U.S. Coast Guard Ship	FL	Monroe	44-2	325	U.S. Naval Stat. and Hosp.
CA	San Diego	37-55	191	U.S. Marine Corps Base	FL	Nassau	45-2	326	U.S. Coast Guard Base No. 20
CA	San Diego	37-223	193	U.S. Naval Air Stat.	GA	Catoosa	24-8	343	Fort Oglethorpe
CA	San Diego	37-213	193	U.S. Naval Radio Stat.	GA	Chatham	26-48	345	Ft. Screven and U.S. Army Post Hosp.
CA	San Diego	37-56	191	U.S. Naval Training Stat.					
CA	San Diego	37-128	192	U.S. Navy Hosp.	GA	Chattahoochee	27-5	345	Fort Benning
CA	San Francisco	38-107	198	Fort Funston Military Res.	GA	Chattahoochee	27-5	345	U.S. Army Post Hosp.
CA	San Francisco	38-304	206	Fort Mason Military Res.	GA	Fulton	61-144	357	Camp Jessup
CA	San Francisco	38-256	204	Fort Miley Military Res.	GA	Fulton	61-138	365	Confederate Soldiers Home
CA	San Francisco	38-309	206	Fort Winfield Scott	GA	Fulton	61-145	357	Fort McPherson
CA	San Francisco	38-1	194	Sailors Home	GA	Muscogee	108-32	377	Fort Benning
CA	San Francisco	38-2	194	U.S. Naval Training Stat. At Yerba Buena (Goat) Island	GA	Muscogee	108-34	377	Fort Benning
					GA	Muscogee	108-30	378	Fort Benning
CA	San Francisco	38-1	194	Y.M.C.A. (Army and Navy Hotel Branch)	GA	Richmond	123-22	382	U.S. Veterans Hosp. (Insane)
					GA	Walker	148-18	390	Fort Oglethorpe
CA	San Mateo	41-53	217	Camp Fremont	GA	Walker	148-18	390	U.S. Army Hosp.
CA	Solano	48-42	221	Navy Yard	HI	Honolulu	2-110	2632	Military and Naval Res. (Ford Island/Luke Field)
CA	Solano	48-42	221	U.S. Naval Hosp.					
CO	Bent	6-16	230	United States Veterans Hosp. No. 80	HI	Honolulu	2-113	2632	Pearl Harbor Naval Res.
					HI	Honolulu	2-114	2632	Pearl Harbor Naval Res.
CO	Rio Grande	53-16	251	Colorado State Soldiers and Sailors Home	HI	Honolulu	2-115	2632	Pearl Harbor Naval Res.

ST	County	E.D.	Roll	Installation/Institution	ST	County	E.D.	Roll	Installation/Institution
IA	Henry	44-13	658	Henry County Soldiers and Sailors Home	MA	Barnstable	1-16	883	Peaked Hill Bars Coast Guard Stat.
IA	Marion	63-10	668	U.S Veterans Hosp. No. 57	MA	Barnstable	1-15	883	Provincetown Coast Guard Stat.
IA	Marshall	64-16	668	Iowa Soldiers Home					
IA	Marshall	64-15	668	Iowa Soldiers Home Hosp.	MA	Barnstable	1-15	883	Race Point Coast Guard Stat.
IA	Polk	77-94	673	Fort Des Moines	MA	Barnstable	1-15	883	Wood End Coast Guard Stat.
IA	Polk	77-48	675	Sailors and Soldiers Home	MA	Bristol	3-158	892	Fort Rodman
IA	Polk	77-94	673	U.S. Army Post Hosp.	MA	Bristol	3-158	892	U.S. Army Post Hosp.
IA	Webster	94-36	687	Fort Dodge City Jail	MA	Dukes	4-4	894	Cuttyhunk Coast Guard Stat.
ID	Ada	1-24	395	U.S. Veterans' Hosp. No. 52	MA	Dukes	4-3	894	Gay Head Coast Guard Stat.
IL	Adams	1-62	405	Soldiers and Sailors Home	MA	Essex	5-49	896	Gloucester Coast Guard Stat.
IL	Cook	16-2378	416	(City of Chicago), Academies Only: Northwestern Military and Naval Academy	MA	Essex	5-211	901	Nahant Coast Guard Stat.
					MA	Essex	5-80	895	Plum Island Coast Guard Stat.
					MA	Essex	5-268	903	Salisbury Beach Coast Guard Stat.
IL	Cook	16-1576	484	(City of Chicago), All Others: Army Post Navy Pier	MA	Essex	5-240	902	Stratsmouth Coast Guard Stat.
IL	Lake	49-40	528	Fort Sheridan Military Res.	MA	Hampshire	8-40	912	Veterans Hosp.
IL	Lake	49-64	529	Great Lakes Naval Training Stat.	MA	Middlesex	9-176	914	Camp Devens
					MA	Middlesex	9-406	927	Camp Devens
IL	Lake	49-64	529	U.S. Veterans Hosp.	MA	Middlesex	9-366	926	John A. Andrew Soldiers Home
IL	Livingston	53-11	533	U. S. Veterans Hosp. No. 53	MA	Middlesex	9-178	914	U.S. Veterans Hosp.
IL	Vermilion	92-39	564	National Home For Disabled Volunteer Soldiers	MA	Nantucket	10-2	932	Coskata Coast Guard Stat.
					MA	Nantucket	10-1	932	Maddaket Coast Guard Stat.
IL	Winnebago	101-59	572	Camp Grant	MA	Norfolk	11-111	936	National Sailors Home
IN	Grant	27-19	589	National Home For Disabled Volunteer Soldiers (Marion Branch)	MA	Norfolk	11-90	936	Sailors Snug Harbor
					MA	Plymouth	12-75	940	Brant Rock Coast Guard Stat.
					MA	Plymouth	12-68	940	Fort Andrews (Peddocks Island)
IN	Marion	49-240	616	Fort Benjamin Harrison	MA	Plymouth	12-69	940	Fort Revere
IN	Marion	49-357	611	Grand Army of The Republic Home	MA	Plymouth	12-86	940	Gurnet Coast Guard Stat.
IN	Rush	70-3	625	Indiana Soldiers and Sailors Orphans Home	MA	Plymouth	12-90	940	Manomet Coast Guard Stat.
					MA	Plymouth	12-98	941	North Scituate Coast Guard Stat.
IN	Tippecanoe	79-33	630	Indiana State Soldiers Home and Hosp.	MA	Plymouth	12-67	940	Point Allerton Coast Guard Stat.
KS	Ford	29-16	702	Kansas State Soldiers Home	MA	Plymouth	12-64	940	U.S. Naval Ammunition Depot and Marine Barracks
KS	Geary	31-12	702	Fort Riley Military Res. (Part)	MA	Suffolk	13-21	942	Boston City Hosp. (East Boston Relief Stat.)
KS	Geary	31-14	702	U.S. Army Post Hosp.					
KS	Leavenworth	52-13	707	Fort Leavenworth Military Res.	MA	Suffolk	13-38	942	Fort Standish
KS	Leavenworth	52-4	707	National Military Home For Disabled Volunteer Soldiers	MA	Suffolk	13-38	942	Fort Strong
					MA	Suffolk	13-40	942	Fort Warren
KS	Leavenworth	52-14	707	U.S. Army Post Hosp.	MA	Suffolk	13-43	942	U.S. Navy Yard
KS	Riley	81-20	718	Fort Riley Military Res.	MA	Suffolk	13-583	943	Y.M.C.A. (Army & Navy Dept.)
KY	Bullitt	15-4	735	Camp Knox	MA	Suffolk	13-484	956	Y.M.C.A. (Army & Navy Dept.)
KY	Campbell	19-36	738	Fort Thomas	MA	Worcester	14-205	963	Camp Devens
KY	Campbell	19-36	738	U.S. Veterans Hosp. No. 69	MA	Worcester	14-259	965	U.S. Veterans Hosp.
KY	Christian	24-25	740	U.S. Veterans Tuberculosis Hosp.	MD	Anne Arundel	2-16	844	Fort George C. Meade
					MD	Anne Arundel	2-10	845	U.S. Naval Academy
KY	Hardin	47-19	747	Fort Knox (Part)	MD	Anne Arundel	2-10	845	U.S. Navy Hosp.
KY	Hardin	47-24	747	Fort Knox (Part)	MD	Baltimore	3-21	846	Confederate Soldiers Home
KY	Hardin	47-19	747	U.S. Army Post Hosp.	MD	Baltimore	3-70	847	Fort Howard
KY	Meade	82-3	768	Fort Knox (Part)	MD	Baltimore City	4-184	856	Army and Navy Preparatory School
LA	Orleans	36-155	808	Jackson Barracks U.S. Army Post	MD	Baltimore City	4-405	867	Camp Holabird
					MD	Baltimore City	4-386	866	Fort McHenry
LA	Orleans	36-101	804	Louisiana State Soldiers Home	MD	Baltimore City	4-398	866	Quarantine Stat.
LA	Rapides	40-47	817	U. S. Veterans Hosp. (Tuberculosis)	MD	Baltimore City	4-379	865	U.S. Coast Guard (Cutters)
					MD	Baltimore City	4-379	865	U.S. Coast Guard (Lighthouse Service)
LA	St. Tammany	52-18	820	Camp Hygeia (Tuberculosis)	MD	Baltimore City	4-41	849	U.S. Coast Guard (Recruiting)
MA	Barnstable	1-19	883	Cahoons Hollow Coast Guard Stat.	MD	Cecil	8-15	873	Veterans Administration Facility
MA	Barnstable	1-7	883	Chatham Coast Guard Stat.	MD	Charles	9-10	872	Indian Head Naval Proving Ground and Marine Camp
MA	Barnstable	1-17	883	Highland Stat. Coast Guard Stat.					
MA	Barnstable	1-7	883	Monomay Point Coast Guard Stat.	MD	Harford	13-22	875	Aberdeen Proving Ground (Part) (Fort Hoyle)
MA	Barnstable	1-9	883	Nauset Coast Guard Stat.	MD	Prince George's	17-13	877	Fort Washington
MA	Barnstable	1-7	883	Old Harbor Coast Guard Stat.	ME	Cumberland	3-93	832	Fort Preble
MA	Barnstable	1-14	883	Orleans Coast Guard Stat.					
MA	Barnstable	1-18	883	Parnet River Coast Guard Stat.					

ST	County	E.D.	Roll	Installation/Institution	ST	County	E.D.	Roll	Installation/Institution
ME	Cumberland	3-9	830	Fort Williams	NC	Dare	28-5	1684	Cape Hatteras U. S. Coast Guard Stat.
ME	Kennebec	6-15	833	National Soldiers' Home (Eastern Branch)	NC	Dare	28-8	1684	Coffeys Inlet U. S. Coast Guard Stat.
ME	Knox	7-16	835	U.S. Coast Guard Cutter, Kickapoo	NC	Dare	28-5	1684	Creeds Hill U. S. Coast Guard Stat.
ME	Sagadahoc	12-3	838	Military and Naval Asylum	NC	Dare	28-5	1684	Durants U. S. Coast Guard Stat.
ME	York	16-4	841	Fletchers Neck Coast Guard Stat.	NC	Dare	28-7	1684	Nags Head U. S. Coast Guard Stat.
ME	York	16-29	841	Fort Foster	NC	Dare	28-7	1684	Oregon Inlet U.S. Coast Guard Stat.
ME	York	16-27	841	U.S. Navy Yard	NC	Dare	28-7	1684	Pea Island U.S. Coast Guard Stat.
MI	Calhoun	13-37	979	Camp Custer	NC	Henderson	45-13	1699	Military Naval Academy
MI	Chippewa	17-15	980	Fort Brady	NC	Hoke	47-5	1699	Fort Bragg (Part)
MI	Kalamazoo	39-54	997	Camp Custer	NC	Hoke	47-7	1699	Fort Bragg (Part)
MI	Kalamazoo	39-62	997	Camp Custer	NC	Hoke	47-9	1699	Fort Bragg (Part)
MI	Kent	41-117	1004	Michigan Soldiers Home	NC	Hyde	48-9	1699	Ocracoke U. S. Coast Guard Stat.
MI	Macomb	50-20	1009	U.S. Army Post Hosp.	NC	Onslow	67-9	1711	Bogue Inlet U.S. Coast Guard Stat.
MI	Wayne	82-370	1046	U.S. Coast Guard	NC	Wake	92-40	1726	Soldiers Home and Hosp.
MN	Cook	16-3	1083	North Superior U.S. Coast Guard Stat.	ND	Burleigh	8-54	1732	Fort Lincoln
MN	Hennepin	27-303	1101	Fort Snelling	ND	Burleigh	8-54	1732	U.S. Army Post Hosp.
MN	Hennepin	27-236	1099	Minnesota State Soldiers Home	ND	Cass	9-46	1733	U.S. Veterans' Hosp.
MN	Hennepin	27-303	1101	U.S. Army Post Hosp.	ND	Ransom	37-16	1741	North Dakota State Soldiers Home and Hosp.
MN	Hennepin	27-303	1101	U.S. Veterans Hosp. No. 106	NE	Dawes	23-11	1271	Fort Robinson
MN	Kittson	35-11	1103	Kittson War Veterans Memorial Hosp.	NE	Douglas	28-132	1279	Fort Omaha (U.S. Army Balloon School)
MN	Lake	38-6	1104	Coast Guard Cutter Crawford	NE	Hall	40-14	1282	Nebraska State Soldiers and Sailors Home and Hosp.
MN	Ramsey	62-79	1118	U.S. Veteran Hosp.	NE	Lancaster	55-15	1285	Veterans Hosp.
MN	St. Louis	69-58	1126	Duluth U.S. Coast Guard Stat.	NE	Sarpy	77-3	1292	Fort Crook
MN	Stearns	73-61	1130	U.S. Veterans Hosp. No. 101	NE	Sarpy	77-3	1292	U.S. Army Post Hosp.
MO	Clay	24-2	1183	U.S. Veterans Hosp. No. 99	NE	Seward	80-27	1292	Nebraska Soldiers and Sailors Home
MO	Jackson	48-76	1195	U.S. Veterans Hosp.	NH	Belknap	1-19	1298	New Hampshire Soldier's Home
MO	Jackson	48-76	1195	U.S. Veterans Hosp. Home For Nurses	NJ	Atlantic	1-79	1309	Absecon Coast Guard Stat.
MO	Lafayette	54-14	1208	Confederate Soldiers Home and Hosp. of Missouri	NJ	Atlantic	1-3	1308	Atlantic Coast Guard Stat.
					NJ	Atlantic	1-36	1309	Brigantine Coast Guard Stat.
MO	Phelps	81-14	1216	Federal Soldiers Home of Missouri and Soldiers Home Hosp.	NJ	Atlantic	1-56	1309	Great Egg Coast Guard Stat.
					NJ	Atlantic	1-48	1309	Little Beach Coast Guard Stat.
MO	St. Louis	95-22	1223	U.S. Veterans Hosp. No. 92	NJ	Atlantic	1-36	1309	South Brigantine Coast Guard Stat.
MO	Vernon	109-13	1250	Camp Clark	NJ	Burlington	3-51	1318	Camp Dix
MO	Vernon	109-5	1250	Camp Clark	NJ	Cape May	5-1	1325	Avalon Coast Guard Stat.
MS	Harrison	24-9	1146	Gulf Quarantine Hosp. and Detention Stat. (Ship Island)	NJ	Cape May	5-6	1325	Cape May Point Coast Guard Stat.
MS	Harrison	24-8	1146	Jefferson Davis Beauvoir Soldiers Home	NJ	Cape May	5-15	1325	Carsons Inlet Coast Guard Stat.
					NJ	Cape May	5-3	1325	Cold Spring Coast Guard Stat.
MS	Harrison	24-4	1146	U.S. Coast Guard Section Base No. 15	NJ	Cape May	5-6	1325	Five Fathom Coast Guard Stat.
MS	Harrison	24-6	1146	U.S. Naval Reserve Park	NJ	Cape May	5-10	1325	Hereford Inlet Coast Guard Stat.
MS	Harrison	24-12	1146	U.S. Veterans Hosp. No. 74	NJ	Cape May	5-12	1325	Ocean City Coast Guard Stat.
MS	Jackson	30-8	1150	U.S. Coast Guard Stat.	NJ	Cape May	5-15	1325	Pecks Beach Coast Guard Stat.
MT	Flathead	15-7	1256	Montana Soldiers Home	NJ	Cape May	5-16	1325	Sea Isle City Coast Guard Stat.
MT	Lewis & Clark	25-17	1258	U.S. Veterans' Hosp.	NJ	Cape May	5-18	1325	Stone Harbor Coast Guard Stat.
NC	Brunswick	10-7	1675	Cape Fear U.S. Coast Guard Stat.	NJ	Cape May	5-16	1325	Townsend Inlet Coast Guard Stat.
NC	Brunswick	10-7	1675	Oak Island U.S. Coast Guard Stat.	NJ	Cape May	5-3	1325	U.S. Coast Guard Cutter Crew
					NJ	Cape May	5-3	1325	U.S. Coast Guard Stat. (Section Base 9)
NC	Buncombe	11-60	1676	Veterans Administration Facility	NJ	Cape May	5-26	1325	Wildwood Coast Guard Stat.
NC	Carteret	16-16	1679	Cape Lookout U. S. Coast Guard Stat.	NJ	Cumberland	6-27	1326	New Jersey Memorial Home For Disabled Soldiers, Sailors, Marines, and Their Wives and Widows
NC	Carteret	16-10	1679	Core Bank U. S. Coast Guard Stat.					
NC	Carteret	16-6	1679	Fort Mason U. S. Coast Guard Stat.					
NC	Carteret	16-12	1679	Portsmouth U. S. Coast Guard Stat.					
NC	Cumberland	26-26	1684	Fort Bragg (Part)					
NC	Cumberland	26-26	1684	U.S. Army Post Hosp.					

ST	County	E.D.	Roll	Installation/Institution	ST	County	E.D.	Roll	Installation/Institution
NJ	Hudson	9-301	1357	New Jersey Home For Disabled Soldiers	NY	New York	31-281	1548	Sailors Home and Institute
NJ	Monmouth	13-95	1372	Deal Coast Guard Stat.	NY	Niagara	32-98	1619	Niagara Coast Guard Stat.
NJ	Monmouth	13-80	1371	Fort Hancock and Sandy Hook Proving Grounds	NY	Oswego	38-34	1635	Fort Ontario Military Res.
NJ	Monmouth	13-97	1372	Fort Monmouth	NY	Oswego	38-37	1635	Oswego Coast Guard Stat.
NJ	Monmouth	13-60	1371	Long Branch Coast Guard Stat.	NY	Queens	41-266	1593	Fort Totten
NJ	Monmouth	13-84	1372	Monmouth Beach Coast Guard Stat.	NY	Richmond	43-53	1614	Fort Wadsworth
NJ	Monmouth	13-79	1371	Sandy Hook Coast Guard Stat.	NY	Richmond	43-52	1614	New York Quarantine Stat.
NJ	Monmouth	13-107	1372	Seabright Coast Guard Stat.	NY	Richmond	43-103	1612	U.S. Coast Guard Boats and Cutters
NJ	Monmouth	13-26	1370	Shark River Coast Guard Stat.	NY	Richmond	43-63	1615	U.S. Quarantine Stat. (Hoffman Island)
NJ	Monmouth	13-79	1371	Spermarti Cove Coast Guard Stat.	NY	Rockland	44-43	1641	Naval Ammunition Depot
NJ	Monmouth	13-113	1372	Spring Lake Coast Guard Stat.	NY	Steuben	51-10	1648	New York State Camp For Veterans
NJ	Monmouth	13-72	1371	Squaw Beach Coast Guard Stat.	NY	Suffolk	52-41	1650	Camp Upton
NJ	Morris	14-70	1374	U. S. Naval Ammunition Depot and Marine Barracks	NY	Suffolk	52-79	1650	Coast Guard Patrol Boat
NJ	Ocean	15-1	1375	Barnegat Coast Guard Stat.	NY	Suffolk	52-96	1651	Coast Guard Patrol Boat (No. 207)
NJ	Ocean	15-2	1375	Bay Head Coast Guard Stat.	NY	Suffolk	52-79	1650	Coast Guard Stations (4th Dist.)
NJ	Ocean	15-24	1375	Bonds Coast Guard Stat.	NY	Suffolk	52-50	1650	Coast Guard Stations (Amagansett)
NJ	Ocean	15-16	1375	Cedar Creek Coast Guard Stat.	NY	Suffolk	52-45	1650	Coast Guard Stations (Bellport)
NJ	Ocean	15-9	1375	Chadwick Coast Guard Stat.	NY	Suffolk	52-45	1650	Coast Guard Stations (Blue Point)
NJ	Ocean	15-28	1375	Forked River Coast Guard Stat.	NY	Suffolk	52-51	1650	Coast Guard Stations (Ditch Plains)
NJ	Ocean	15-43	1375	Harvey Cedars Coast Guard Stat.	NY	Suffolk	52-59	1651	Coast Guard Stations (Eatons Neck)
NJ	Ocean	15-5	1375	Island Beach Coast Guard Stat.	NY	Suffolk	52-96	1651	Coast Guard Stations (Fire Island)
NJ	Ocean	15-24	1375	Little Egg Coast Guard Stat.	NY	Suffolk	52-45	1650	Coast Guard Stations (Forge River)
NJ	Ocean	15-24	1375	Long Beach Coast Guard Stat.	NY	Suffolk	52-46	1650	Coast Guard Stations (Georgica)
NJ	Ocean	15-24	1375	Loveladies Island Coast Guard Stat.	NY	Suffolk	52-51	1650	Coast Guard Stations (Hither Plain)
NJ	Ocean	15-7	1375	Mantoloking Coast Guard Stat.	NY	Suffolk	52-45	1650	Coast Guard Stations (Lone Hill)
NJ	Ocean	15-14	1375	Naval Air Stat.	NY	Suffolk	52-123	1652	Coast Guard Stations (Mecox)
NJ	Ocean	15-26	1375	Naval Air Stat.	NY	Suffolk	52-125	1652	Coast Guard Stations (Moriches)
NJ	Ocean	15-24	1375	Ship Bottom Coast Guard Stat.	NY	Suffolk	52-51	1650	Coast Guard Stations (Napeague)
NJ	Ocean	15-36	1375	Toms River Coast Guard Stat.	NY	Suffolk	52-18	1649	Coast Guard Stations (Oak Island)
NJ	Salem	17-6	1382	Fort Mott	NY	Suffolk	52-125	1652	Coast Guard Stations (Petunk)
NM	Grant	9-2	1395	U.S. Army General Hosp.	NY	Suffolk	52-45	1650	Coast Guard Stations (Point of Woods)
NM	Grant	9-2	1395	U.S. Veterans' Hosp.	NY	Suffolk	52-125	1652	Coast Guard Stations (Quoque)
NY	Allegany	2-24	1406	Soldiers and Sailors Memorial Hosp.	NY	Suffolk	52-131	1652	Coast Guard Stations (Rocky Point)
NY	Bronx	3-387	1476	Fort Schuyler	NY	Suffolk	52-125	1652	Coast Guard Stations (Shinnecock)
NY	Bronx	3-105	1465	Home For Friendless and American Female Guardian Society	NY	Suffolk	52-45	1650	Coast Guard Stations (Smiths Point)
NY	Bronx	3-622	1487	U.S. Veterans Hosp. No. 81	NY	Suffolk	52-117	1652	Coast Guard Stations (Southampton)
NY	Chenango	9-31	1416	New York State Women's Relief Corps Home	NY	Suffolk	52-125	1652	Coast Guard Stations (Tiona Coast)
NY	Dutchess	14-26	1419	U.S. Veterans Hosp.	NY	Suffolk	52-135	1652	Fort H. G. Wright
NY	Erie	15-30	1424	U.S. Coast Guard (Office)	NY	Suffolk	52-132	1652	Fort Michie
NY	Erie	15-34	1424	U.S. Coast Guard (Stat., Base, and Crews On Vessels)	NY	Suffolk	52-133	1652	Fort Terry
NY	Franklin	17-5	1438	U.S. Veterans Hosp.	NY	Suffolk	52-69	1651	U.S. Veterans Hosp.
NY	Jefferson	23-23	1443	Big Sandy Coast Guard Stat.	NY	Ulster	56-63	1656	Veterans Memorial Hosp.
NY	Kings	24-39	1501	Naval Hosp.	NY	Westchester	60-256	1663	Fort Slocum
NY	Kings	24-107	1514	Soldiers Home	NY	Yates	62-2	1670	Soldiers and Sailors Hosp.
NY	Nassau	30-213	1462	Coast Guard Stations (Jones Beach)	OH	Erie	22-13	1791	Ohio Soldiers and Sailors Home
NY	Nassau	30-215	1460	Coast Guard Stations (Long Beach)	OH	Franklin	25-114	1799	Fort Hayes ("columbus Barracks")
NY	Nassau	30-122	1460	Coast Guard Stations (Point Lookout)					
NY	Nassau	30-134	1460	Coast Guard Stations (Short Beach)					
NY	Nassau	30-213	1462	Coast Guard Stations (Zacks Inlet)					
NY	New York	31-36	1545	Fort Jay Including Post Hosp.					
NY	New York	31-35	1545	Fort Wood Including Post Hosp.					

ST	County	E.D.	Roll	Installation/Institution	ST	County	E.D.	Roll	Installation/Institution
OH	Greene	29-30	1804	Soldiers and Sailors Orphans Home	RI	Washington	5-6	2182	Point Judith Coast Guard Stat.
OH	Greene	29-1	1804	U.S. Stat. Hosp.	RI	Washington	5-1	2181	Quonochontaug Coast Guard Stat.
OH	Montgomery	57-154	1856	National Military Home For Disabled Volunteer Soldiers	RI	Washington	5-14	2182	U.S. Coast Guard 3d District Office
OH	Ottawa	62-23	1860	Camp Perry	RI	Washington	5-22	2182	Watch Hill Coast Guard Stat.
OH	Ross	71-28	1865	U.S. Veterans Hosp. No. 97	SC	Beaufort	7-6	2188	Beaufort Co. Jail
OK	Carter	10-27	1896	Confederate Soldiers Home	SC	Beaufort	7-3	2188	Beaufort Town Jail
OK	Comanche	16-36	1899	Fort Sill Military Res.	SC	Beaufort	7-11	2188	U. S. Marine Camp and Hosp.
OK	Murray	50-12	1914	Oklahoma Soldiers Tubercular Sanitarium	SC	Beaufort	7-11	2188	U.S. Navy Prison
					SC	Charleston	10-50	2190	Navy Hosp.
OK	Muskogee	51-4	1915	Oklahoma Soldiers Memorial Hosp.	SC	Charleston	10-50	2190	U. S. Navy Yard
					SC	Charleston	10-64	2190	U. S. Navy Yard
OR	Clatsop	4-26	1941	Point Adams U.S. Coast Guard Stat.	SC	Richland	40-56	2211	Camp Jackson
					SC	Sumter	43-32	2214	Camp Alice
OR	Clatsop	4-2	1941	U.S. Coast Guard Cutter Redwing	SD	Fall River	24-16	2223	South Dakota Soldiers Home
					SD	Harding	32-4	2224	Camp Crook Hosp.
OR	Coos	6-25	1942	Coos Bay U.S. Coast Guard Stat.	SD	Meade	47-109	2227	Fort Meade Military Res. and Post Hosp.
OR	Coos	6-47	1942	Coquille River U.S. Coast Guard Stat.	SD	Meade	47-51	2227	Fort Meade Timber Res.,
					SD	Meade	47-62	2227	Fort Meade Timber Res.
OR	Coos	6-20	1942	U.S. Public Health Relief Stat. No. 274	TN	Davidson	19-209	2243	Confederate Veterans Home and Hosp.
OR	Douglas	10-68	1943	Oregon Soldiers' Home and Hosp.	TN	Knox	47-20	2258	Fort Sanders Hosp.
OR	Douglas	10-69	1943	Umpqua River U.S. Coast Guard Stat.	TN	Knox	47-20	2258	Fort Sanders Hosp. Nurses' Home
					TN	Shelby	79-115	2277	U.S. Veterans Hosp. No. 88
OR	Lane	20-65	1946	Siuslaw U.S. Coast Guard Stat.	TX	Bexar	15-187	2299	Air Corps Primary Flying School
OR	Lincoln	21-20	1944	Yaquina Bay U.S. Coast Guard Stat.	TX	Bexar	15-195	2299	Camp Bullis
					TX	Bexar	15-173	2299	Camp Normoyle
OR	Multnomah	26-39	1949	U.S. Coast Guard Stat.	TX	Bexar	15-196	2292	Camp Stanley
OR	Multnomah	26-101	1950	U.S. Veteran's Hosp.	TX	Bexar	15-103	2296	Fort Sam Houston
OR	Tillamook	29-38	1955	Tillamook Bay U.S. Coast Guard Stat.	TX	Bexar	15-161	2299	Fort Sam Houston
					TX	Bexar	15-225	2299	Fort Sam Houston
PA	Erie	25-24	2035	Pennsylvania Soldiers and Sailors Home	TX	Cameron	31-22	2304	Camp San Benito
					TX	Cameron	31-11	2305	Fort Brown
PA	Franklin	28-13	2042	Soldiers Orphans Industrial School	TX	Cameron	31-11	2305	U.S. Army Post Hosp.
					TX	Dallas	57-62	2317	Dallas Baby Camp Hosp.
PA	Monroe	45-3	2080	Fort Tobyhanna	TX	El Paso	71-76	2329	Fort Bliss Military Res. (Part)
PA	Philadelphia	51-194	2128	League Island: U.S. Navy Yard, Marine Reserve, U.S. Naval Hosp., and U.S. Coast Guard Units	TX	El Paso	71-78	2329	Fort Bliss Military Res. (Part)
					TX	Galveston	84-25	2335	Fort Crockett
					TX	Galveston	84-2	2334	Fort San Jacinto
					TX	Galveston	84-45	2335	Fort Travis
PA	Philadelphia	51-281	2095	Nurses Naval Home	TX	Galveston	84-25	2335	U.S. Army Post Hosp.
PA	Philadelphia	51-262	2094	Sailors Home	TX	Harris	101-44	2344	Texas National Guard Headquarters
PA	Philadelphia	51-286	2096	U.S.M.C. Recruiting Stat.					
PA	Philadelphia	51-98	2114	U.S. Naval Home	TX	Hays	105-1	2340	Soldiers, Sailors, and Marines Memorial Hosp.
PA	Philadelphia	51-98	2114	U.S. Veterans Bureau Hosp.					
PA	York	67-119	2167	Army Reserve Depot	TX	Hidalgo	108-24	2356	Camp McAllen
PR	Cayey Mun.	57-16	2645	Naval Radio Stat.	TX	Kerr	133-6	2367	U.S. Veterans Hosp. No. 93
RI	Bristol	1-5	2168	Rhode Island Soldiers Home	TX	Kinney	136-3	2367	Fort Clark
RI	Newport	3-8	2170	Block Island Coast Guard Stat.	TX	Kinney	136-3	2367	U.S. Army Post Hosp.
RI	Newport	3-30	2170	Brenton Point Coast Guard Stat.	TX	Presidio	189-4	2385	Fort D.A. Russell
					TX	Presidio	189-4	2385	U.S. Army Post Hosp..
RI	Newport	3-31	2170	Fort Adams	TX	Starr	214-4	2391	Fort Ringold
RI	Newport	3-2	2169	Fort Getty	TX	Starr	214-4	2391	U.S. Army Post Hosp.
RI	Newport	3-2	2169	Fort Greble	TX	Terrell	222-2	2399	Army Air Service Border Patrol
RI	Newport	3-4	2169	Fort Wetherell	TX	Webb	240-15	2407	Fort McIntosh
RI	Newport	3-8	2170	New Shoreham Coast Guard Stat.	TX	Webb	240-15	2407	U.S. Army Post Hosp.
					UT	Salt Lake	18-85	2420	Fort Douglas
RI	Newport	3-10	2169	U.S. Naval Hosp.	UT	Salt Lake	18-85	2420	Fort Douglas Hosp.
RI	Newport	3-39	2169	U.S. Naval Magazine	VA	Arlington	7-12	2436	Fort Myer Military Res.
RI	Newport	3-38	2169	U.S. Naval Sea Plane Base	VA	Elizabeth City	28-8	2442	Fort Monroe
RI	Newport	3-19	2169	U.S. Naval Torpedo Stat.	VA	Elizabeth City	28-10	2442	National Home For Disabled Soldiers
RI	Newport	3-11	2169	U.S. Navel Training Stat.					
RI	Washington	5-7	2182	Fort Phillip Kearney	VA	Elizabeth City	28-8	2442	U.S. Army Hosp.
RI	Washington	5-12	2182	Green Hill Coast Guard Stat.	VA	Fairfax	30-19	2442	Camp Humphreys Military Res.
RI	Washington	5-6	2182	Narragansett Coast Guard Stat.	VA	Fairfax	30-20	2442	Fort Hunt Military Res.

ST	County	E.D.	Roll	Installation/Institution	ST	County	E.D.	Roll	Installation/Institution
VA	King George	50-3	2448	Naval Proving Grounds	WA	Kitsap	18-27	2506	U.S. Torpedo Stat.
VA	Nansemond	62-13	2451	U.S. Army Base	WA	Kitsap	18-50	2506	Veterans Home
VA	Norfolk City	112-6	2469	St. Helena Government Res. (U.S. Navy Yard)	WA	Kitsap	18-51	2506	Veterans Home
VA	Norfolk City	112-99	2472	U.S. Army Supply Base	WA	Lincoln	22-30	2508	Fort Spokane Indian Hosp.
VA	Norfolk City	112-28	2470	U.S. Coast Guard	WA	Pacific	25-12	2509	Fort Canby
VA	Norfolk City	112-100	2472	U.S. Naval Base	WA	Pacific	25-4	2509	Fort Columbia
VA	Portsmouth City	114-33	2474	U.S. Navy Hosp.	WA	Pacific	25-18	2509	Klipsan Beach Coast Guard Stat.
VA	Portsmouth City	114-34	2473	U.S. Navy Yard	WA	Pacific	25-34	2509	U.S. Coast Guard (Patrol Boat)
VA	Prince George	75-5	2456	Camp Lee	WA	Pacific	25-22	2509	U.S. Coast Guard (Stat.)
VA	Princess Anne	77-8	2456	Fort Story Military Res.	WA	Pacific	25-35	2509	U.S.Public Health Service 3d Class Relief Stat. No. 334
VA	Princess Anne	77-7	2456	U.S Naval Rifle Range	WA	Pierce	27-4	2509	Fort Lewis Military Res.
VA	Richmond City	116-29	2476	Soldier's Home (R.E. Lee Camp No. 1)	WA	Pierce	27-139	2511	U.S. Veterans Hosp. No. 94 (No. 57)
VA	Warwick	95-8	2464	Camp Eustis	WA	Pierce	27-4	2509	U.S. Veterans Hosp. No. 94 (No. 94)
VA	York	100-3	2464	Navy Mine Depot	WA	Pierce	27-81	2510	Washington State Soldiers Home
VI	St. Croix Island	0-4	2668	U.S. Army and Navy Reservations	WA	Skagit	29-3	2513	Coast Guard Stat. Base No. 12
VI	St. Thomas Island	0-24	2668	U.S. Army and Navy Reservations	WA	Spokane	32-173	2518	Fort George Wright
VT	Bennington	2-3	2426	Vermont Soldiers and Sailors Home	WA	Spokane	32-173	2518	U.S. Army Post Hosp.
VT	Bennington	2-4	2426	Vermont Soldiers and Sailors Home	WA	Spokane	32-84	2517	U.S. Veterans Bureau
WA	Clallam	5-21	2486	U.S. Coast Guard Stat.	WA	Walla Walla	36-52	2523	Fort Walla Walla
WA	Clallam	5-28	2486	U.S. Coast Guard Stat.	WA	Walla Walla	36-43	2523	U.S. Veterans Hosp. No. 85
WA	Clallam	5-28	2486	U.S. Coast Guard Stat.	WI	Milwaukee	40-311	2598	National Home For Disabled Soldiers
WA	Clark	6-53	2485	U.S. Army Post Hosp.	WI	Monroe	41-3	2601	Camp McCoy U.S. Military Res.
WA	Grays Harbor	14-68	2489	Grays Harbor Coast Guard Stat.	WI	Walworth	64-20	2615	Northwestern Military and Naval Academy
WA	Island	15-15	2489	Fort Casey	WI	Waukesha	67-46	2617	U.S. Veterans Hosp. No. 37
WA	Island	15-15	2489	U.S. Army Post Hosp.	WI	Waupaca	68-12	2617	Wisconsin Veterans Home
WA	Jefferson	16-13	2487	Fort Flagler	WY	Albany	1-1	2621	Fort Francis K. Warren Maneuver and Target Range
WA	Jefferson	16-22	2487	Fort Worden	WY	Albany	1-2	2621	Fort Francis K. Warren Maneuver and Target Range
WA	Jefferson	16-13	2487	U.S. Army Post Hosp.	WY	Albany	1-24	2621	Fort Francis K. Warren Maneuver and Target Range
WA	Jefferson	16-22	2487	U.S. Army Post Hosp.	WY	Fremont	7-18	2622	Fort Washakie Hosp.
WA	Jefferson	16-19	2487	U.S. Quarantine Stat.	WY	Johnson	10-4	2622	Wyoming Soldiers and Sailors Home Hosp.
WA	King	17-39	2494	Fort Lawton	WY	Laramie	11-15	2623	Fort Francis E. Warren Military Res.
WA	King	17-39	2494	U.S. Army Post Hosp.	WY	Laramie	11-15	2623	U.S. Army Post Hosp.
WA	King	17-163	2500	U.S. Coast Guard (Cutters and Lighthouse Ships)	WY	Sheridan	17-6	2624	U.S. Veterans Hosp. No. 86 (For Insane)
WA	King	17-167	2500	U.S. Coast Guard (Office)					
WA	Kitsap	18-38	2506	Fort Ward					
WA	Kitsap	18-16	2506	Naval Ammunition Depot					
WA	Kitsap	18-38	2506	U.S. Army Post Hosp.					
WA	Kitsap	18-53	2506	U.S. Naval Hosp.					
WA	Kitsap	18-53	2506	U.S. Navy Yard					

Descriptions of Native American Tribes

Eastern Algonquians – This group includes all of the Algonquian tribes formerly inhabiting the area of the present New England States, Long Island, and other parts of New York adjacent to the New England States. These Indians are now widely scattered and practically all have large admixtures of white or Negro blood. The total number enumerated in 1930 was 2,015, of whom 813 were in Wisconsin and 761 in Maine. In 1910, the corresponding total was 2,027, with 693 in Wisconsin and 634 in Maine. Those in Wisconsin in 1910 were mainly Stockbridges, a tribe formerly living in western Massachusetts, and Brothertons, a name applied to a group of fragments of Eastern Algonquian tribes which united to form a community in Oneida County, New York, and later moved to Wisconsin. The Maine Algonquians belong mainly to the Passamaquoddy and Penobscot tribes and are located in Penobscot and Washington Counties. The Indians of Massachusetts and Rhode Island, of whom 184 were reported as Eastern Algonquians and 937 without tribal designation, were probably of the Mashpee and Wampanoag tribes. These tribes are all of mixed Indian, white, and Negro blood. Of all the Eastern Algonquians returned in 1930, only 144, or 7.1 percent, were reported as full blood, and it is very doubtful if any are entirely free from white or Negro blood.

Assiniboin – This tribe is probably a detached fragment of the Yanktonai Sioux. The early habitat of the tribe was about Rainy Lake and Lake of the Woods. They moved gradually westwards to Montana and Saskatchewan. The Assiniboin were estimated before 1836 to number from 8,000 to 10,000. This number was reduced by epidemics and wars to 2,365 in 1880, after their location on the Fort Belknap and Fort Peck Reservations in Montana. In 1930 the number enumerated was 1,581, of which number 1,467 were in Montana, mainly in Blaine, Roosevelt, and Valley Counties. This represents an increase from 1,253 in 1910. In 1930, 39.5 percent of the Assinboin were reported as full blood.

Bannock – This is one of the northern tribes of the Shoshonean family whose early habitat was in southern Idaho, southwestern Montana, and northwestern Wyoming. The tribal name has been rather loosely applied in the past and in some estimates of numbers may have covered a large part of the related Shoshoni. The Bannock are now mostly located with a part of the Shoshoni on the Fort Hall Reservation in Idaho. The number returned as Bannock in 1930 was 415, of whom 313 were in Idaho, mainly in Bingham and Bannock Counties. The 1910 census tabulated 413 as Bannock, of whom 363 were in Idaho. In 1930, 199, or 48.0 percent, of the Bannock were returned as full blood.

Catawba – The Catawba tribe is the surviving remnant of all the detached tribes of the Siouan stock. The early habitat of the tribe was in North and South Carolina in the vicinity of the upper and middle Catawba and Wateree Rivers. At present, the Catawba are located on a small reservation in York and Lancaster Counties, South Carolina. In 1930 the number returned as Catawba was 166, of which number 159 were in South Carolina. In 1910 the Catawba numbered 124, with 99 in South Carolina. Nearly all are now of mixed blood.

Cayuse and Molala – These two tribes constituted the Waiilatpuan stock as shown in the 1910 census tabulation. The Cayuse formerly occupied an area in northeastern Oregon and a portion of southern Walla Walla County, Washington, almost surrounded by the Shahaptians, particularly the Nez Perces, with whom they were closely associated. The Molala, when first known to Europeans, lived on the west slope of the Cascades in Clackamas and Marion Counties, Oregon. The Cayuse are now mainly on the Umatilla Reservation in Oregon, while the remnant of the Molala, numbering only 31 in 1910, are scattered through the Cascade Mountains. The total number enumerated in the tribal group in 1930 was 199, of whom 193 were in Oregon, with 163 in Umatilla County. In 1910 there were 329 in the two tribes, of whom 302 were in Oregon. Of those reported in 1930, 169, or 84.9 percent, were returned as full blood.

Cherokee – In gross numbers, the Cherokee is the largest Indian tribe in the United States and is geographically by far the most widely distributed. However, even in 1910, only 21.9 percent of the Cherokee claimed to be full-blood Indians and nearly 62 percent were reported as more than one-half white. As a strictly "Indian" tribe, the Navaho, with a tribal membership of over 40,000, nearly all of whom are of full blood, is more significant than the Cherokee, with 45,238 members, of whom only 17.8 percent claim to be full-blood Indians. The Cherokee were driven forcibly out of their early habitat in the southern Alleghenies in 1838 and settled on a large reservation in Indian Territory. A few hundred who eluded the military dragnet remained in the Alleghenies and were eventually settled on the Qualla Reservation in Swain County, North Carolina. The number of Indians returned as Cherokee on the schedules from North Carolina in 1930 was 14,094, but this number was arbitrarily reduced to 1,963 by assigning those returned from the eastern counties to the group of "Virginia-Carolina Indians." This smaller number still represents an increase of nearly 40 percent in the 20-year period. The Cherokee of Oklahoma in the same period have increased from 29,610 to 40,904, an increase of 11,294, or 38.1 percent. Indians were returned as Cherokee in 1930 from 44 states, or all except Maine, New Hampshire, Rhode Island, Delaware, and the District of Columbia.

Chickasaw – The Chickasaw were first known to the whites in the northern part of the present State of Mississippi. They began to move west of the Mississippi River early in the nineteenth century and in 1855 were given a separate reservation in Indian Territory. The number enumerated as Chickasaw in 1930 was 4,745, an increase from 4,204 in 1910. Of the population in 1930, the number in Oklahoma was 4,685. Of these, 829 were enumerated in Johnston County, 764 in Pontotoc County, and 611 in Bryan County. The

Chickasaw are now mainly of mixed blood, only 24.6 percent having claimed to be of full blood in 1930.

Chippewa – This is the largest of the Algonquian tribes and the fourth largest Indian tribe within the boundaries of the United States. The Chippewa were woodland Indians and originally occupied much of the present State of Michigan and parts of the northern shores of Lakes Superior and Huron. Many of the tribe moved westward after their first contact with Europeans and are at present scattered over a large area, in a number of reservations, and mixed with the white population. The number of Chippewa Indians showed an increase in Minnesota, Wisconsin, North Dakota, and Montana, but a considerable decrease in Michigan. The decrease in Michigan, however, was probably due to failure to return the Indian population of many areas by tribe. The Chippewa have had a large admixture of white blood ever since the early days of French settlement in the region of the Great Lakes. As compared with 34.5 percent in 1910, only 18.7 percent are now reported as full blood. Even this probably includes as full blood many who are only predominantly of Indian blood.

Choctaw – This tribe is the largest of the Muskhogean stock, and with the exception of the Cherokee, the largest of the "Five Civilized Tribes." The early habitat of the Choctaw was in southern Mississippi and Alabama. The greater part of the tribe moved to the west when their lands were opened for white settlement, but a few remained behind. The total number enumerated in 1930 was 17,757, an increase from 15,917 in 1910. Of these, 16,641 were in Oklahoma, with the largest numbers in McCurtain, Pittsburg, Bryan, Choctaw, and Le Flore Counties. There were also 624 in Mississippi, 190 in Louisiana, and the remainder scattered over 25 other States. The Choctaw are largely of mixed blood, although 32.3 percent claimed to be of full blood in 1930. There is a considerable admixture of Negro blood. Many of the Indians of Muskhogean stock acquired Negro slaves before their migration westward, and the descendants of these slaves have remained in close association with the Indian tribes to which the masters of their ancestors belonged.

Chumashan Stock – This is a small linguistic stock which at an early date occupied a considerable area of the coast of Santa Barbara and Ventura Counties in California, and some of the islands off the coast. There were formerly several tribes, but all except the Santa Ynez are either extinct or practically so. The number returned as belonging to this stock was 14 in 1930 and 38 in 1910. It is possible that others were returned as "Mission" Indians and so lost to the tribal classification.

Cocopa – This is one of the southern tribes of the Yuman stock, occupying the region around the mouth of the Colorado River in Arizona, California, and Lower California. A part of the survivors of the tribe are gathered on small reservations in the extreme southwestern corner of Yuma County, Arizona. Others are scattered through their old habitat. The number of Cocopa enumerated in 1930 was 99, of which number 89 were in Arizona, with 88 in Yuma County. The other 10 were all in Imperial County, California. The number returned in 1930 represents a sharp decrease from the Cocopa population of 245 in 1910.

Comanche – This is one of the best known of the Shoshonean tribes, because of its easterly range, which brought its members into frequent conflict with the white settlers. The Comanche separated at an early date from the Shoshoni and moved southeastward to the Great Plains, where they formed an alliance with the Kiowa and the Kiowa Apache. In the early part of the nineteenth century, they, with their allies, occupied a large area from western Kansas south to the Mexican border. Since 1875, they have been located with the Kiowa and Kiowa Apache on a reservation in Oklahoma. The number returned as Comanche in 1930 was 1,423, of whom 1,390 were in Oklahoma, mainly in Comanche, Cotton, and Caddo Counties. In 1910, there were 1,171, of whom 1,160 were in Oklahoma. In 1930 there were 602, or 42.3 percent, who were returned as full blood.

Costanoan Stock – The Costanoan Indians, known locally as Santa Cruz, constituted an independent linguistic stock. Their habitat extended along the California Coast from San Francisco Bay to Monterey and west to the San Joaquin River. Provision was made in the tribal code for the enumeration of the Santa Cruz Indians in 1930, but none were returned under that name. It is possible that a few were returned as "Mission" Indians and so could not be classified by tribe. In 1910, 17 of the tribe were enumerated, of whom four were of full blood.

Creek – The Creek constituted originally a confederacy rather than a single tribe. Their habitat was south and east of that of the Choctaws in Alabama, Georgia, and Florida. They moved to Indian Territory between 1836 and 1840. The Alibamu of Texas and Louisiana and the Koasati of Louisiana, two small Muskhogean tribes, were combined for convenience with the Creek in 1930. The total number enumerated in 1930 was 9,083, as compared with 7,341 in 1910. This number in 1910 included 298 Alibamu and 98 Koasati. In 1930 there were 8,607 Creek in Oklahoma, most of whom were in the counties of McIntosh, Hughes, Okmulgee, and Okfuskee. There were also 180 in Texas, of whom 176 were in Polk County, and 134 in Louisiana, most of whom were probably Alibamu and Koasati. More than half of the Creek claimed full blood in 1930, the same proportion as in 1910. In 1910 there were 565 with Negro blood.

Crow – The tribe formed the extreme northwest extension of the Siouan stock. The tribal habitat was originally in eastern Montana and the Dakotas, but before they were first known to the whites they had moved westward to the base of the Rocky Mountains. They have for many years been located on the Crow Reservation in Montana. In 1930 there were 1,674 Indians enumerated as Crow, of whom 1,625 were in Montana, with 1,593 in Big Horn County. The Office of Indian Affairs in 1932 enumerated 1,760 on the Crow Reservation. The number enumerated in 1910 was 1,799, indicating a decrease in the 20-year period, continuing a downward trend in population which has been apparent over a period of nearly 70 years. In the 1930 enumeration, 61.6 percent were returned as full blood.

Dakota – Including all tribes or divisions of tribes commonly known as Sioux or Dakota, this is the third largest of all the Indian tribes in the United States, exceeded in number only by the Cherokee and the Navaho. The habitat of the Dakota, when first known to the white settlers, covered the greater part of the present states of Minnesota and North and South Dakota, with at least one division ranging north into Canada. The Dakota is properly a group of seven tribes, to which the Assiniboin are sometimes added as an eighth tribe. Of the tribes of the Dakota, the Mdewakanton and the Wahpekute, generally considered together as the Santee Sioux, are now located on the Santee Reservation in Knox County, Nebraska, and in the Flandeau Jurisdiction in South Dakota, with scattered groups in Minnesota. The Sisseton Sioux are now mainly on the Sisseton Reservation in eastern North and South Dakota. The Wahpeton Sioux have long been closely associated with the Sisseton, and are located with them on the Sisseton Reservation. The Yankton Sioux were formerly in Minnesota, but moved southwest into South Dakota and parts of Iowa. They are now mainly on the Yankton Reservation in South Dakota. The Yanktonai Sioux were perhaps originally a part of the Yankton tribe. They moved west from Minnesota into North and South Dakota. They are now located on several reservations in North and South Dakota and Montana. The Teton Sioux are the largest of the seven Dakota tribes and exceed in number all of the other six combined. This great tribe, when first known, occupied a large area from the Mississippi River in Minnesota, west through North and South Dakota, and northern Nebraska. The Teton Sioux are now located on various reservations, mainly in North and South Dakota. The total number of Dakota enumerated in 1930 was 25, 934. Of these, 20,918 were in South Dakota, with the largest numbers in Shannon, Todd, Corson, and Dewey Counties; 2,307 in North Dakota, mainly in Sioux and Benson Counties; 1,251 in Montana, with 1,079 in Roosevelt County; 690 in Nebraska, mainly in Knox County; 311 in Minnesota; and 144 in Oklahoma. Altogether, there were 29 States which reported at least one Indian of the Dakota group. In 1910 the number enumerated in all of the Dakota tribes combined was 22,778, of whom 14,284 were Teton, 1,539 Santee, 2,514 Sisseton and Wahpeton, 2,088 Yankton, 1,357 Yanktonai, and 996 reported as Sioux without other tribal designations of the Dakota in 1930, 53.3 percent were reported as full blood. In 1910 the Santee Sioux reported proportionally the greatest and the Yanktonai the least admixture of white blood.

Delaware – The Delaware confederacy at the time of white settlement occupied a large area in Delaware, eastern Pennsylvania, New Jersey, and southern New York. They moved successively west to Ohio, Indiana, Missouri, and finally to Kansas, Oklahoma, and Texas. The great majority of the remaining members of the tribe are now in Oklahoma, mainly in Craig, Nowata, and Washington Counties. The number enumerated in 1930, including the related Munsee, was 971, as compared with 985 in 1910. Only 20.2 percent were reported as full blood, as compared with 29.7 percent in 1910.

Diegueno – The habitat of this tribe was in the extreme southwestern corner of the United States, in the western part of San Diego County, California. In 1930 the Census enumerated 322 Indians as Diegueno, of whom 321 were in California, and of these, 306 were in San Diego County. This number represents a decrease from 756 in 1910, all in California. This decrease, however, may not be quite as great as indicated, as the Diegueno should be considered as a group of small tribes rather than a single tribe, and some may have been returned under local names or simply as "Mission" Indians. In contrast to the other tribes of the Yuman stock, the Diegueno in 1930 were to a considerable extent mixed with white blood. Only 57.8 percent were returned as of full blood in 1930, as compared with more than 90 percent of the Northern Yumans, the Maricopa, and the Mohave.

Gros Ventres (Atsina) – This tribe is probably an offshoot of the Arapaho. The Gros Ventres, since their first contact with the white race, have always lived in the present area of Montana. For some 60 years they have been located on the Fort Belknap Reservation in Blaine and Phillips Counties, Montana. The name Gros Ventres has been applied to two wholly distinct tribes, the Atsina, the Gros Ventres of the Prairie, and the Hidatsa, the Gros Ventres of the Missouri. At the census of 1930, both tribes were indiscriminately returned as Gros Ventres, and the separation was made entirely on a geographic basis. The number classed as Gros Ventres (Atsina) was 631, as compared with 510 in 1910. Of these, 615 in 1930 and 503 in 1910 were in Montana.

Hidatsa – The Hidatsa and the Crow were perhaps originally one tribe, with a habitat in North Dakota. After the separation of the Crow from the Hidatas, the latter moved southwest and allied themselves with the Mandan. The Hidatsa are popularly known by the name of Gros Ventres, thus confusing them with the Atsina, an Algonquian tribe which has the same popular name. In the 1930 census, both of these tribes were returned as Gros Ventres, and it was necessary to separate them on a geographical basis. Those in North and South Dakota were separately tabulated as Hidatsa, while those in Montana and other states were assumed to be Atsina. Since the scattered Indians returned as Gros Ventres were mostly south and west of the State, this separation was probably the best that could have been made. The two Indians reported as "Gros Ventres" in Oklahoma, however, may be Hidatsa. The number so tabulated as Hidatsa was 528, with 519 in North Dakota. This corresponds reasonably well with the 644 "Gros Ventres" enumerated in 1932 by the Office of Indian Affairs on the Fort Berthold Reservation in North Dakota and also with the 547 Hidatsa enumerated by the Census in 1910. the Hidatsa population has changed very little since 1875, when they were supposed to number about 600. The Hidatsa claiming full blood numbered 310 in 1930, or 58.7 percent of the total.

Hopi – The Hopi are Pueblo Indians who have occupied their present villages in Arizona for at least 300 or 400 years. They are peaceful and industrious, and have become famous for their artistic pottery, basketry, and weaving. These characteristics are in striking contrast to those of the war-like Comanche. The number of Hopi enumerated in 1930 was 2,752, of whom 2,701 were in Arizona, with 2,292 in Navajo County. The number returned as Hopi in 1910 was 2,009. In 1932, the Office of Indian Affairs enumerated 2,786 as Hopi and before 1910 the Indian Office estimated the number in the tribe variously from 1,800 to 2,100. The increase of 36.9 percent in 20 years may

therefore be accepted as actual. The Hopi have very little admixture of white blood, 97.2 percent in 1930 having been returned as full-blood Indians.

Iowa – Next to the Catawba, this is the smallest of the Siouan tribes separately tabulated in 1930, numbering only 176, with 83 in Richardson County, Nebraska, and 71 in Oklahoma, mainly in Lincoln and Noble Counties. The traditional habitat of the Iowa was in southern Wisconsin, but when first known to Europeans they were located in Iowa. After several migrations, the greater part of the Iowa were located on the Iowa Reservation in Brown County, Kansas, from which between 1910 and 1930 the majority appear to have crossed the State line into Nebraska. All of the Iowa in Nebraska are of mixed blood, while of those in Oklahoma, 52 still claim to be of full blood.

Iroquoian Stock – Including those enumerated as Iroquoians who are predominantly of white blood, this is the largest of all the linguistic stocks in the United States. All tribes of this stock are, however, civilized and are rapidly becoming absorbed in the white population. At the beginning of the seventeenth century, the Iroquoians occupied two separate areas, the northern comprising most of the states of New York, western New Jersey, and parts of Pennsylvania, West Virginia, and Ohio, also parts of the Province of Ontario west to Lake Huron. The southern habitat extended over the southern Alleghenies in Virginia, the Carolinas, Georgia, and eastern Tennessee. In the North, the western Iroquoians, the Erie and Huron, were broken up and absorbed or dispersed at an early date by their kinsmen of the Iroquois Confederacy in western New York. The New York tribes are now located in New York and Wisconsin. The remnant of the Huron, known as the Wyandot, are in Oklahoma. The southern Iroquoians were of two separate groups, the Tuscarora, Meherrin, and Nottoway of eastern North Carolina and southeastern Virginia, and the Cherokee of the southern Alleghenies and eastern Tennessee. The Tuscarora later united with the Iroquois in New York. The Meherrin and Nottoway have been absorbed in other tribes. Of the Cherokee, a part still remains in their old habitat, but the great majority are in Oklahoma.

Iroquois – In this tribal group are included the five nations of the once powerful Iroquois Confederacy—the Cayuga, the Mohawk, the Oneida, the Onondaga, and the Seneca—together with the Tuscorora, which was at first itself a confederacy of tribes and later was incorporated with the Iroquois confederacy to form the "Six Nations." Of these six tribes, the Seneca in 1910 was the largest, with an enumerated population of 2,907. Of these, 2,485 were in New York. There were 2,436 of the Oneida, of whom 2,107 were in Wisconsin, and 211 in New York. There were 81 Cayuga, with 53 in New York; 368 Mohawk with 320 in New York; 365 Onondaga with 327 in New York; and 400 Tuscarora with 382 in New York. In addition, there were 1,219 St. Regis Indians, a group of mixed Iroquois living on the International boundary between St. Lawrence and Franklin Counties, New York, and Canada. In all, the Iroquois group comprising the descendants of the "Six Nations," numbered 7,837 in 1910. By 1930, the Indian population enumerated as Iroquois had declined to 6,866, but the number of Indians in New York not reported by tribe increased from 886 to 1,875. Of the Indians in Cattaraugus County who are mainly Seneca and Cayuga, 80 were returned as Iroquois, three as of other tribes, and 883 without tribal designation. It is probable, therefore, that the Iroquois population remianed practically the same as in 1910. Of the Iroquois in New York, 36.1 percent, and of those in Wisconsin, 74.5 percent, were returned in 1930 as full blood. Outside of New York and Wisconsin, there were 340 Iroquois returned from Oklahoma, 81 from Pennsylvania, and 78 from Michigan. Geographically, the Iroquois are more widely distributed than any other tribal group except the Cherokee. In 1930, members of the tribal group were reported from 36 different States and the District of Columbia.

Kalapooian Stock – The tribes of this linguistic stock formerly occupied the greater part of the Willamette Valley in Oregon. At the census of 1910, seven tribes of this stock were enumerated, with a combined population of only 106. In 1930 the stock was tabulated only as a whole, and only 45 were reported. Of these, only 11 were returned as full blood.

Kansa – The traditional habitat of the Kansa was in southern Illinois and Indiana, but in the eighteenth century they were living in Kansas. In 1873 the tribe was removed to the Kaw Reservation in Oklahoma. The number enumerated in 1930 was 318, of which number 313 were in Oklahoma, with 237 in Kay County. In 1910 there were 238 enumerated as Kansa, 232 in Oklahoma and six in Kansas. Of these, 71 in 1910 and 76 in 1930 claimed full blood.

Karok Stock – This linguistic stock is represented by only one tribe, known as Karok or Orleans. Their habitat in historic times has always been in the valley of the Klamath River. The number returned as belonging to this tribe was 755 in 1930, as compared with 775 in 1910. Of these, 475 were in Siskiyou and 230 in Humboldt Counties in California. Nearly all are of mixed blood.

Keresan Stock – The Keresan is one of the three "pueblo" stocks of the southwest. The stock is composed of seven pueblos or tribes which have been established in the same locations in northern New Mexico for at least 400 years. The largest of these pueblos is the Laguna in Valencia County. The population of Keresan stock in 1930 was 4,134, an increase from 4,027 in 1910. Of these, 4,092 were in the three counties of Valencia, Sandoval, and McKinley in New Mexico. The population has shown very little change, at least since 1860. the Keresans have a comparatively little admixture of white or Negro blood.

Kickapoo – This is a small but well-known tribe formerly living in Wisconsin, but now located in the Kickapoo Reservation in Brown County, Kansas, and in Lincoln and Pottawatomie Counties, Oklahoma. The number enumerated in 1930 was 523, as compared with 348 in 1910. Perhaps as many more are located in the State of Chihuahua in Mexico. Of the Kickapoo in Kansas, only 14.7 percent were returned as full blood, but of those in Oklahoma, 95.0 percent were so returned.

Kiowan Stock – The Kiowa, an important tribe of Plains Indians, has been considered as an independent linguistic stock, although it is now classed by many ethnologists with the Tanoans of New Mexico. The early habitat of the Kiowa was in southern Montana and northwestern Wyoming, but they later moved to western Nebraska and eastern Colorado. They have long been intimately associated with the Kiowa Apache, an Athapaskan tribe. Early in the nineteenth century, these tribes formed a confederacy with the Shoshonean Comanche, and in 1863 they were settled with the Comanche on a reservation in Oklahoma. The number returned at the census of 1930 was 1,050, a decrease from 1,126 in 1910. This is, however, probably an under-enumeration, as the Office of Indian Affairs reports 1,951 Kiowa on the reservation in 1932. There were 1,259

Indians of "tribe not reported" in Caddo, Comanche, and Kiowa Counties, some of whom were undoubtedly of the Kiowa tribe. The Kiowa have a considerable admixture of white blood, but the majority were returned as full blood Indians in 1930.

Klamath and Modoc – These two tribes, separately shown in the 1910 tabulation, but combined in 1930, constituted the Lutuamian stock in the earlier classification of stocks and tribes. The Klamath Indians formerly lived in Klamath County, Oregon, around Klamath Lake. The Modoc formed the most southerly tribe of the stock, with a habitat in northern California and southern Oregon. The Klamath are now divided between the Klamath Reservation in Oregon and the Hoopa Valley Reservation in California. The Modoc are mainly on the Klamath Reservation in Oregon, although a few were taken in 1872-73 to the Quapaw Reservation in Oklahoma. The number enumerated in 1930 in the two tribes combined was 2,034, as compared with a total of 978 in 1910. The numbers, both in 1910 and in 1930, correspond approximately with the enumerations of the Office of Indian Affairs in 1909 and 1932. These tribes both have a large admixture of white blood, and the 1910 report indicated some Negro admixture in the Klamath tribe. The 1930 enumeration showed 37.8 percent of full blood.

Kusan Stock – This stock is represented by a single small tribe, the Kusa, or Coos Bay Indians. The earliest known habitat of this tribe was near Coos Bay in Oregon. The number enumerated in 1930 was 107, as compared with 93 in 1910. Of these, 99 were in Oregon, with 83 in Coos County. Only eight were returned as full blood.

Kutenaian Stock – The Kutenai tribe is considered as an independent linguistic stock. Their traditional home was east of the Rocky Mountains in Montana and Alberta, but for more than a hundred years they have lived west of the mountains in British Columbia, Idaho, and western Montana. Most of the tribe in the United States are now located in the Kootenai Reservation in Boundary County in Idaho, and on the Flathead Reservation in Lake County, Montana. The number enumerated in 1930 was 287, a sharp decrease from 538 in 1910. Of the 1930 population, 185 were in Montana and 101 in Idaho. The Idaho Kutenai were nearly all returned as full blood, but of those in Montana only 30.8 percent were full blood.

Maidu Stock – The Maidu are classed as a separate linguistic stock. Their habitat in the past, as in the present, has been in northeastern California. They are now widely scattered throughout this area and the great majority have been lost to the tribal designation in the census classification. Only 93 were returned as Maidu in 1930, as compared with 1,100 in 1910. The Office of Indian Affairs enumerated 195 Maidu in 1932, most of whom were on the Round Valley Reservation in Mendocino County. As none were returned by the census enumerators from this county, these at least should be added to the census figure. The Maidu are mostly of mixed blood, and many enumerated as Indians in 1910 may have been enumerated as white in 1930.

Mandan – The Mandan, when first known to the white settlers, were living on the Missouri River in central North Dakota, but their traditional habitat was east of the Mississippi, perhaps in northern Wisconsin. They are now located with the Arikara and Hidatsa on the Fort Berthold Reservation in Dunn and McLean Counties, North Dakota.

The Mandan numbered 271 in 1930. Of this number, 258 were in North Dakota. There were 209 of the tribe enumerated in 1910, of whom 197 were in North Dakota. Of the total in 1930, 176 were returned as full blood.

Maricopa – The Maricopa lived along the lower portion of the Gila River in Arizona, in close association with the Pima. They have been located with the Pima for many years on the Gila River Reservation. There were 310 enumerated as Maricopa in 1930, of whom 295 were in Arizona and of these, 287 were in Maricopa County. In 1910 there were 386, of whom 382 were in Arizona. The Office of Indian Affairs, however, reported 579 as Maricopa in 1932, of whom 565 were resident on the Gila River Reservation.

Menominee – This tribe in the seventeenth century lived in northern Michigan and Wisconsin, just south of the lands of the Chippewa, although they appear to have been more closely related to the Sauk, Fox, and Kickapoo than to the Chippewa and Ottawa. Nearly all of the tribe now live on the Menominee Reservation in Shawano and Oconto Counties, Wisconsin. The number enumerated in 1930 was 1,969, as compared with 1,422 in 1910. These numbers check very closely with the enumerations of the Office of Indian Affairs. In 1930 the number of Menominee enumerated in Shawano and Oconto Counties was 1,889, as compared with 1,855 enumerated in 1932 on the Menominee Reservation. The tribe is no larger than at any other time in the last 70 years, but only 25.2 percent were returned as full blood in 1930, as compared with 49.5 percent in 1910.

Miami and Illinois – This is a group of small Algonquian tribes made up of the Miami and the remnants of the Wea, Piankashaw, and Peoria. The number enumerated in 1930 was 284, as compared with 360 in 1910. Of these, 173 in 1930 were located in Ottawa County, Oklahoma, and 47 in Indiana. Only 21 of this group of tribes (17 in Oklahoma and 4 in Indiana) were returned as full blood.

Miwok Stock – In the 1910 census, three tribes of this stock were separately enumerated as the Marin, Middle Town, and Miwok. These tribes occupied three separate areas in central California. The total number returned in 1930 was 491, a decrease from 699 in 1910. The largest groups in 1930 were in Kern and Tuolumne Counties. The Miwok tribes are largely of mixed blood and are probably approaching extinction as distinguishable Indian tribes.

Mohave – The habitat of the Mohave was along the Colorado River in the present area of Mohave County, Arizona. They are now located mainly on the Colorado River and Fort Mohave Reservations in Arizona. There were 854 of the tribe enumerated in 1930, of whom 574 were in Arizona, with 345 in Yuma County and 112 in Mohave County; and 277 in California, of whom 255 were in San Bernardino County. The Census of 1910 reported 1,058 Mohave, 667 in Arizona, and 389 in California. The Indian Office enumerated 769 Mohave in Arizona in 1932, not including Indians of Mohave and other tribal mixture. Nearly all of the Mohave were returned as of full racial blood in 1930.

Mono-Paviotso – This tribal group was reported in 1910 as three tribes, the Mono, Panamint, and Paviotso. The early habitat of the Mono was in Mono and Inyo Counties, California, and Esmeralda County, Nevada. The Mono still range through this area and have never been gathered on a reservation. The Panamint were represented in 1910 by a small band of 10 Indians in Inyo County, California. The Paviotso is one of the largest tribes or tribal groups of the Shoshonean stock. The Paviotso occupied, and still occupy, a wide range in southeastern Oregon, western Nevada, and northeastern California. Some of them are locally known as Snakes and others are indiscriminately called Paiute. In the 1910 tabulation, the Paviotso were arbitrarily separated from the Paiute by geographic location, but in 1930 this group includes only those returned on the schedules as Mono or Paviotso. These are shown separately in the tables for age, blood, school attendance, and illiteracy, and combined with the Paiute in the tables showing geographic distribution. In 1930 only 406 were actually returned in the Mono-Paviotso group. Of these, 382 were in California, mainly in Fresno County. In 1910 the number classified as Paviotso alone was 3,038. The greater part of these were obviously returned as Paiute in 1930.

Muskhogean Stock – The Muskhogeans constitute the fifth largest of the Indian linguistic stocks in the United States. The early habitat of the Muskhogean tribes was in Mississippi, Alabama, western and southern Georgia, and northern Florida. The Census of 1930 differentiated four tribes of this stock, the Chickasaw, Choctaw, Creek, and Seminole. In 1910 the Alibamu and Koasati were shown separately, but in 1930 they were tabulated with the Creek.

Omaha – The Omaha belong to the Dhegiha group of the Siouan stock, with the Kansa, Osage, Ponca, and Quapaw. Their traditional habitat was in southern Illinois, but they were found by Europeans in northwestern Iowa, eastern Nebraska, and southern South Dakota. Since about 1860, they have been located on the Omaha Reservation in Thurston County, Nebraska. The census of 1930 enumerated 1,103 Omaha, of whom 1,027 were in Nebraska, and 48 in Oklahoma with the Osage. In 1910 there were 1,105 in the Omaha tribe, with 1,075 in Nebraska and only 5 in Oklahoma.

Osage – The largest tribe of the Dhegiha group of the Siouans was first known to Europeans in the present State of Missouri, although the traditional home of the tribe was in southern Illinois and Indiana. In 1870 the Osage were located on their own reservation in Oklahoma. The discovery of oil on this reservation brought wealth to the Osage tribe and hastened the process of assimilation into the white population. In 1930 there were 2,344 enumerated as Osage, of whom 2,106 were in Oklahoma, with 1,559 in Osage County. The tribe has been widely scattered in recent years, and in 1930 Indians were enumerated as Osage in 21 different states. In 1910 there were only 1,373 Osage classified as such by the Federal Census, but this was probably an under-enumeration, as the Office of Indian Affairs reported 2,100 in the same year. According to the reports of the Indian Office, the Osage population appears to have decreased rapidly from 4,481 in 1870 to 1,509 in 1890. At that time the mixed bloods had reached about 33 percent of the total. Since then, the population has steadily increased, but the number of full bloods has continued to decline. In 1910, 591, or 43.0 percent, claimed to be of full blood, but by 1930 the number of full bloods had declined to 545, or 23.3 percent.

Oto and Missouri – These two tribes with the Iowa come from what is known as the Chiwere group of the Siouan stock. The Missouri are now practically extinct or absorbed into the Oto tribe. The Missouri, when first known to the whites, had moved from their traditional habitat, probably in Wisconsin, to Missouri. The Oto are also supposed to have moved westward before the coming of the white men to Iowa and Nebraska. The Oto, with the remnant of the Missouri, were located on the Otoe Reservation in Oklahoma in 1882. In 1930 the number enumerated in the two tribes was 627, of which number 614 were in Oklahoma, with 376 in Noble County and 170 in Pawnee County. In 1910 the census enumerated 332 Oto and 13 Missouri. The Office of Indian Affairs enumerated 523 on the Otoe Reservation in 1932, including 492 Oto and 31 of mixed Oto and other tribal blood. Of the Oto and Missouri in 1930, more than half were returned as of full blood.

Ottawa – The habitat of the Ottawa when first met by Europeans was along the northern shore of Georgian Bay in Canada. In consequence of Indian wars in the seventeenth century, the Ottawa moved west into Wisconsin, but later many of them moved back into the Lower Peninsula of Michigan. They are now mainly located in Emmet, Charlevoix, and Leelanau Counties, Michigan. A smaller band is located with the Quapaw in Ottawa County, Oklahoma. Another small band was enumerated in Vilas County, Wisconsin. The total number of the Ottawa enumerated in 1930 was 1,745, as compared with 2,717 in 1910. There were also 359 Indians with tribe not reported in Emmet, Charlevoix, and Leelanau Counties, who should probably be added to the number of Ottawa. There has, however, undoubtedly been a definite decrease in the Ottawa population in 20 years. The Ottawa, like the Chippewa and Menominee, are largely mixed with white blood.

Paiute – The tribal name of Paiute has been very loosely applied to several Shoshonean tribes of the interior plateau. It is properly restricted to the Indians of southwestern Utah, southern Nevada, and adjacent portions of California and Arizona. Because of the impossibility of restricting the term in a census enumeration to those properly known by the name, the figures shown for the Paiute should be considered as representing the large group of tribes including the Paviotso. In the 1930 classification, the Chemehuevi, a tribe formerly living along the Colorado River from Needles to Bill Williams Fork, were included with the Paiute. The total number returned in 1930 as Mono, Panamint, Paviotso, Snake, Paiute, or Chemehuevi was 5,060, as compared with 5,631 in 1910. In 1930 the Indians of this group were widely scattered. There were 2,660 in Nevada, mostly in Washoe, Mineral, Lyon, Churchill and Humboldt Counties; 1,531 in California, mainly in Inyo, Fresno, and Mono Counties; 291 in Oregon; 249 in Arizona; 193 in Utah; and 112 in Idaho. Of the total in 1930, 71.4 percent were returned as full blood.

Piman Stock – The habitat of the Indians of Piman stock is in southern Arizona and the States of Sonora and Chihuahua in Mexico. This stock is now grouped by many ethnologists with the Shoshonean and the Mexican Nahuatlan as the Uto-Aztecan family. The most important of the Piman tribes in Arizona are the Papago and the Pima. At the census of 1910, in addition to these two tribes, the Mayo, the Opata, and the Yaqui, were separately shown in the published report. Since these are primarily Mexican tribes, they were included in 1930 in the group designated as Canadian and Mexican tribes.

Papago – The early habitat of the Papago was in southern Arizona from Tucson south across the Mexican border into the State of Sonora. The Papago in the United States have been located for many years on reservations in Pima, Pinal, and Maricopa Counties in Arizona. The number enumerated in 1930 was 5,205, of whom 5,163 were in Arizona. The number enumerated in 1910 was 3,798, of whom all but 13 were in Arizona. Nearly all of the tribe are of full blood.

Pima – The Pima were closely associated with the Papago, and were their neighbors on the north and west in the valleys of the Salt and Gila Rivers. They are now gathered in reservations in Pinal and Maricopa Counties in Arizona. The number enumerated in 1930 was 4,382, of whom 4,322 were in Arizona. In 1910 the number enumerated was 4,236. Nearly all of the Pima were of full blood.

Pomo Stock – The habitat of the Indians of the Pomo stock is in the Coast ranges in the northern part of California. In 1910, five tribes or bands of the Pomo stock were separately tabulated. These were the Pomo, Clear Lake, Gynomehro, Little Lake, and Lower Lake Indians. The number enumerated in 1930 was 1,143, as compared with a total of 1,193, including all five tribes, in 1910. All but nine in 1930 were in California, mainly in Mendocino, Lake, and Sonoma Counties. Slightly more than half were reported as full blood.

Ponca – The traditional habitat of the Ponca was in southern Illinois and Indiana, with the other tribes of the Dhegiha group. Their association with the Omaha was particularly close. The Ponca moved northwest to the Missouri River in Iowa, South Dakota, and Minnesota. They are now located on two reservations, one in Kay County, Oklahoma, and the other in Knox County, Nebraska. The total number enumerated in 1930 was 939, of which number 743 were in Oklahoma. This represents an increase from 875 in 1910. This increase, however, has been entirely in the Oklahoma division, as the Nebraska band declined in numbers from 193 in 1910 to 161 in 1930. Of the Ponca in Oklahoma, 204, or 27.5 percent, were reported as full blood, while of the Nebraska band only 13.7 percent claimed full blood.

Potawatomi – This tribe, when first known, inhabited what is now the Lower Peninsula of Michigan. Later they moved to the Upper Peninsula and then gradually to the south and west to their present locations in Kansas and Oklahoma. The tribe is widely scattered. The greatest concentration is in Jackson County, Kansas, where 573 were enumerated. There were 347 Potawatomi in Pottawatomie County, Oklahoma, and 288 in Forest County, Wisconsin. Indians were returned as Potawatomi from 19 different states, from New York to California. The total number enumerated in 1930 was 1,854, as compared with 2,440 in 1910. Of the total number in 1930, 38.0 percent were returned as full blood. The largest proportion of full bloods was in the Wisconsin band, the Oklahoma and Kansas Potawatomi being mainly of mixed blood.

Quapaw – After the removal of the Dhegiha from Illinois and Indiana, the Quapaw settled in northeastern Arkansas and southeastern Missouri. Before the Civil War, they were located on the Quapaw Reservation in what is now Ottawa County, Oklahoma. The number enumerated in 1930 was 222, with 212 in Oklahoma. In 1910 the census enumerated 231 of the tribe, with 221 in Oklahoma. The Office of Indian Affairs, however, reported 307 in 1910 and 313 in 1930. This may have represented the total population of the reservation, including scattered representatives of other tribes. The reports of the Indian Office show that the Quapaw population has remained fairly constant ever since their removal to the reservation. Only 62, or 27.9 percent, of the Quapaw were returned as full blood in 1930.

Salinan Stock – This is a small independent linguistic stock now practically extinct. They were formerly connected with the Mission of San Antonio in Monterey County, California, and were known as San Antonio Indians. In 1910 there were 16 reported as belonging to this tribe and stock. In 1930 none were reported. It may be, however, that there are a few survivors who were enumerated in Monterey County as "Mission" Indians and so lost to the tribal classification.

Salish (Interior) – This tribal group is made up of the Salishan tribes in western Washington, Montana, and Idaho. Of these, 12 were separately distinguished in 1910, the most important, numerically, being the Colville, Spokan, Kalispel, Flathead, Columbia, and Coeur d'Alene. The total number enumerated in 1930 was 5,211, of whom 2,607 were in Washington, mainly in Okanogan, Ferry, and Stevens Counties, 2,036 in Montana, mainly in Lake and Sanders Counties, and 480 in Idaho, with 354 in Benewah County alone. These figures agree approximately with the figures of the Office of Indian Affairs, which for 1932 show 2,588 on the Colville Reservation and 581 on the Spokane Reservation in Washington, 440 on the Coeur d'Alene Reservation in Idaho, and 2,174 on the Flathead Reservation in Montana. In 1910 the total number in the 12 interior tribes was 3,780, of whom 2,242 were in Washington, 939 in Montana, 419 in Idaho, and 151 in Oregon. Of the Interior Salish, only 32.3 percent were reported as full blood in 1932.

Salish (Washington Coast) – This tribal group is a combination of 18 tribes for which separate tabulations were made in 1910. The former habitat of these tribes was in western Washington, along the Pacific Coast and the coast and islands of Puget Sound. The largest of these tribes in 1910 were the Snohomish, Clallam, Lummi, Swinomish, Suquamish, and Puyallup. The total number enumerated in 1930 was 4,106, of which 4,055 were in Washington. These Indians were most numerous in Whatcom, Snohomish, and Grays Harbor Counties, but were widely distributed over the entire western half of the State. The total number in these same tribes in 1910 was 3,918, of whom 3,850 were in Washington. In 1930, 54.3 percent of the Washington Coast Salish were returned as full blood.

Salishan Stock – The numerous tribes of the important Salishan stock formerly ranged over most of northern and western Washington, northern Idaho, northwestern Oregon, and southern British Columbia. The tribes tabulated as Salishans in 1910 were grouped in 1930 into three tribal divisions, namely, the Washington Coast Salish, the Interior Salish, and the Tillamook. Other Salishan tribes, the Bellacoola, Comox, Cowichan, Shuswap, and Songish were included with the "Canadian and Mexican Tribes." In the comparative figures for 1910, shown in this report, these tribes have been excluded from the stock total.

Sauk and Fox – The Sauk and the Fox are two separate tribes, but they have been so closely associated for over a century that they are usually considered together. Their original habitat was probably the Lower Peninsula of Michigan. They moved early to Wisconsin and then beyond the Mississippi. In 1930 the total number enumerated was 887, as compared with 724 in 1910. The largest band, mainly of the Fox tribe, is located in Tama County, Iowa. The number in Iowa was 344 in 1930, as compared with 257 in 1910. The Office of Indian Affairs enumerated 363 of the tribe on the Iowa Reservation in 1932. There were 478 in Oklahoma in 1930, mainly in Lincoln, Payne, and Pottawatomie Counties.

Seminole – The name Seminole is applied to a part of the Creek tribe which during the eighteenth century separated from the main body and settled in Florida. Here they were joined by remnants of other tribes, including the Yuchi, and a large Negro element from run-away slaves. After the second Seminole war, one of the most disastrous and costly of the Indian wars, the greater part of the tribe were removed to Indian Territory. A few refugees escaped to the Everglades, where their descendants still live. The number enumerated in 1930 was 2,048, of whom 1,789 were in Oklahoma and 227 in Florida. In 1910 the number in Oklahoma was 1,503, but only 16 were enumerated in Florida. The actual number in Florida was, however, probably at least as large as in 1930. Of the Seminole in Oklahoma, 1,521 were enumerated in 1930 in Seminole County and 120 in Hughes County. Of the Seminole in Florida, 53.3 percent, and of those in Oklahoma, 74.5 percent, were returned in 1930 as full blood. In view of the history of the tribe, and especially their acceptance of hundreds of Negro fugitives while still in Florida, it is difficult to accept these figures as to blood at their face value.

Shahaptians – This tribal group includes all of the eight tribes included in 1910 in the Shahaptian stock. The largest of these tribes were the Nez Perces, Yakima, Warm Springs, Klickitat, and Walla Walla. The Shahaptians formerly ranged from central Oregon and southern Washington, east to central Idaho. The Nez Perces are now mainly on their own reservation in Idaho, The Yakima also have their own reservation in Washington which they share with the Klickitat, while the Warm Springs or Tenino share a reservation in Oregon with other tribes. The Walla Walla and Umatilla are located on the Umatilla Reservation in Oregon. The total number enumerated as Shahaptians in 1930 was 4,119, of whom 1,890 were in Washington, chiefly in Yakima and Klickitat Counties; 1,091 in Idaho, mainly in Nez Perces, Idaho, and Lewis Counties; and 1,054 in Oregon, mainly in Umatilla, Wasco, and Jefferson Counties. The 1910 tabulation showed a total of 4,374 in the eight tribes of this group, of whom 1,984 were in Washington, 1,206 in Oregon, and 1,074 in Idaho. Of the Shahaptians in 1930, 65.9 percent were returned as full blood.

Shapwailutan Stock – In the 1910 census classification, this stock was shown as three separate stocks, the Lutuamian, the Shahaptian, and the Waiilatpuan stocks. Linguistic studies in recent years have now led to the grouping of these three stocks into one. The former habitat of the Shapwailutans extended from northern California north through central Oregon and east along both banks of the Columbia River and the Snake River into central Idaho, adjoining the Salishans on the north, the Shoshoneans on the east and south, and the Kalapooians, Athapaskans, and Shastans on the west and southwest. The total number enumerated in the stock was 6,352 in 1930, as compared with 5,698 in 1910.

Shastan Stock – This stock, originally composed of several tribes, occupied an area south and west of the habitat of the Shapwailutans in northern California and southern Oregon. Many of the tribes are now extinct. In 1910 the stock was represented by three tribes, the Shasta, Pit River, and Hat Creek. The Shasta are mainly scattered through their old habitat, although a few are located on the Klamath, Grande Ronde, and Siletz Reservations in Oregon. A part of the Shasta tribe has at times been confused with the Klamath Indians. This confusion may possibly account for some of the apparent decrease in the Shastans and the large increase in the Shapwailutans. The Pit River is the largest of the Shastan tribes. Many remain in their early habitat in the drainage basin of the Pit River. Others are on the Round Valley Reservation in California and in the Klamath Reservation in Oregon. The Hat Creek is the smallest of the Shastan tribes and occupies a portion of the Pit River basin. The number enumerated as of the Shastan stock in 1930 was 844. Of these, 693 were in California, mainly in Shasta and Modoc counties, and 138 in Oregon. The total number of Shastans returned in 1910 was 1,578. Of these, 1,383 were in California and 177 in Oregon. In 1930, 70 percent of the Shastans were returned as full blood. In 1910 the Pit River and Hat Creek Indians were largely of full blood, while the Shasta were mainly of mixed blood.

Shawnee – This is the southernmost tribe of the Algonquian stock. The history of the tribe is very complicated and in some details uncertain. It is probable that they had moved from the north to the habitat on the Cumberland River where they were first known to Europeans. Later, a part of the tribe settled on the Savannah River. Some of the Shawnee were in Pennsylvania early in the nineteenth century, and others among the Creeks in the South. All were eventually pushed west across the Mississippi River. The greater part of the tribe is now in Oklahoma, mainly in Cleveland, Craig, Ottawa, and Pottawatomie Counties. The number enumerated as Shawnee in 1930 was 1,161, as compared with 1,338 in 1910. In 1930, 412, or 35.5 percent of the Shawnee were returned as full blood.

Shoshoni – The Shoshoni are the most northerly and constitute the largest single tribe of the Shoshonean stock. The habitat of the tribe when first known to the whites was in central and southern Idaho and adjacent portions of Montana, Wyoming, Utah, and Nevada. The Shoshoni are now mainly located on the Fort Hall Reservation in Idaho, the western Shoshoni Reservation in Nevada and Idaho, and the Wind River Reservation in Wyoming. The number enumerated in 1930 was 3,994, of whom 1,633 were in Nevada, mainly in Elko, Nye, Lander, and White Pine Counties; 1,251 in Idaho, chiefly in Bingham and Bannock Counties; 787 in Wyoming, of whom 767 were in Fremont County; 177 in California, of whom 145 were in Inyo County; and 107 in Utah, mainly in Box Elder County. This distribution has changed very little since 1910, when there were 3,840 Shoshoni, of whom 1,555 were in Nevada, 1,259 in Idaho, 700 in Wyoming, and 248 in Utah. There were only 33 in California in 1910, thus suggesting some migration in the 20-year period from Nye County, Nevada, to that part of Inyo County east of Death Valley. Of the Shoshoni returned in 1930, there were 2,750, or 68.9 percent, who claimed to be of full blood.

Shoshonean Stock – The important Shoshonean stock ranks sixth among the linguistic families of the American Indians. The former habitat of the stock covered practically the whole of the States of Nevada and Utah, a part of eastern Oregon, southern Idaho, western Colorado, and southern California, extending at times into Arizona, New Mexico, and Texas. If the Pimans and Nahuatlans are included, the habitat of the Uto-Aztecan family extends far south into Mexico. In the census of 1910, separate tabulations were made for 19 tribes of this stock, of which the largest were the Shoshoni, Paviotso, Ute, and Hopi. In the 1930 enumeration, these tribes were combined into eight tribal groups. The total number in the Shoshonean stock in 1930 was 15,985, representing a decrease from 16,842 in 1910.

Southern California Shoshoneans – This tribal group is made up of eight tribes, which were separately reported in 1910. The most important of these tribes were the Kawia and San Luiseno. The Southern California Shoshoneans occupied scattered areas in several counties. The Gabrieleno were formerly in Los Angeles County and parts of Orange and San Bernardino Counties; the Juaneno were in Orange County; the Kawaiisu, mainly in southern Kern County; the Kawia, in eastern San Bernardino and northern Riverside Counties; the Kern River, in Kern County; the San Luiseno, in western Riverside and northwestern San Diego Counties; and the Serrano, in San Bernardino County. The eighth tribe, the Tehachapi, were either identical with or closely associated with the Kawiisu in Kern County. The total number returned in this group in 1930 was 361, of whom 350 were in California, with 290 in Riverside County. In 1910 the number returned in the eight tribes combined was 1,497. It seems probable that in 1930 most of these Indians were returned as "Mission" Indians or otherwise without tribal designation. About half were reported as full blood in 1930.

Siouan Stock – This is one of the largest and at one time was perhaps the most powerful of all the Indian stocks in North America. The early habitat of the stock was in the northern and central plains and the region of the upper Mississippi River in Minnesota. Detached tribes were located east of the southern Allegheny Mountains, on the upper Ohio, and on the Gulf Coast. In the 1910 tabulation this stock was separated into 20 tribes, of which the largest—the Teton Sioux—was again separated into seven subdivisions. In 1930 the Siouans were grouped into 14 tribes and tribal groups. The total number of the Siouan stock in 1930 was 37,329, as compared with 32,941 in 1910. The Siouan tribes have given names to the five States of North and South Dakota, Kansas, Iowa, and Missouri.

Tanoan Stock – This is one of the important stocks of New Mexico, usually grouped with the Keresan and Zunian stocks and the Shoshonean Hopi, as Pueblo Indians. The Tanoans have lived, at least since the sixteenth century, in the southern part of New Mexico, with extensions into Old Mexico. The Tanoans were separated in the 1910 census tabulation into 13 tribes or pueblos, of which those of Isleta, Taos, and San Juan were the most important. In 1930, all were combined into one tribal group. The number returned as Tanoans in 1930 was 3,412, of which number 3,348 were in New Mexico. This represents an increase from 3,140 in 1910. Nearly all of the Tanoans are of full blood.

Tillamook – The Tillamook was the most southerly tribe of the Coast Salish. Their habitat was along the Pacific Coast in Tillamook County, Oregon. The remnants of the tribe have for many years lived on the Grande Ronde and the Siletz Reservations in Oregon. Only 16 were returned as Tillamook in 1930, of whom nine were in Oregon. In 1910, there were 25 reported, with 18 in Oregon.

Tonkawan Stock – This is an independent linguistic stock represented by only one tribe, the Tonkawa, whose early habitat was in central Texas. In 1884 the Tonkawa were located on the Oakland Reservation in Kay County, Oklahoma. Although small in numbers, the Tonkawa have maintained their tribal identity and apparently have associated little with other tribes. There were 48 Tonkawa returned as such in 1930, of whom 46 were in Oklahoma, and of these, 42 were in Kay County. These figures must be approximately correct, as the Office of Indian Affairs reported 46 Tonkawa enrolled in 1932, of which 35 were resident on the reservation. In 1930, 33 of the 48 were reported as full blood.

Tunican Stock – The Tunica tribe, forming an independent linguistic stock, formerly occupied the region along the lower Yazoo River in Mississippi. The Tunicans are probably related to the Chitimachans. The remnant of the tribe, 43 in number, were enumerated in 1910 in northern Louisiana. In 1930 only one Indian was reported as a Tunica, a female in Rapides Parish, Louisiana. The survivors in 1910 were largely of mixed blood, with some Negro admixture.

Ute – This important tribe or confederacy in former times ranged over central and western Colorado, eastern Utah, and the northern edge of New Mexico. The Ute are now located on various reservations in Utah and Colorado. In the 1930 tabulations, the Pahvant, a related tribe, is included with the Ute. This tribe formerly occupied an area south and east of Great Salt Lake in Utah. Only 37 Pahvant were so reported in 1910. It is probable that the tribe has now completely lost its identity through intermarriage with the Ute. The number enumerated as Ute in 1930 was 1,980, of whom 1,269 were in Utah, chiefly in Uinta, Duchesne, Juab, and San Juan Counties; and 669 in Colorado, in La Plata and Montezuma Counties. This is a decrease of 13.2 percent from the 2,281 returned as Ute and Pahvant in 1910. In 1930, 85.1 percent of the Ute were returned as full blood.

Virginia-Carolina Indians – These Indians, residing in the lowland counties of Virginia, North Carolina, and South Carolina, are almost entirely of mixed origin. Those in Virginia were classed as Algonquians in 1910 and shown under the tribal names of Pamunkey, Mattapony, Chickahominy, and Powhatan. The Indians of the southeastern part of North Carolina are officially designed as Croatans and are not definitely assigned to any linguistic stock. A better designation for this group would be Cheraw, as they are undoubtedly descended in part from the important tribe of that name, probably of Siouan stock, which formerly inhabited this region. The greater part of the North Carolina Indians were returned on the schedules in 1930 as Cherokee, but those in the lowland counties were arbitrarily deducted from the Cherokee tribe and assigned to the Virginia-Carolina group. The total number assigned to this group in 1930 was 12,975, as compared with 6,195 in 1910. Of these, 10,452 were returned from Robeson County, North Carolina. The rapid increase in numbers may be accounted for in part by a desire on the part of those of the younger generation with even a trace of Indian blood to be classed as Indians rather than Negroes. There has, however, been a definite natural increase, as indicated by the fact that in 1930, 4,468 were under 10 years old, and 7,932, or 61.1 percent, were under 20. The returns showing 43.4 percent of Virginia-Carolina Indians as "full-blood" may be ascribed either to ignorance of racial admixture or to a desire to conceal the fact of admixture from the enumerator.

Washoan Stock – This stock is represented by only one tribe, the Washo, which, since first known, has lived near Lake Tahoe and eastward in California and Nevada. The number enumerated in 1930 was 668. Of this number, 389 were in Nevada, mainly in Douglas, Washoe, and Ormsby Counties, and 275 in California, chiefly in Alpine and Mono Counties. In 1930, 79.5 percent of the Washo were returned as of full blood.

Winnebago – When first known to the white explorers, the Winnebago were settled in the vicinity of Green Bay, Wisconsin. Part of the tribe moved westward with the Dakota and were finally located on a reservation in Thurston County, Nebraska. Another portion of the Winnebago remained in Wisconsin and are now under the Tomah School Jurisdiction in Jackson, Monroe, Shawano, and Wood Counties. The number enumerated in 1930 was 1,446, including 937 in Wisconsin and 423 in Nebraska. In 1910 the number of Winnebago was given by the Census as 1,820, with 1,007 in Nebraska and 735 in Wisconsin. The number returned in Wisconsin in 1910 was probably too small, as the Office of Indian Affairs enumerated 1,270 in that State in 1910. On the other hand, the 1930 enumeration in Nebraska is certainly too low. The Office of Indian Affairs reported 802 on the Winnebago Reservation in 1932, and the Census Bureau enumerated 426 in Thurston County, Nebraska, without tribal designation. Of the Wisconsin Winnebago, 84.1 percent were returned as full blood, but of those in Nebraska only 61.7 percent claimed full blood.

Wintun Stock – The Wintun stock was subdivided in the 1910 census into three tribes, the Nomelaki, Patwin, and Wintun. The habitat of the stock was in the western half of the Sacramento Valley and in part of Trinity County. The Nomelaki, really a subgroup of the Wintun, are mainly located on the Round Valley Reservation in California. The others are scattered over their traditional habitat. The number returned in 1930 was

512, mainly in Shasta and Trinity Counties. In 1910 the total number reported was 710, including 399 Wintun, 186 Patwin, and 125 Nomelaki. Only 21.1 percent were returned in 1930 as full blood.

Wiyot Stock – The Indians of this stock have no definite tribal subdivisions and are generally known as the Humboldt Bay Indians. As far as known, they have always lived on the northern California coast in the vicinity of Humboldt Bay. In 1930 the number so reported was 236, with 230 in California and 214 in Humboldt County. This is an apparent increase from 152 in 1910. Of the number returned in 1930, only 74 claimed full blood.

Wyandot – Early in the seventeenth century, the Huron Confederacy was one of the largest and most powerful tribal groups on the North American continent. Champlain estimated their population in 1615 as 30,000, and Hewitt gives a more conservative estimate of 20,000 in 1648.[ii] In this latter year, desperate warfare began between the Huron and the Iroquois confederacies, and after two years the Huron power was completely destroyed. The survivors were driven from their habitat in the present Province of Ontario and most of them were adopted into other tribes. A small band fled to northern Michigan and then to Wisconsin, where they were associated with the Potawatomi and Ottawa. Many years later, they returned eastward and settled around the western end of Lake Erie where they became known as Wyandot. In 1842 they sold the last of their lands in Ohio and moved to Kansas, and in 1867 were finally located in Ottawa County, Oklahoma. The number enumerated in 1930 was 353, exactly the same number as enumerated in 1910. Practically all of these were of mixed blood. Even in 1910, 242, or 68.6 percent were returned as "more than half white."

Yakonan Stock – This stock is made up of three small tribes, the Alsea, Siuslaw, and Yaquina, and is now almost extinct. The traditional habitat of the stock was along the Oregon Coast in Lincoln, Lane, and Douglas Counties. Most of the survivors are on the Siletz Reservation in Oregon. Only nine were returned as Yakonans in 1930, of whom seven were in Oregon and two in Washington. The report of the Office of Indian Affairs for 1932 shows 13 Alsea and Yaquina enrolled at the Siletz Reservation, of whom five are residing there and eight elsewhere. In 1910 the census enumeration showed 55 of the stock, including 29 Alsea, seven Siuslaw, and 19 Yaquina.

Yanan Stock – This California stock is almost extinct and is now represented by a remnant of one tribe, the Yana. The former habitat of the Yana was in Tehama and Shasta Counties. Almost the entire tribe, then estimated at about 3,000, was massacred by white miners in 1864. In 1930 only nine Indians were returned as Yana, five in Mendocino County, three in Shasta County, and one in Sacramento County. In 1910 there were 39 enumerated as belonging to this tribe.

Yokuts Stock – The habitat of the Indians of the Yokuts stock has been, since first known, in the southeastern part of the Sacramento Valley and the adjacent foothills of the Sierra Nevada. In the 1910 Indian tabulation, eight tribes of the Yokuts stock were separately shown, of which only two, the Chukchansi and the Yokuts, were of numerical importance. Over 100 of the stock are enrolled at the Tule River Reservation in California, but the majority are widely scattered. In 1930 the total number enumerated as of the stock was 1,145. Of this number, 1,085 were in California, with more than 100 in each of Butte, Fresno, Kings, Madera, and Mendocino Counties. There were also 29 in Nevada and 13 in Oregon. In 1910 only 533 were returned in all eight of the Yokuts tribes, with 530 in California. Of those returned as of Yokuts stock in 1930, 41.4 percent were of full blood.

Yuchean Stock – This stock is represented by only one tribe, the Yuchi, formerly living on the Savannah River in Georgia. The entire tribe was removed to Indian Territory in 1836. In 1930 there were 216 Indians enumerated as Yuchi, of whom 195 were in Oklahoma, with 140 in Creek County. In addition, there were 50 returned as Yuchi in California and 16 in Oregon. These were arbitrarily assumed to be Yuki and assigned to that tribe. There were only 78 Yuchi so returned in 1910, of which number 74 were in Oklahoma. Of those who in 1930 were classified as Yuchi, 100, or 46.3 percent, were reported as full blood.

Yukian Stock – This California stock occupied three small, separate areas in Mendocino, Sonoma, Lake, and Napa Counties. In the 1910 tabulations, the stock was separated into four tribes, the Coast Yuki, Redwood (Huchnom), Wappo, and Yuki. In 1930 the number enumerated as Yuki, including 66 reassigned from those reported as Yuchi, was 17, of which number 150 were in California, mainly in Mendocino and Sonoma Counties, and 24 in Oregon. In 1910 there were 198 returned as of the Yukian stock, including 95 Yuki, 73 Wappo, 15 Coast Yuki, and 15 Redwood. Of the total number included in the 1930 tabulation, 74, or 41.8 percent, were reported as full blood.

Yuman Stock – The habitat of the Yuman stock is southwestern Arizona, the southern end of California, and the northern half of Lower California in Mexico, In 1930 the enumerated population of Yuman stock was 4,537, as compared with 4,267 in 1910. The Yuman stock in the United States is represented by nine tribes and tribal groups, for which statistics were separately presented in 1910. In 1930, five of these tribes and groups were kept separate, while the other four were combined into a single tribal group.

Yuma – This is the largest tribe of Yuman stock. Their early habitat was near that of the Cocopa in southwestern Arizona. A large part of the Yuma are now located on the Fort Yuma Reservation in California on the Colorado River, just above the Mexican boundary. There were 2,306 Yuma enumerated in 1930, of whom 2,231 were in California, with 1,160 in San Diego County, 676 in Imperial County, and 377 in Riverside County. This is a very large increase from the 834 enumerated in 1910, which may or may not be actual, as in neither of the two enumerations were the tribal designations of California Indians very accurately returned. In 1930 the number returned as full blood was 1,636, or 70.9 percent of the total number.

Northern Yumans – This is a collective name applied to four small Yuman tribes which occupied the northern part of the habitat of the Yuman stock in the present State of Arizona. The first of these tribes, the Havasupai, lived in central Arizona, but in 1882 were moved to their own reservation in Coconino County. The number enumerated as Havasupai in 1910 was 174. the Office of Indian Affairs in 1932 enumerated 197 of the tribe, of whom 190 were on the reservation. The Walapai (or Hualapai) formerly occupied a large area in northern Arizona, eastward from the great bend in the Colorado River. A part of the tribe now live on the Hualapai Reservation in Arizona. The number enumerated in 1910 was 501. In 1932 the Bureau of Indian Affairs enumerated 449 as Walapai and of Walapai and other tribal mixtures. The Yavapai have been moved from their early home in southwestern Arizona in 1875 to the San Carlos Reservation in Gila and Graham Counties. From their association here with the Apache, they became known as the Mohave-Apache Indians. There were 289 of the tribe in 1910. In 1932 the Office of Indian Affairs enumerated 193 as Mohave-Apache, of whom 191 were on the Fort McDowell Reservation. The Yuma Apache, a small mixed group of Indians mainly of Yavapai origin, were located in 1910 with the Apache on the San Carlos Reservation. Only 24 were enumerated under the name in that year. The total number of the four tribes combined in 1930 was 646. Of these, 639 were in Arizona, 396 in Mohave County and 206 in Coconino County.

Yurok Stock – The Indians of the Yurok stock appear to have had no tribal subdivisions. A part of the stock is locally known as the Weitspek, but others are indiscriminately known, along with Indians of other northern California tribes, as Klamath Indians. They are thus confused with the Klamath Indians of Shapwailutan stock. The number enumerated in 1930 as of this stock was 471, of whom 440 were in California, with 428 in Humboldt County. In 1910, 668 Indians were returned as Yurok, but there is no way of determining whether the decrease indicated is actual or due only to errors in reporting tribal designations. Of those returned in 1930, 43.5 percent were of full blood, as compared with 79.0 percent so returned in 1910.

Zunian Stock – This is the smallest in number, but one of the best known of the pueblo stocks of New Mexico. They have lived for many centuries in the same region in McKinley and Valencia Counties, New Mexico. The stock is composed of only one pueblo or tribe. The number tabulated as Zuni in 1930 was 1,749, of which number 1,726 were in New Mexico, with 1,715 in McKinley County.[iii] The number returned at the Census of 1910 was 1,667, with 1,664 in New Mexico. In 1910 all but 15 of the Zuni were reported as of full blood, but in 1930 no report was obtained as to blood, except for a very few members of the tribe.

ALL OTHER TRIBES OF THE UNITED STATES
AND TRIBES NOT REPORTED

On the Census schedules in 1930, there were 35,150 persons returned as Indians, either with no tribe reported or with some tribal name not included in the code list of tribes. By far the greater part of these were returned with no tribal designation. Many of these Indians were undoubtedly so far removed from their tribal relations that they did not know to what tribe their ancestors belonged. In other cases, the enumerator simply neglected to obtain the information. In many cases, it would have been possible to make a fairly good guess as to the tribal affiliation from the place of residence, but it was thought better to publish the list of Indians with tribe not reported by state and county without attempting any arbitrary assignment to tribes. By following this course, the statistics, by tribes, of age, school attendance, etc., are shown only for Indians definitely reported by tribe. Anyone, however, who is familiar with the location of the various tribes will be able to make his own assignment of these miscellaneous groups to tribes. Of all the states, California has the greatest variety of Indian stocks and tribes. Many of these tribes are either extinct or represented by only a few scattered members. Others have been for generations more or less attached to the Spanish Missions, and are popularly known as "Mission" Indians. Others scattered through the mountains are known as "Digger" Indians, without regard to stock or tribe. The Indian Reservations in California, and on the Pacific Coast generally, are inhabited by Indians of many tribes so intermarried that it is difficult to determine to what tribes they should be assigned. Altogether, it is not surprising that out of 19,212 Indians in that State, there should be 5,578 who could not be assigned to any definite tribe or stock. Out of the 92,725 Indians in Oklahoma, all but 4,900 were assigned to stocks and tribes. Here it is possible in some counties to make a good guess as to the tribes to which the unknown should be assigned. For example, of the Indians returned by tribe from Kiowa County the great majority belonged to the Kiowa tribe, and it might be assumed that a majority of the 376 unknown in Kiowa County were also Kiowa. But of the 645 unknown in Caddo County, some are probably Caddo, while others are Kiowa, Kiowa Apache, or Comanche. Of the Michigan Indians of unknown tribe, it may be assumed that most of those in Emmet, Charlevoix, and Leelanau Counties are Ottawa, while those in Chippewa and Mackinac Counties are Chippewa. The North Carolina Indians of unknown tribe undoubtedly belong to the Virginia-Carolina group. Those in New York are probably for the most part Iroquois, particularly those in Cattaraugus and Onondaga Counties. Indians of unknown tribe reported from Arizona and New Mexico may belong to any one of several tribes and stocks whose habitat is in these states. In Washington, it is probable that the unknown in the western counties are largely Coast Salish and those in the eastern counties Interior Salish. The Indians of Barnstable County, Massachusetts, are undoubtedly mainly eastern Algonquians of the Mashpee group. On the other hand, the Indians of Pennsylvania may belong to any one of the tribes, with the possible exceptions of the "Mission" tribes of California. The Carlisle Indian School drew students from all parts of the country, and many of these obtained positions in the East, married, and never returned permanently to their former homes. The Indians in large cities were generally returned without tribal designation. In a certain sense, this is as it should be, for the Indian who lives and works in New York, Chicago, or Detroit, certainly is far removed from his tribal relations and is no longer in any true sense an Apache, a Dakota, or an Iroquois.

CANADIAN AND MEXICAN TRIBES

This classification is made up of Indians belonging to tribes, the great majority of whose members are located in Canada and Mexico. These tribes are often of the same linguistic stocks as other tribes mainly resident in the United States, but for convenience they were all assigned to this one group. Typical of the Canadian tribes, and one of the largest tribes of this group in the United States, is the great Algonquian Cree tribe, of which there are still perhaps 15,000 members in Manitoba and the Prairie Provinces. The Cree are closely related to the Chippewa and many of them have migrated across the border all the way from the Lake region to the Rockies. The Salishan tribes of British Columbia are also well represented in the northwestern States, particularly Washington.[iv] In the East, the Abnaki, Malecite, and Micmac, all of Algonquian stock, are fairly numerous in New York and Maine. In the southwest, there are many Indians of Mexican tribes in Arizona, with smaller numbers in California and New Mexico. Perhaps the most important of these tribes is the Yaqui, probably the largest tribe of the Piman stock, with its habitat in the State of Sonora. The Opata and Mayo, two other large Piman tribes, are also represented north of the Mexican border. The "Mexicans," however, of whom 1,422,533 were enumerated in the United States in 1930, are not considered in the census as Indians, although most of them are to a large extent of Indian blood. Only those persons of Mexican birth or extraction who were definitely Indians and who maintained tribal relations, were classified as Indians. There were in all 5,651 Indians enumerated in 1930 as belonging to Canadian or Mexican tribes, or born in Canada or Mexico without tribal designation. In 1910, as far as can be determined from the report of that year, there were 1,782 in this group. It is apparent that in the 20-year period there had been a considerable migration of Canadian and Mexican Indians across the borders, probably in search of economic opportunities. These Indians were reported mainly from border counties or from cities near the one or the other of the international boundaries.

INDIAN POPULATION OF ALASKA

Alaskan Tribes – In Washington and Oregon, and to a less extent in California and Idaho, Indians were reported as belonging to a number of tribes whose members are mainly located in Alaska. The greater part of these Indians belonged to one or another of the five important Alaskan linguistic stocks, the Athapaskan, the Eskimauan, the Haidan, the Tlingit, and the Tsimshian. The total number of Alaskan Indians was reported as 385, as compared with 85 in 1910.

Athapaskan Stock – The Alaskan extension of the Athapaskan stock occupies a large part of the interior of the Territory, including the valleys of the Yukon River and its tributaries. The Ahtena, one of the best known of the Alaskan tribes of this stock, occupies the basin of the Copper River, and the Knaiakhotana live on the Kenai Peninsula and around Cook Inlet. The report, based upon the special enumeration of Indians, differentiates 11 Athapaskan tribes in Alaska. The number returned in 1930 as Athapaskans was 4,935, as compared with 3,916 in 1910.

Eskimauan Stock – The habitat of the Eskimauan stock includes almost the entire coast line of the North American continent from southern Alaska along the coasts of the Pacific Ocean, Behring Sea, the Arctic Ocean and its islands, including Greenland, to the Atlantic coast of Labrador. At least one group of this stock lives west of Behring Strait in Siberia. The Eskimauans are divided into numerous small tribes, of which 40 are separately mentioned in the special Indian report of 1910. The number of Indians of Eskimauan stock in Alaska in 1930 was 19,028, as compared with 14,087 in 1910.

Haidan Stock – This is mainly a Canadian stock, including only one tribe, the Haida, occupying the Queen Charlotte Islands off the coast of British Columbia. The Alaskan Indians of this stock are mostly on Prince of Wales Island, off the coast at the southern extension of the Territory. The number of Haidans in Alaska in 1930 was 588, representing an increase from 530 in 1910.

Tlingit Stock – The habitat of Tlingit Indians is along the coast and adjacent islands of southern Alaska. The tribes of this stock for which members were reported in Alaska in 1910 were 12 in number, of which the largest were the Chilkat, Huna, Hutsnuwu, and Sitka. The number enumerated in 1930 in the stock as a whole was 4,462, as compared with 4,426 in 1910.

Tsimshian Stock – The habitat of Tsimshians is primarily in British Columbia, and the Tsimshians in the United States are classed with Canadian tribes. A considerable number of Indians of the Tsimshian tribe or division of the Tsimshian stock have in comparatively recent years settled in southern Alaska. In 1930 there were 845 of the tribe in Alaska, an increase from 729 in 1910. In 1910 there were 37 Tsimshians in the State of Washington and 14 in Oregon.

OTHER FOREIGN-BORN INDIANS

In 1930 there were 217 Indians returned as born in foreign countries other than Canada and Mexico. Some of these are properly tabulated as Indians. Those born in the West Indies may be West Indian Negroes who were entered on the schedules as "West Indian." A few born in India were probably "Indians" of an entirely different race. Those of scattered origin may have been children of civilized Indians traveling abroad, or of Indians with traveling shows, but it is probable that some were the result of clerical errors which at the time this report was written could not easily be corrected. In any discussion of the American Indians by tribe, this foreign-born group is entirely without significance.

ALPHABETICAL CODE LIST FOR
INDIAN TRIBES OF THE UNITED STATES

(Each code number is to be followed by "-4" if the Indian is of mixed blood, and by "-5" if a full blood.)

Tribe .... Code		
Abnaki 98	Clallam 50	Jemez 77
Acoma 35	Clatsop 26	Jicarilla Apache 16
Ahtena 99	Clear Lake 48	Juaneno 62
Aleut 99	Coast Yuki 88	Kai-Pomo 20
Alibamu 44	Cochiti 35	Kake 99
Alsea 84	Cocopa 89	Kalapooia 33
Arapaho 01	Coeur d'Alene 51	Kalispel 51
Arikara 21	Columbia 51	Kansas 67
Assiniboin 75	Colville 51	Kashowoo 86
Auk................99	Comanche 56	Kawaiisu 62
Bannock 55	Comox 98	Kawla 62
Bellacoola 98	Cow Creek 19	Kern River 62
Blackfeet...........02	Cowichan 98	Kichai 24
Brotherton 15	Cowlitz 50	Kickapoo 07
Brule Sioux..........74	Coyotero Apache 16	Kiowa 36
Caddo 22	Cree 98	Kiowa Apache 17
Catawba 63	Creek 44	Kitamat 98
Cayuga 30	Croatan 14	Klamath 39
Cayuse 80	Crow 64	Klikitat 53
Chastacosta 19	Delaware 05	Koasati 44
Chehalis 50	Diegueno 90	Kusa 37
Chemehuevi 59	Dwamish 50	Kutenai 38
Cherokee 32	Flathead 51	Kwakiutl 98
Chetco 19	Gabrieleno 62	Laguna 35
Cheyenne 03	Grosventres 06	Lakmiut 33
Chickahominy 14	Gynomehro 48	Lipan Apache 16
Chickasaw 42	Haida 99	Little Lake 48
Chilcat 99	Hano 77	Lower Lake 48
Chimakum 25	Hat Creek 54	Luiseno 62
Chinook 26	Havasupai 91	Lummi 50
Chippewa 04	Hidatsa 65	Maidu 40
Chiricahua Apache ...16	Hoh 25	Malecite 98
Chitimacha 27	Hotavilla 57	Malemiut 99
Choctaw 43	Humboldt Bay 83	Mandan 68
Choinimni 86	Hunkpapa Sioux 74	Maricopa 92
Chukchansi 86	Hupa 20	Marin 41
Chukimina 86	Iowa 66	Mary's River 33
Clackamas 26	Iroquois 30	Mashpee............15
	Isleta 77	Mattapony 14

Mattole	.20	Paiute	.59	Santa Ana	.35
Mayo	.98	Paloos	.53	Santa Barbareno	.28
Menominee	.08	Pamunkey	.14	Santa Clara	.77
Mescalero Apache	.16	Panamint	.58	Santa Cruz	.29
Mathow	.51	Papago	.46	Santa Ynez	.28
Miami	.09	Passamaquoddy	.15	Santee Sioux	.74
Micmac	.98	Patwin	.82	Santiam	.33
Middletown	.41	Paviotso	.58	Santo Domingo	.35
Minniconjou Sioux	.74	Pawnee	.23	Sauk and fox	.12
Mishongnovi	.57	Pecos	.77	Seminole	.45
Missouri	.69	Pend d'Oreilles	.51	Seneca	.30
Miwok	.41	Penobscot	.15	Serrano	.62
Modoc	.39	Peoria	.09	Shasta	.54
Moenkapi	.57	Pequot	.15	Shawnee	.13
Mohave	.93	Piankashaw	.09	Shinnecock	.15
Mohawk	.30	Picuris	.77	Shipaulovi	.57
Mohegan	.15	Piegan	.02	Shongopavi	.57
Molala	.80	Pima	.47	Shoshoni	.60
Mono	.58	Pisquow	.51	Shushwap	.98
Montauk	.15	Pit River	.54	Sia	.35
Muckleshoot	.50	Pojoaque	.77	Sichumovi	.57
Munsee	.05	Pomo	.48	Sihasapa Sioux	.74
Nambe	.77	Ponca	.72	Sisseton Sioux	.74
Narragansett	.15	Poosepatuck	.15	Siuslaw	.84
Navajo	.18	Potawatomi	.11	Skagit	.50
Nespelim	.51	Powhatan	.14	Skokomish	.50
Nez Perces	.53	Puyallup	.50	Snakes	.58
Niantic	.15	Quapaw	.73	Snohomish	.50
Nisqually	.50	Quileute	.25	Snoqualmu	.50
Nomelaki	.82	Quinaielt	.50	Songish	.98
Nooksak	.50	Redwood	.88	Spokane	.51
Nootka	.98	Redwood (Calif.)	.20	Squaxon	.50
Oglala Sioux	.74	Rogue River	.19	Stockbridges	.15
Okinagan	.51	Saiaz	.20	Suquamish	.50
Omaha	.70	St. Regis	.30	Swinomish	.50
Oneida	.30	San Antonio	.49	Tachi	.86
Onondaga	.30	San Carlos Apache	.16	Taos	.77
Opata	.98	Sandia	.77	Tawaskoni	.24
Oraibi	.57	San Felipe	.35	Tehachapi	.62
Orleans	.34	San Ildefonso	.77	Tenankutchin	.99
Osage	.71	San Juan	.77	Tesuque	.77
Oto	.60	San Luis Obispo	.28	Teton Sioux	.74
Ottawa	.10	Sanpoil	.51	Tillamook	.52
Pahvant	.61	Sans Arc Sioux	.74	Tlatskanai	.19

Tolowa 19	Ute 61	Wea 09
Tonkawa 78	Waco 24	Wechikhit 86
Tonto Apache 16	Wailakki 20	Weitspek 95
Topinish 53	Walapai 91	White Mountain Apache
Tsimshian 98	Wallawalla 53	16
Tunica 79	Walpi 57	Wichita 24
Tuscarora 30	Wampanoag 15	Wikchamni 86
Twana 50	Wapato 33	Winnebago 76
Two Kettle Sioux 74	Wappo 88	
Umatilla 52	Warm Springs 53	**Indian born in–**
Umpqua 19	Wasco 26	United States 97
Upper Coquille 19	Washo 81	Canada 98

Endnotes

[i] U.S. Department of Commerce. Bureau of the Census. *Fifteenth Census of the United States:1930. The Indian Population of the United States and Alaska.* Washington, DC: Government Printing Office, 1937. pp. 33-73.

[ii] *Handbook of American Indians*, Vol. 1, p.587.

[iii] An examination of the schedules for the Zuni Indian Reservation shows that the enumerators completely ignored instructions as to reporting tribe and blood. In the coding of the schedules, the Indians in that part of the reservation which is in McKinley County were coded as Zuni, but the Indians in the part of the reservation in Valencia County, 204 in number, were coded as "Tribe not reported." The addition of these 204 Indians in Valencia County would make the total for the tribe 1,953 instead of 1,749.

[iv] The Makah were included with Canadian tribes in 1930, since the Wakashan stock to which they belong is distinctly a Canadian stock with its habitat mainly on Vancouver Island. The Makah, however, have lived, since they were first known to white settlers, in the vicinity of Cape Flattery in Clallam County, Washington, where a reservation was established for them in 1855. A count of the names on the 1930 Census schedules for this reservation showed 305 Indians of the Makah tribe, with a few intermarried Saliah, Nootka, and Quileute, a family of Cheyenne, and one Cherokee. Of the Makah, 218 were returned as full blood, 86 of mixed blood, and one with blood not reported. There were 360 Makah enumerated in 1910, of whom 354 were in Washington and six in Oregon.

1930 Metropolitan Area Maps

The following maps show geographic detail and boundaries for 96 major metropolitan districts in the United States. The maps are arranged alphabetically by U.S. state and by city within each state.

These maps show county lines and other census boundaries (i.e., precincts, wards, districts, etc.) and should help researchers get a broad idea of the geographic layout around a given city. A researcher who is unsure of an exact location of an ancestor's residence can often use these maps alone or in conjunction with NARA's *1930 Census Microfilm Locator* (see pages 51, 60) in understanding proximity and adjacency of a range of enumerated areas.

Alabama – Birmingham

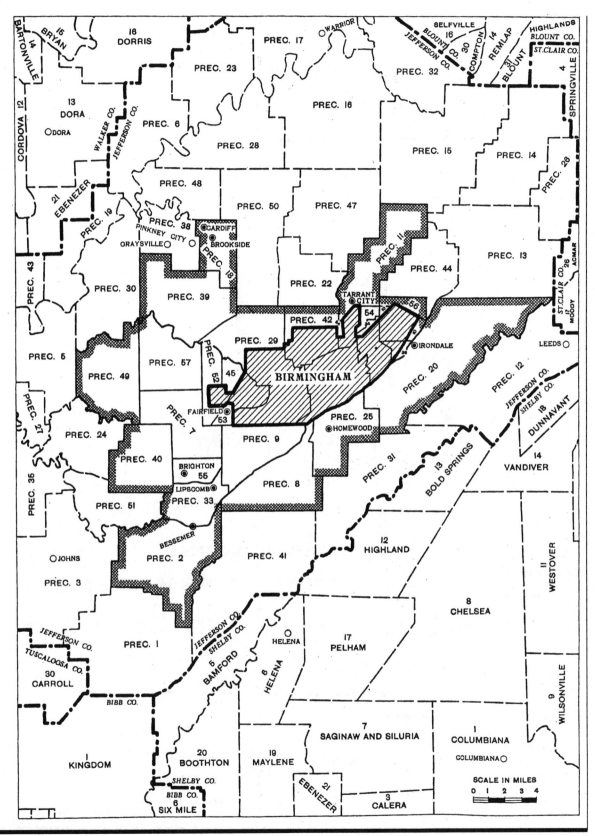

Arkansas – Little Rock

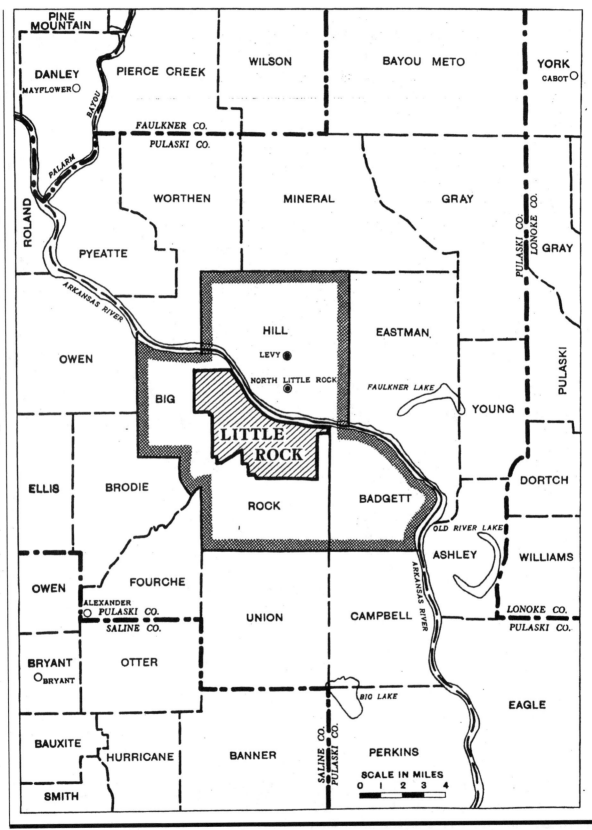

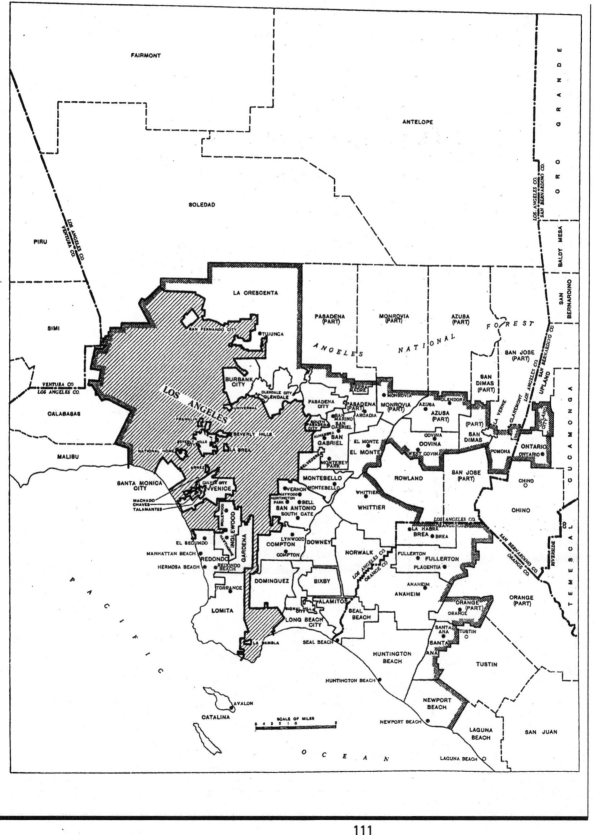

California – Sacramento

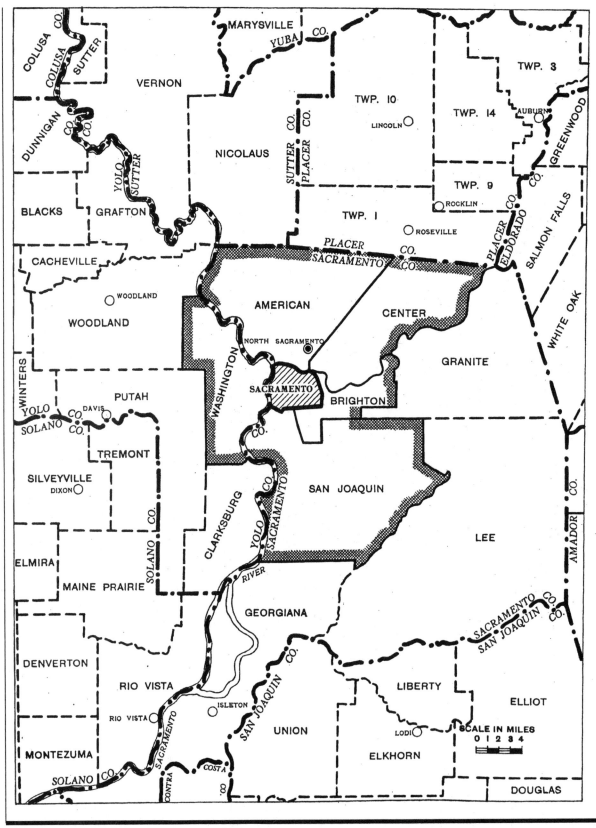

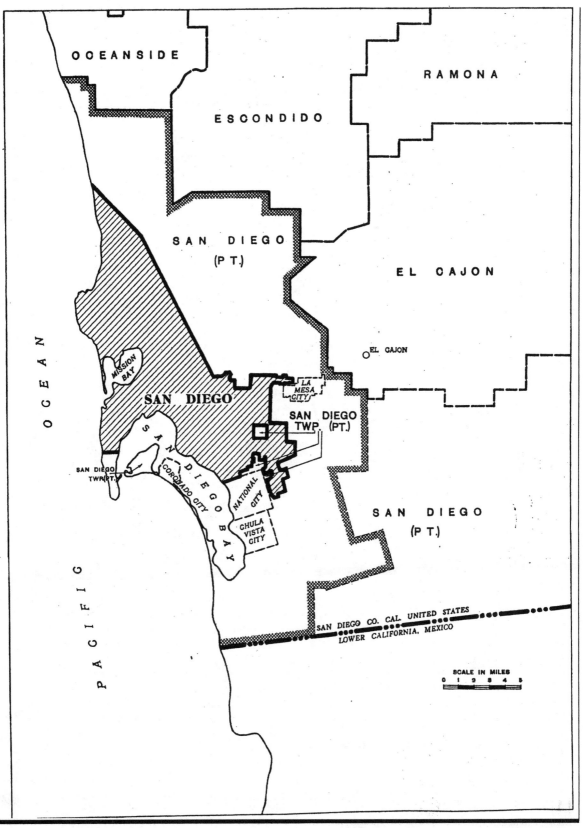

California – San Francisco - Oakland

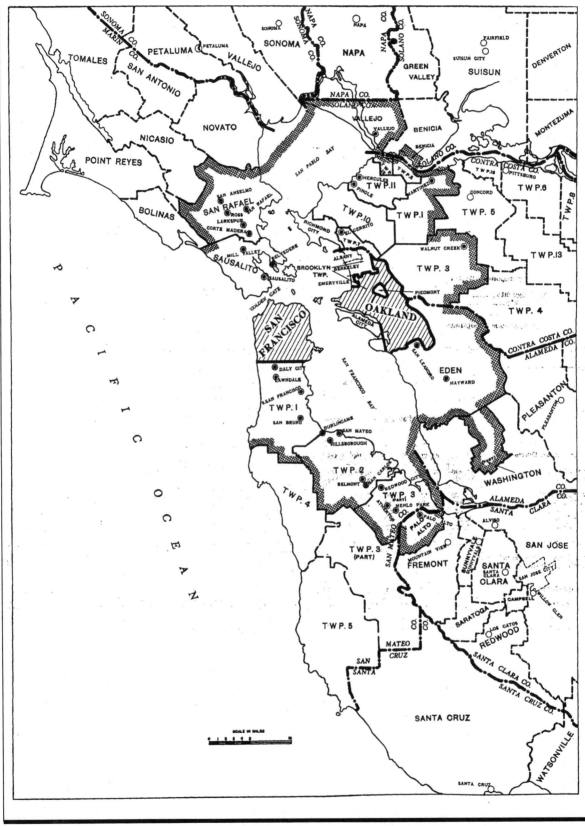

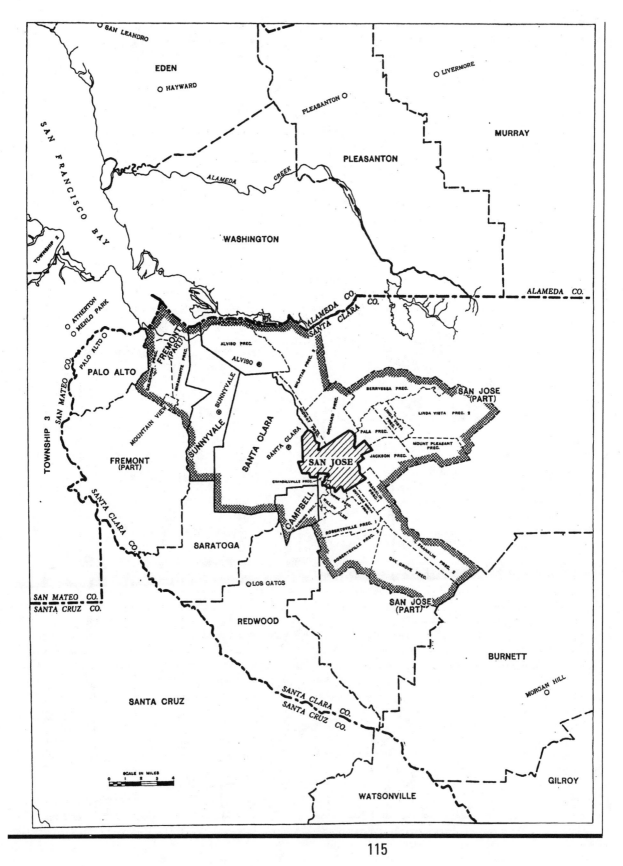

Colorado – Denver

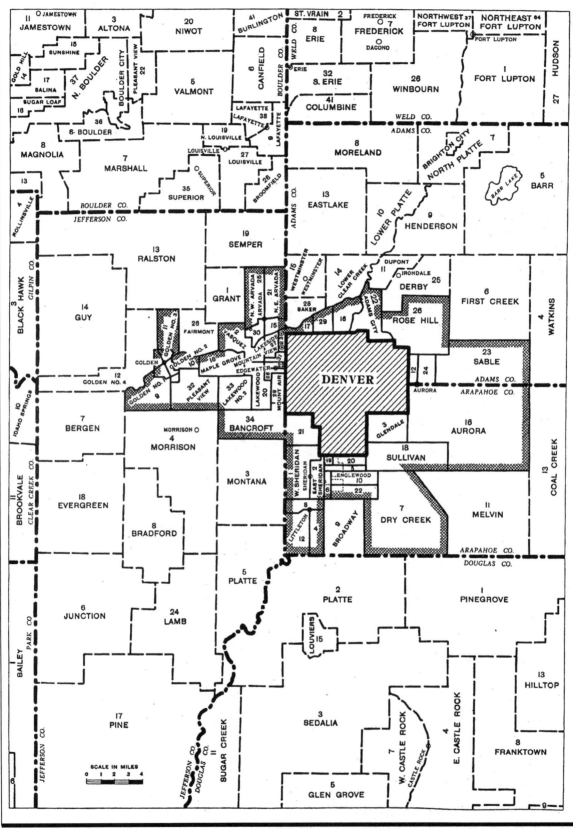

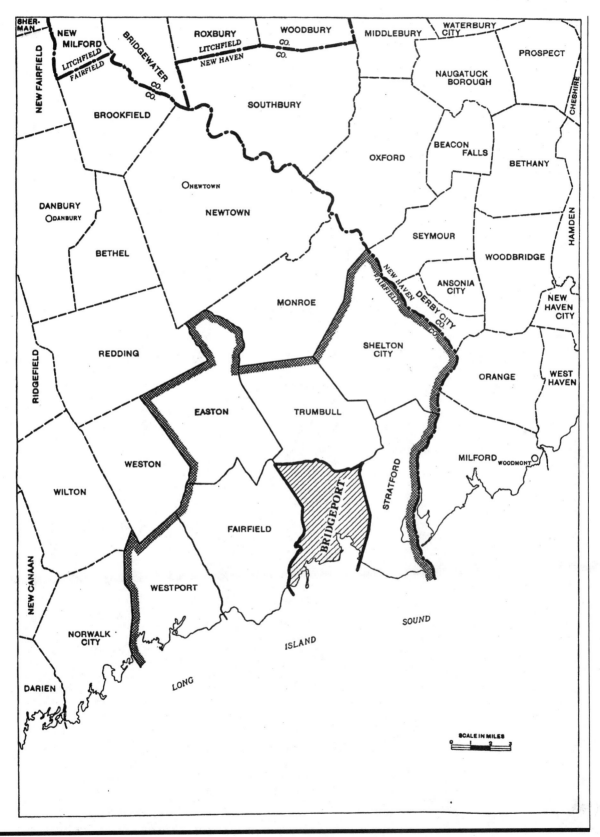

Connecticut – Hartford

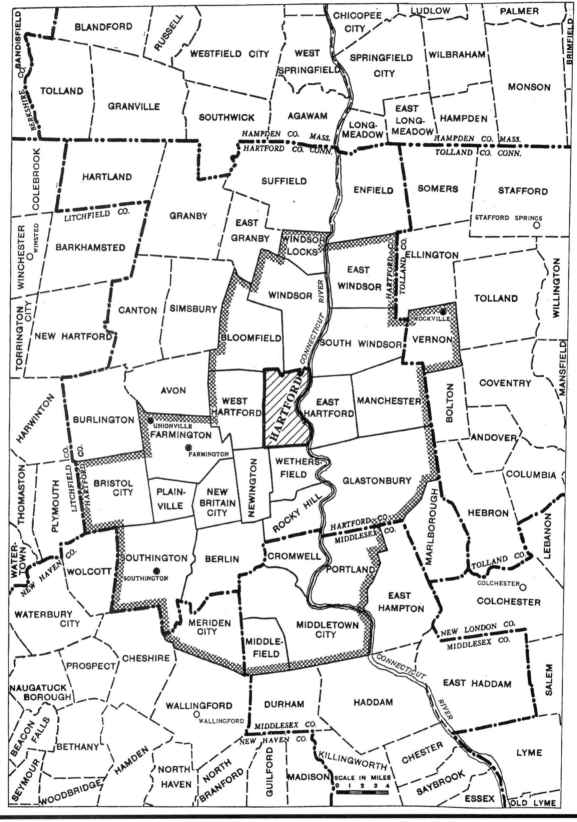

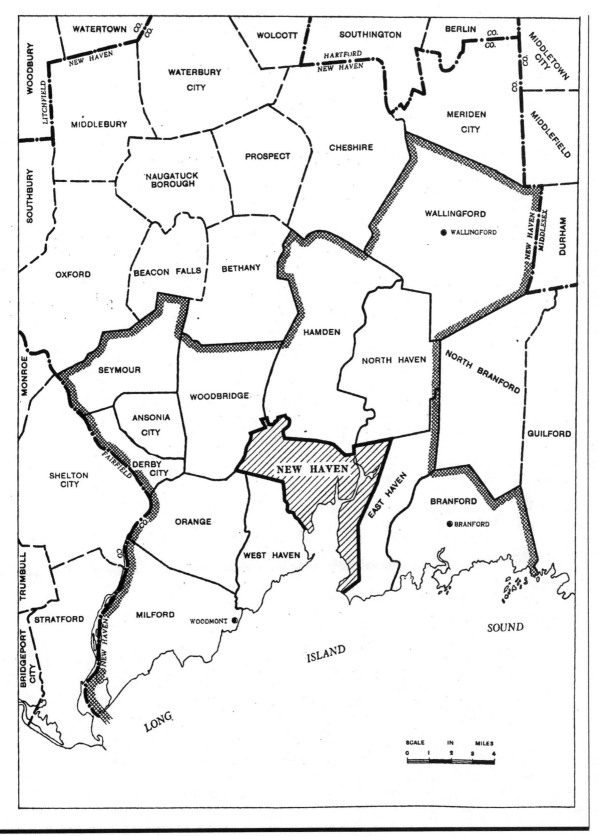

Connecticut – Waterbury

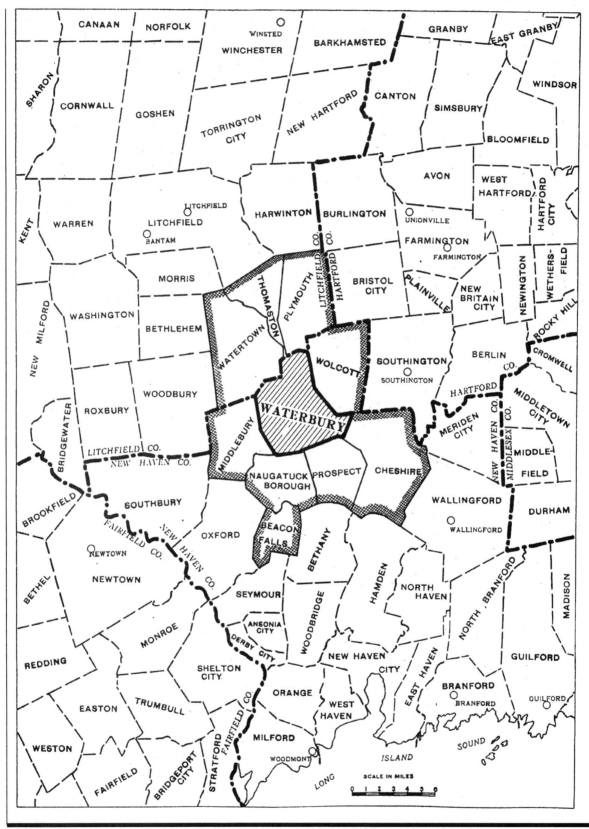

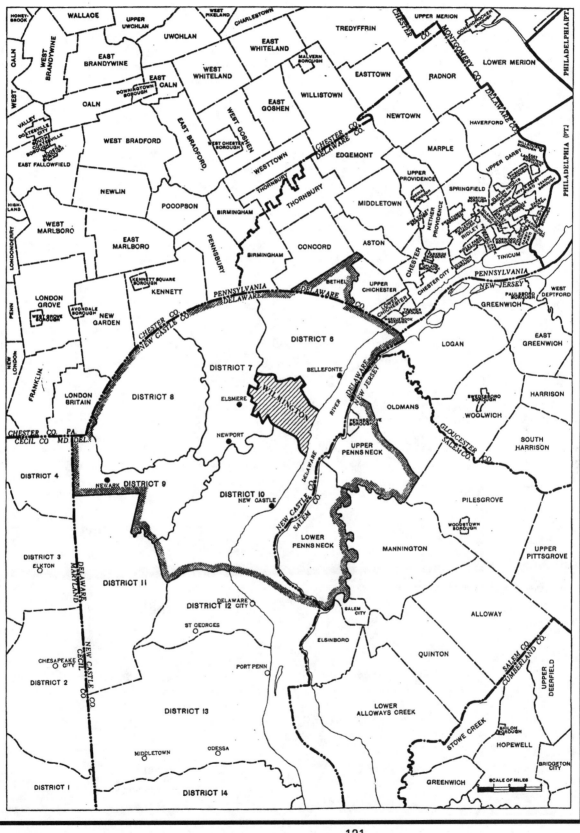

Florida – Jacksonville

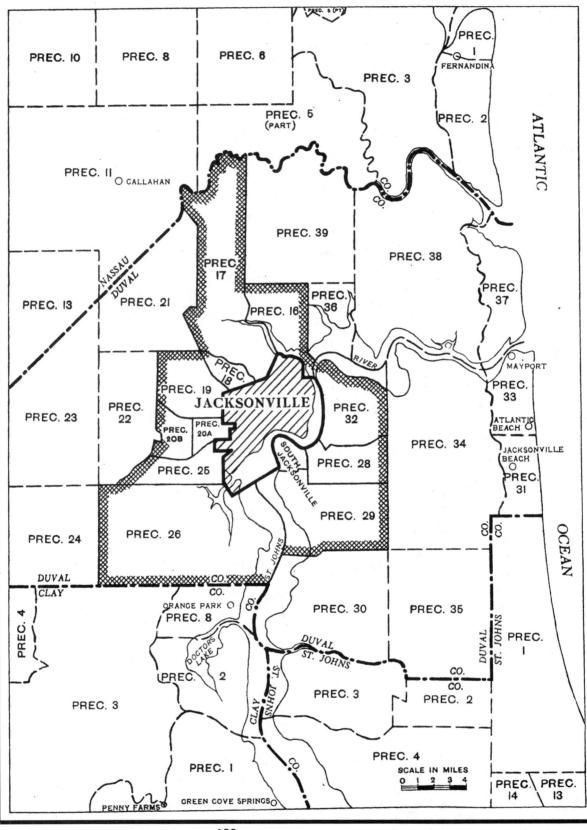

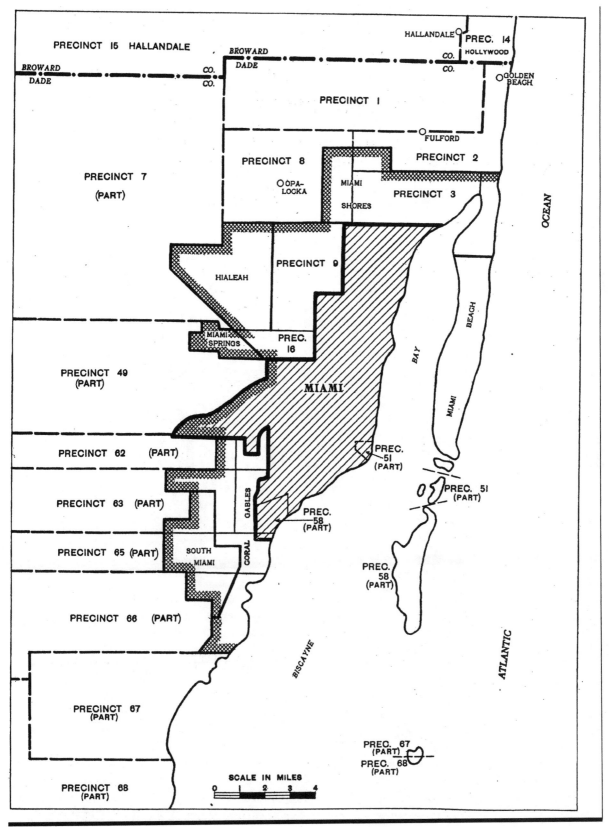

Florida – Tampa - St. Petersburg

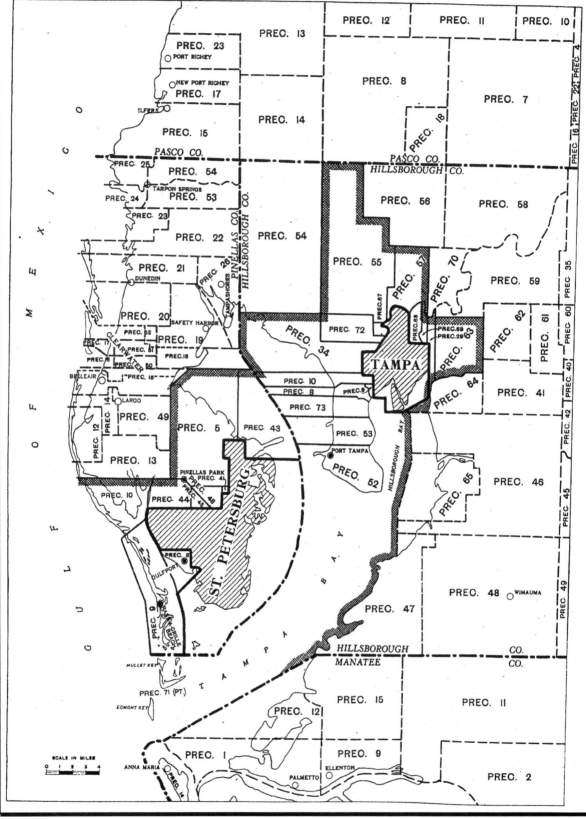

Georgia – Atlanta

DIST. 991
KENNESAW

DIST. 911

DIST. 1319

COBB CO.

MILTON CO.

DIST. 1175

DIST. 1176

DIST. 1227

DIST. 842

DULUTH

DIST. 897

DIST. 845

ROSWELL

DIST. 1172

MILTON CO.

GWINNETT CO.

DIST. 1263

DIST. 1608

MACHINERY CITY

MARIETTA

DIST. 1679

DIST. 1226

DIST. 524

GWINNETT CO.

NORCROSS

DIST. 406

DIST. 544

DIST. 898

COBB CO.

FULTON CO. DIST. 1100

DORA-VILLE

DIST. 1416

DIST. 405

LILBURN

SMYRNA

DIST 1292

DIST. 1568

RIVER

DIST. 1328

DIST. 722

CHAMBLEE

FULTON CO.

DE KALB CO.

DIST. 686

DIST. 572

DE KALB CO.

DIST. 1578

DIST. 895

DIST. 992

DIST. 489

DIST. 1362

DIST. 1327

CLARKSTON

DIST. 1045

STONE MOUNTAIN

DIST. 531

DIST 1378

COBB CO.
DOUGLAS CO.

DIST. 1395

DIST. 1273

DIST. 1511

CHATTAHOOCHEE

DIST. 1289

ATLANTA

DECATUR
DIST. 1379

AVONDALE ESTATES

DIST. 1586

DIST. 637

DIST. 1398

DIST. 784

CAMPBELL CO.

DIST. 1762

DIST. 1666

DE KALB CO.

DIST. 683

DIST. 731

DIST. 479

DIST.
530

EAST POINT
DIST.
1332

DIST.
1589

DIST.
1348

DIST. 1349

DIST. 1422

DE KALB CO.

DIST. 536

DIST. 1448

DIST. 487

DIST. 734

FULTON CO.

CAMPBELL CO.

DIST. 1615

HAPEVILLE

CLAYTON CO.

DE KALB CO.

HENRY CO.

ROCKDALE CO.

HENRY CO.

DIST. 1261

DIST 733

DIST. 499

COLLEGE PARK

CLAYTON CO.

FOREST PARK

DIST. 1446

DIST. 1644

DIST. 1406

DIST. 888

DIST. 622

DIST.
1725

UNION CITY

DIST. 548

RIVERDALE

DIST. 1189

DIST. 491

FAIRBURN

DIST. 1204

DIST. 775

STOCKBRIDGE

DIST. 1134

CAMPBELL CO.
FAYETTE

CO.

FLINT

DIST.

DIST. 1088

JONESBORO

CLAYTON CO.
HENRY CO.

DIST.
652

DIST.
746

COWETA CO.
FAYETTE CO.

DIST. 549

TYRONE

DIST. 1248

1262

RIVER

SCALE IN MILES
0 1 2 3 4

DIST. 709

DIST. 496

DIST. 1651

DIST. 486

DIST. 1477

Georgia – Savannah

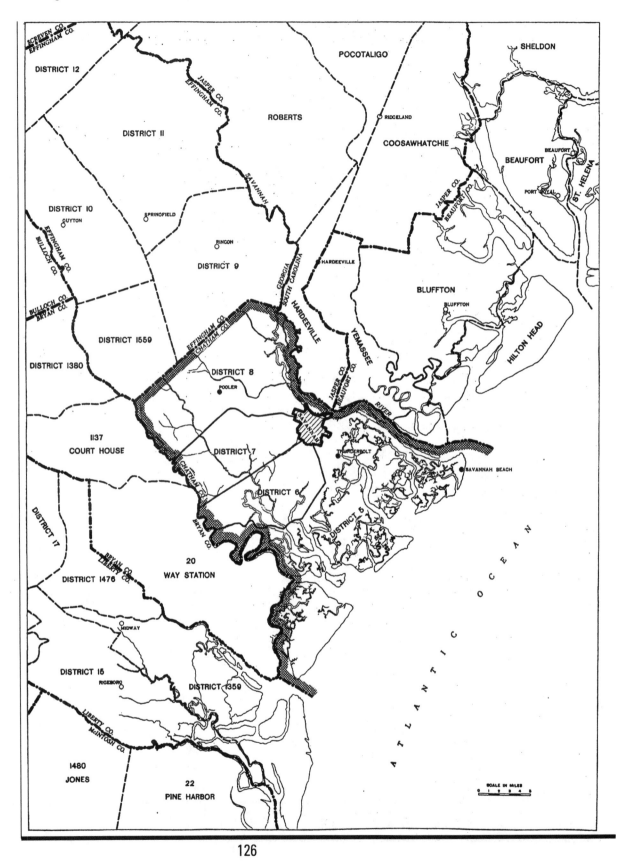

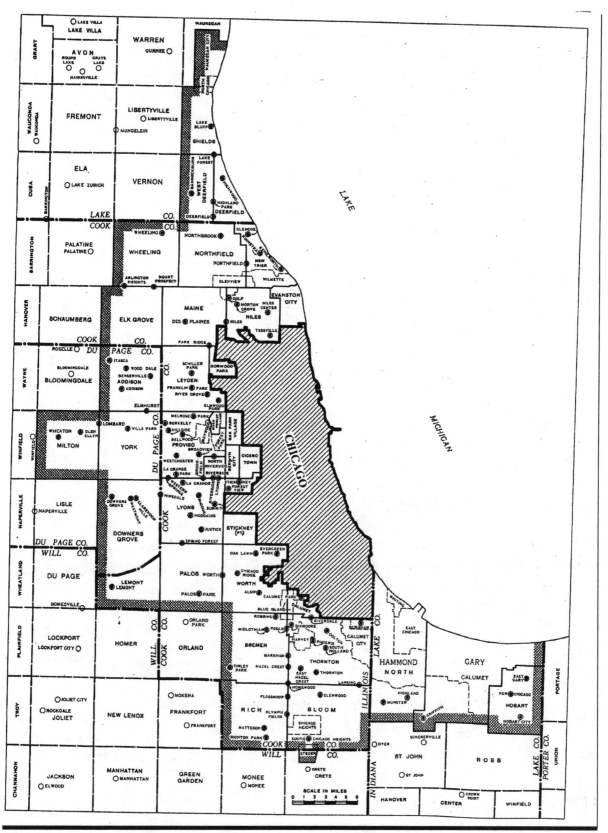

Illinois – Peoria

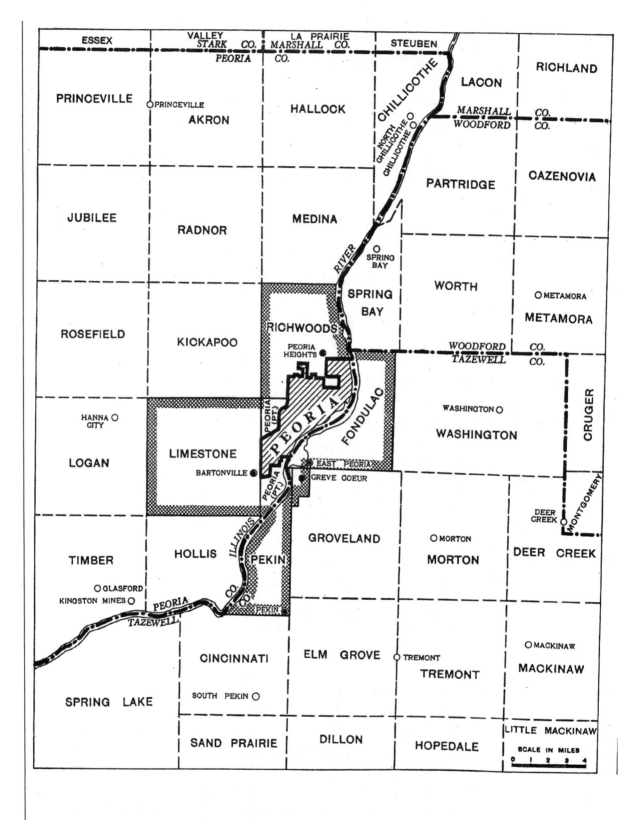

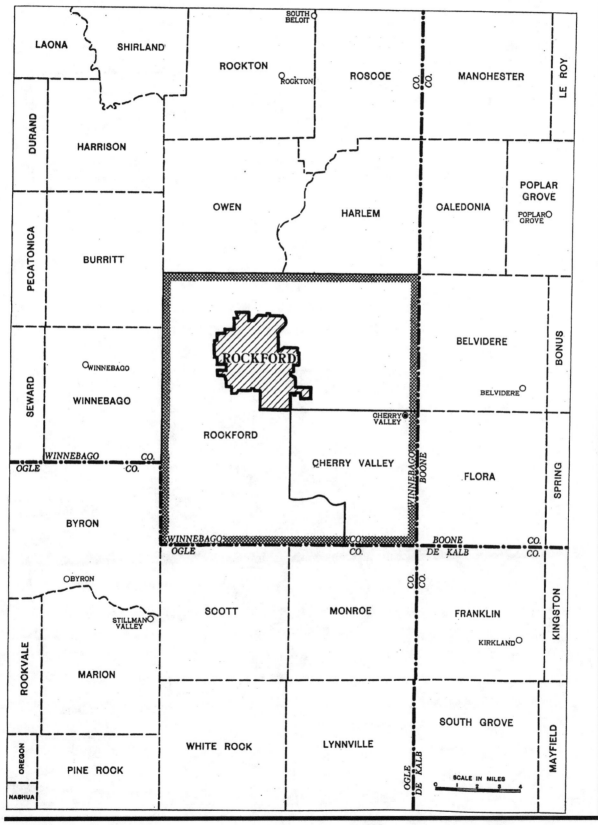

Indiana – Evansville

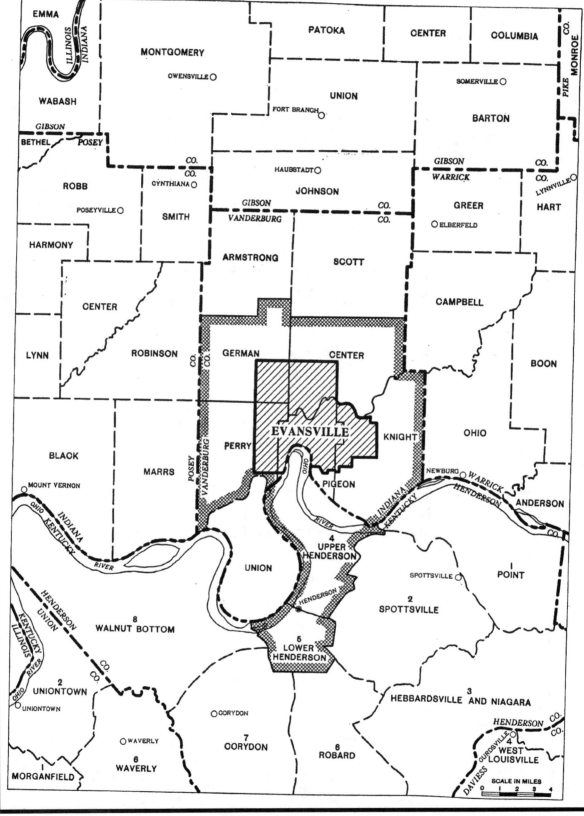

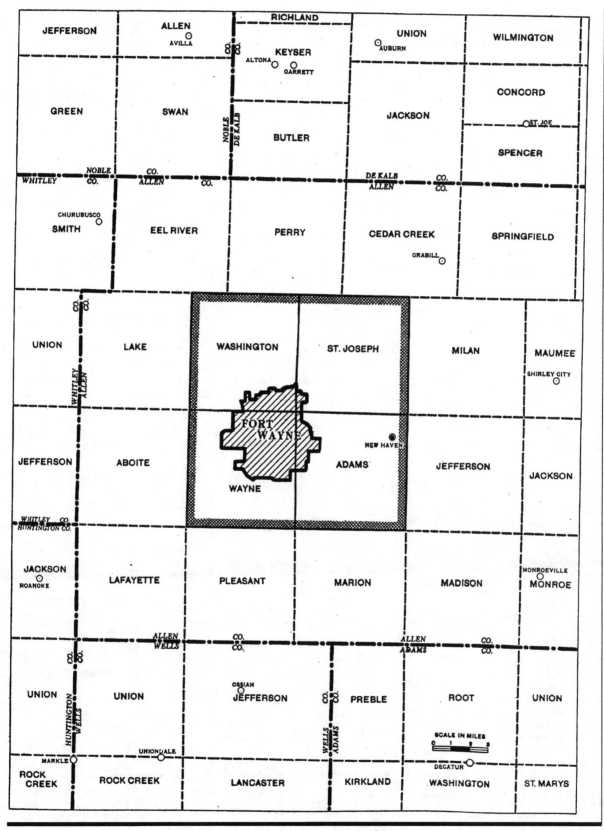

Indiana – Indianapolis

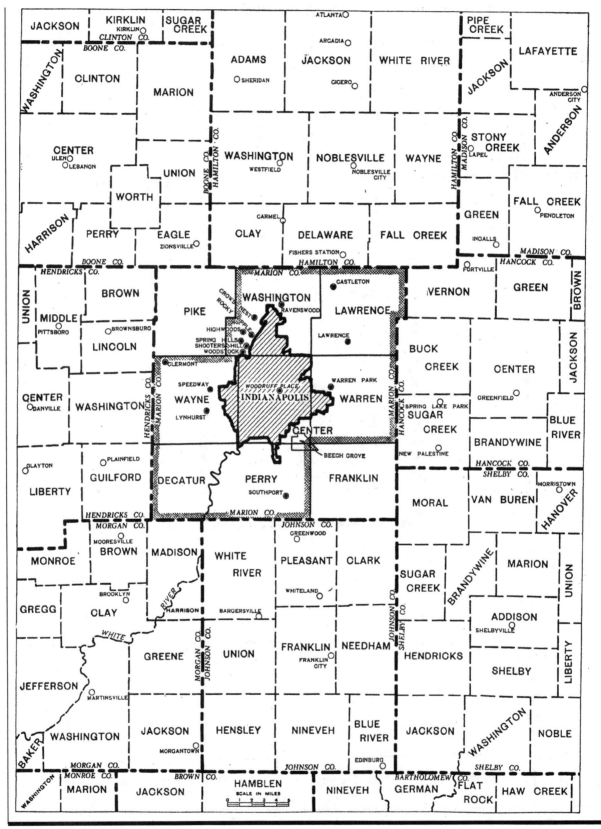

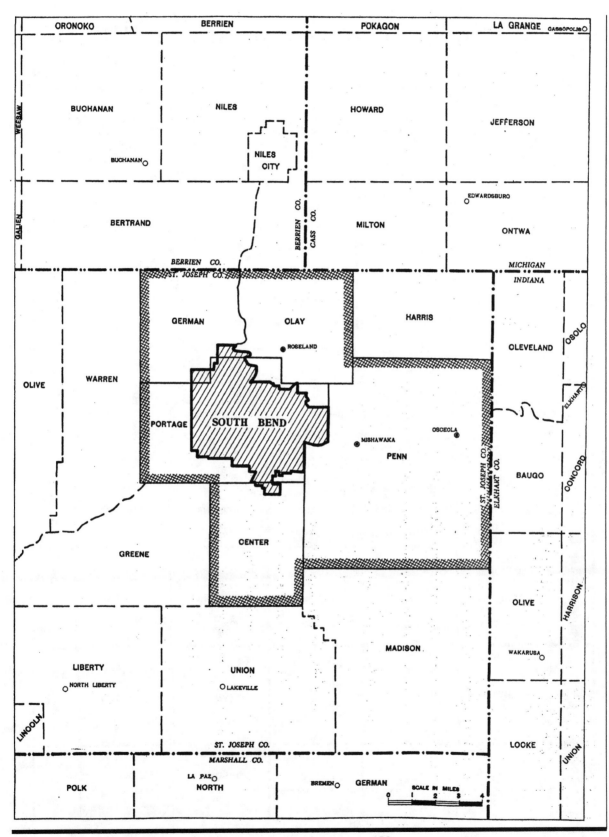

Iowa – Davenport

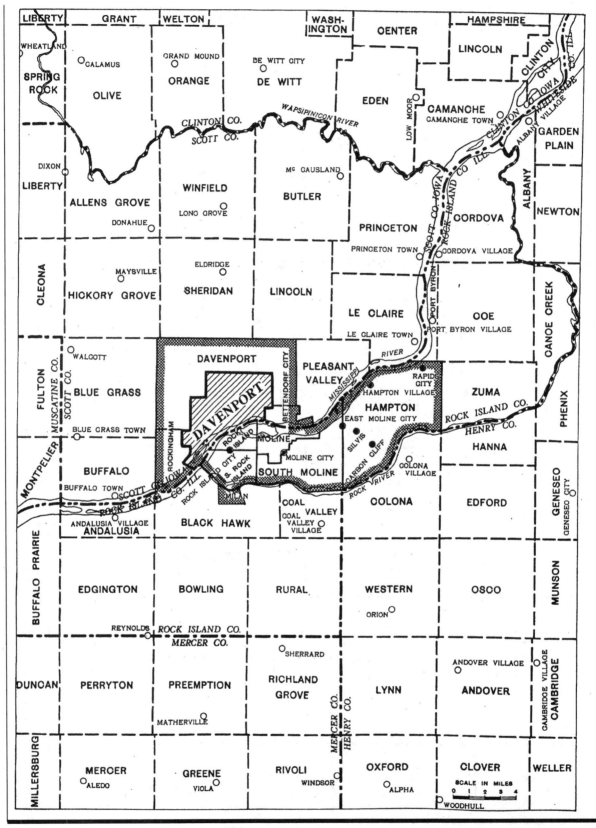

Iowa – Des Moines

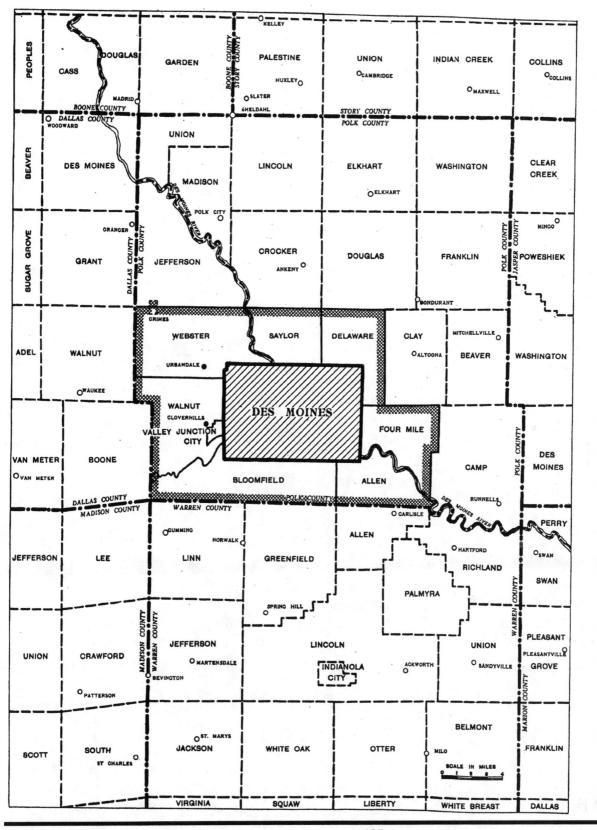

Kansas – Kansas City, KS -- Kansas City, MO

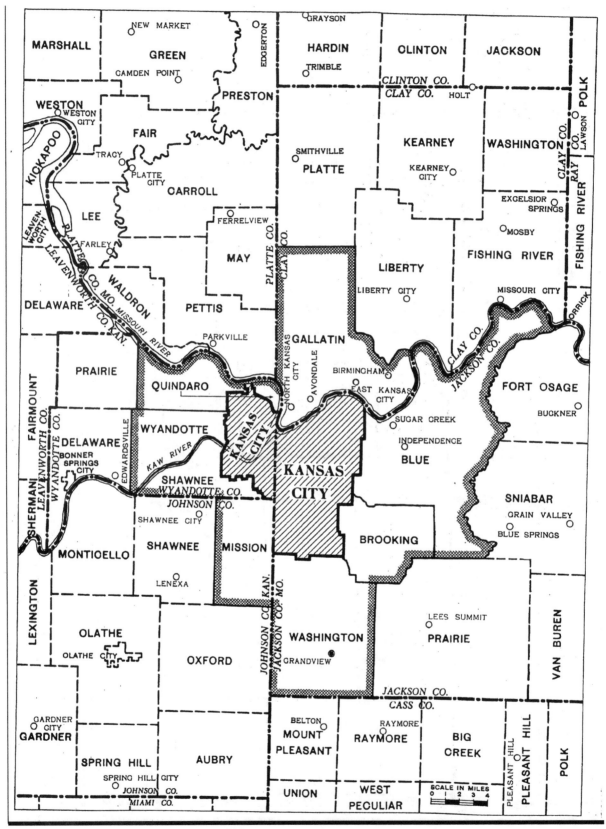

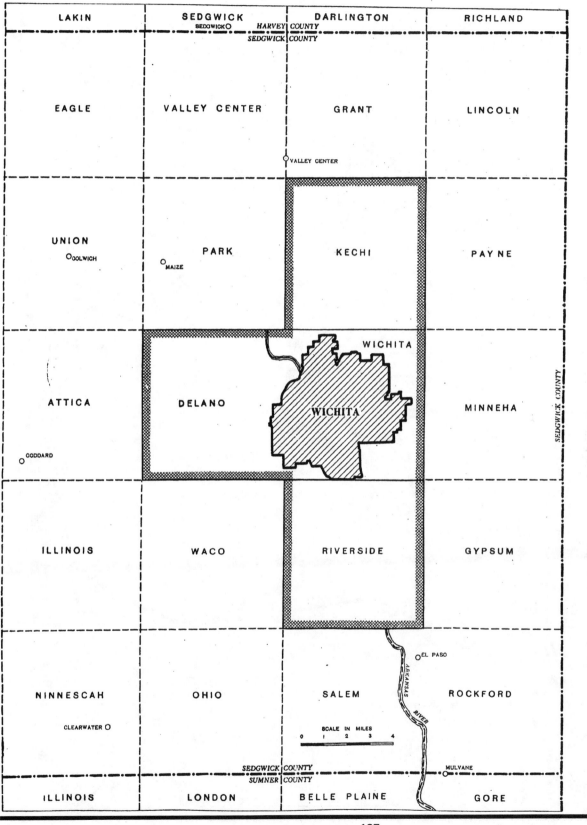

Kentucky – Louisville

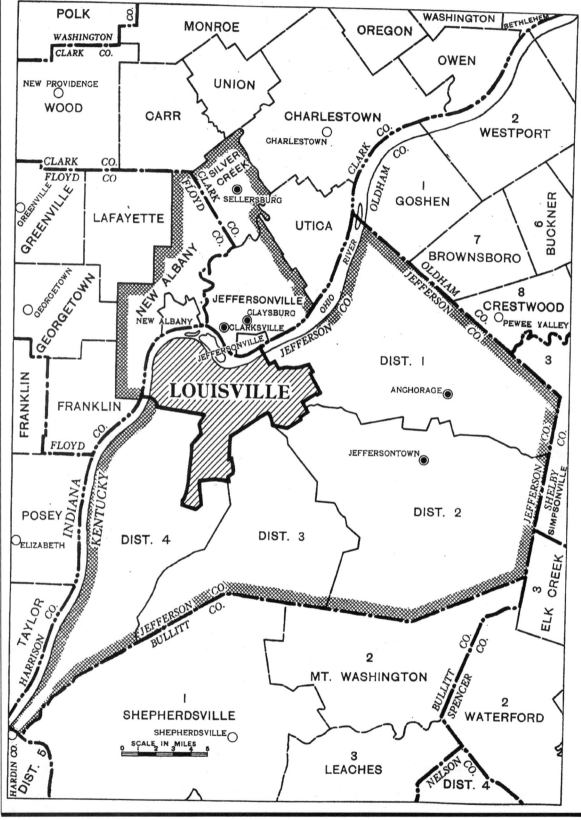

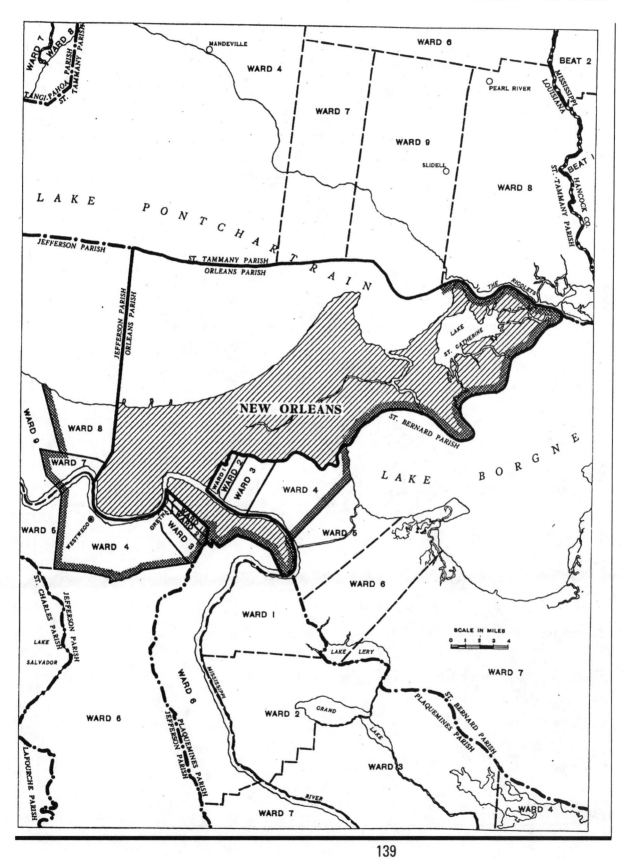

Maryland – Baltimore

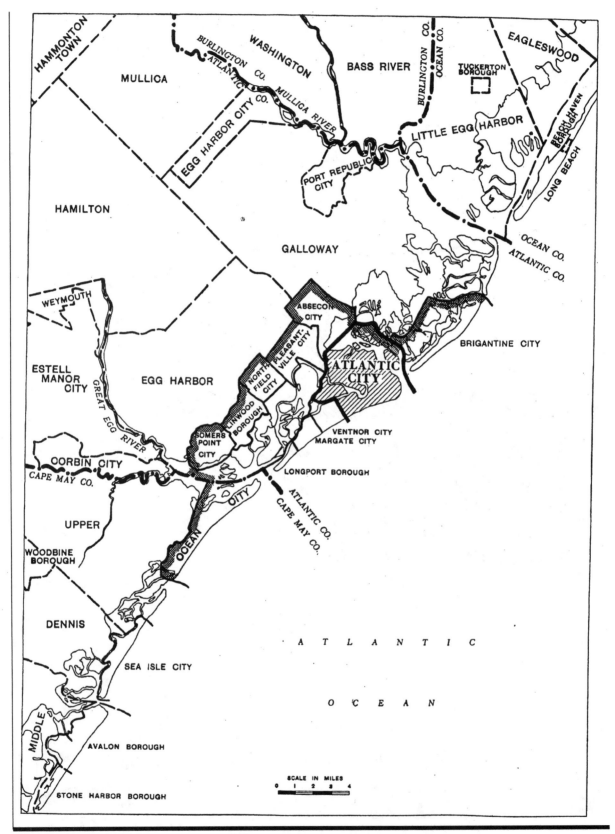

Massachusetts – Lowell - Lawrence

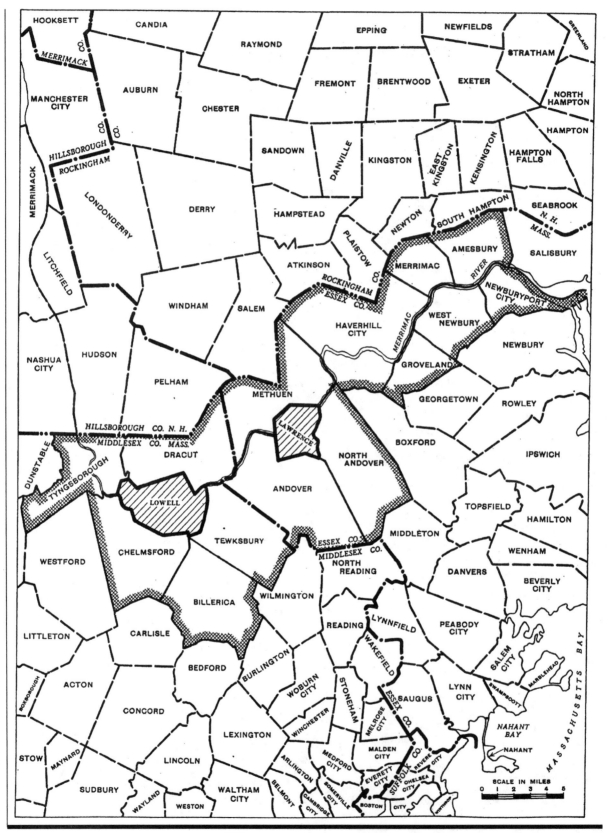

Massachusetts – Springfield - Holyoke

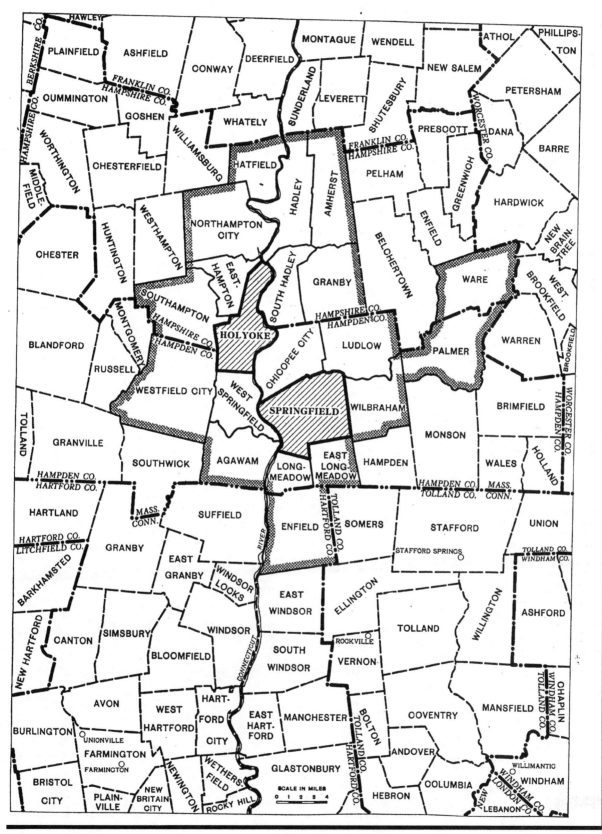

Massachusetts – Worcester

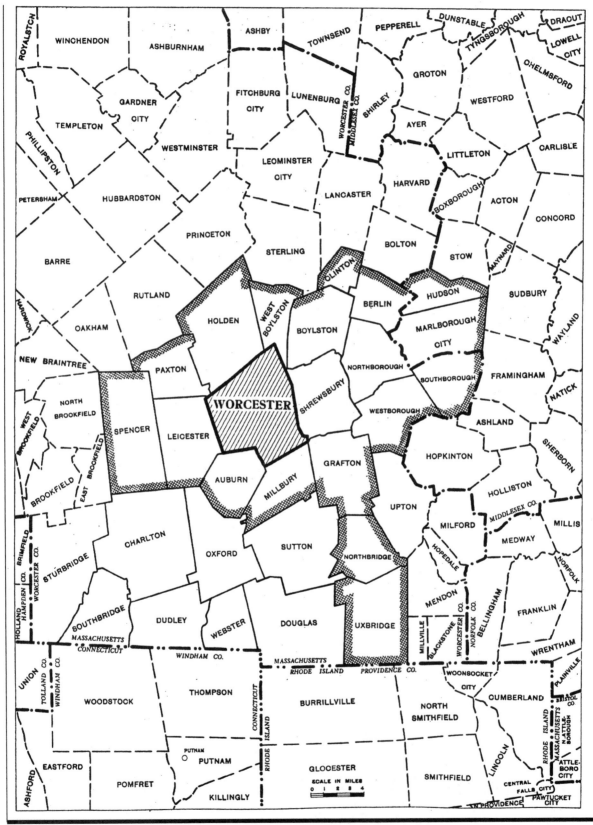

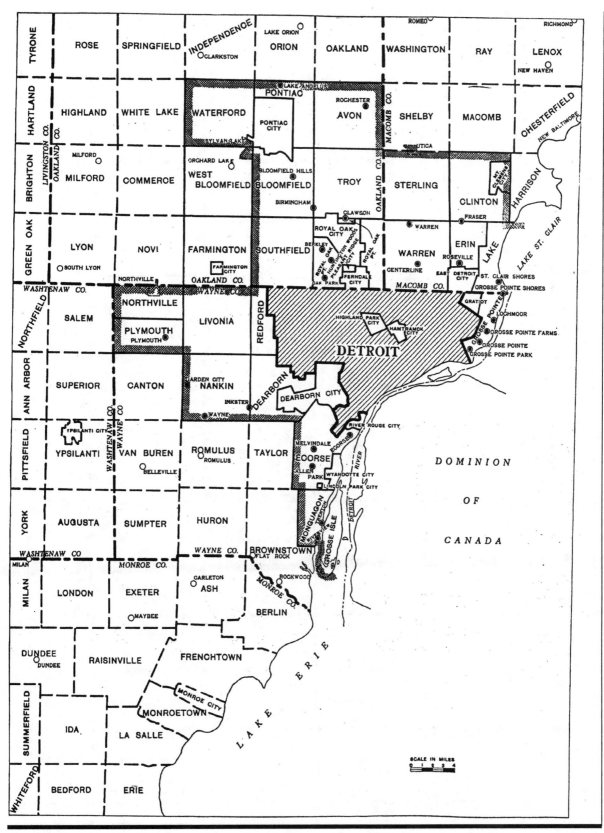

Michigan – Flint

SPAULDING	BRIDGEPORT	FRANKENMUTH ○ FRANKENMUTH	TUSCOLA	VASSAR	FREMONT
ALBEE	TAYMOUTH	BIRCH RUN	TUSCOLA CO. SAGINAW CO. ○○ ARBELA	○MILLINGTON MILLINGTON	WATERTOWN

SAGINAW CO.
GENESEE CO.
TUSCOLA CO.
GENESEE CO.

| MAPLE
GROVE | ○MONTROSE
MONTROSE | PINE RUN
CLIO CITY ○□
VIENNA | THETFORD' | FOREST
○OTISVILLE | ○OTTER LAKE
MARATHON
○COLUMBIAVILLE |

MOUNT MORRIS ○

| HAZELTON | FLUSHING
FLUSHING○ | MOUNT MORRIS | GENESEE | RICHFIELD | OREGON |
| VENICE | CLAYTON | FLINT | **FLINT**
BURTON | ○DAVISON
DAVISON | ELBA |

SHIAWASSEE CO.
GENESEE CO.
LAPEER CO.
GENESEE CO.

| ○DURAND
VERNON | GAINES
○GAINES | MUNDY | GRAND BLANC CITY
GRAND BLANC | ATLAS | HADLEY |

GENESEE CO.
OAKLAND CO.

| BYRON○
BURNS | ARGENTINE
LINDEN○ | FENTON
FENTON○ | HOLLY
HOLLY○ | GROVELAND | ○ORTONVILLE
BRANDON |

GENESEE CO.
LIVINGSTON CO.

| COHOCTAH | DEERFIELD | TYRONE | OAKLAND CO.
ROSE | SPRINGFIELD
SCALE IN MILES
0 1 2 3 4 | INDEPENDENCE |

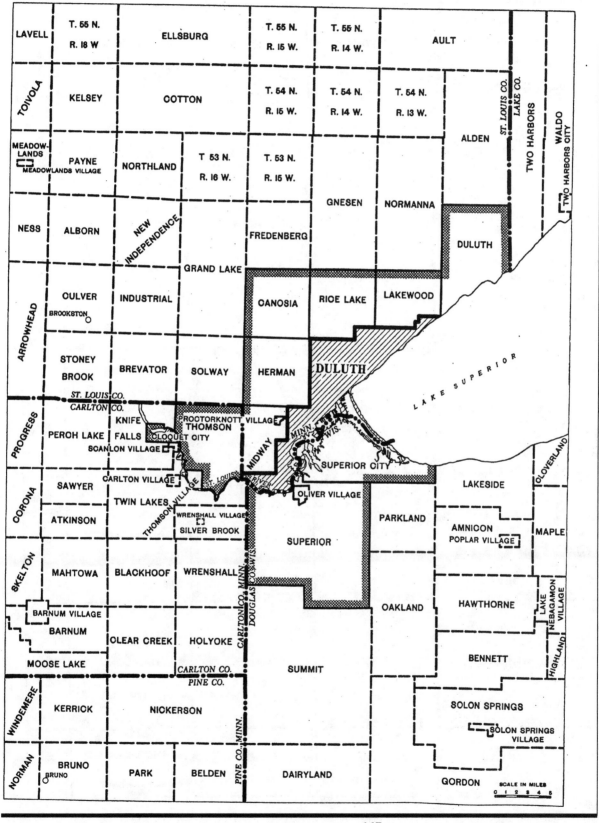

Minnesota – Grand Rapids

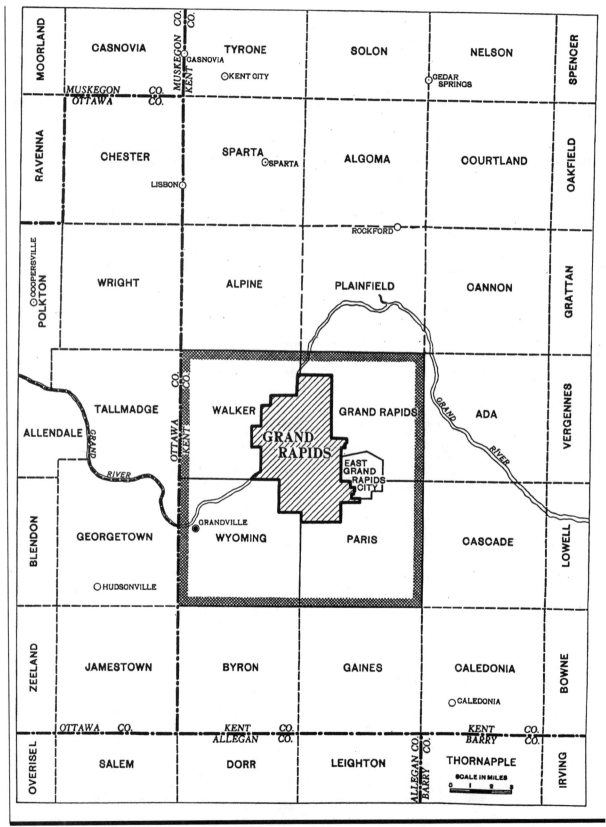

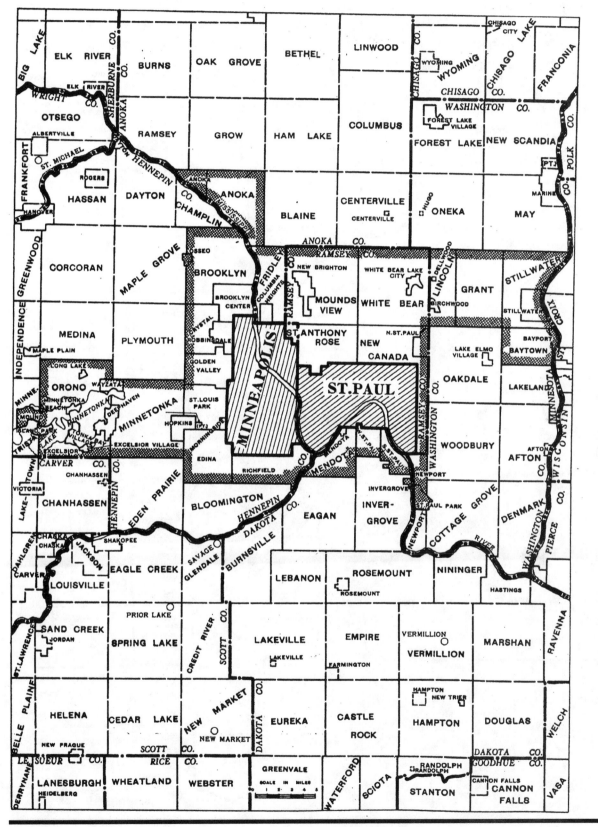

Missouri – St. Louis

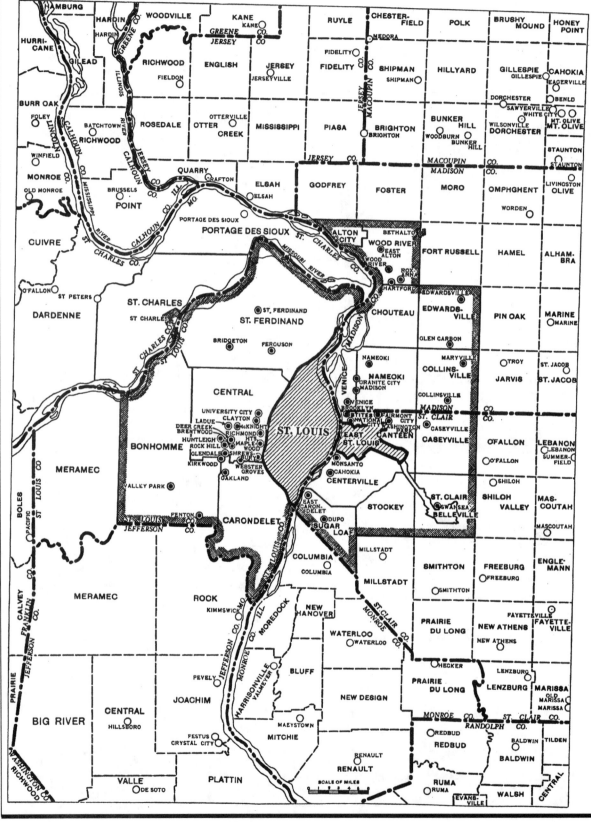

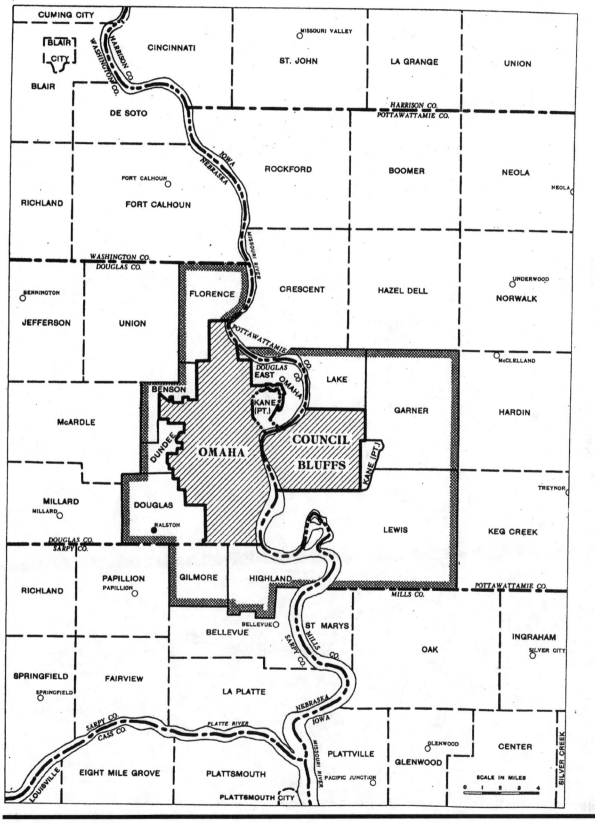

New Jersey – Atlantic City

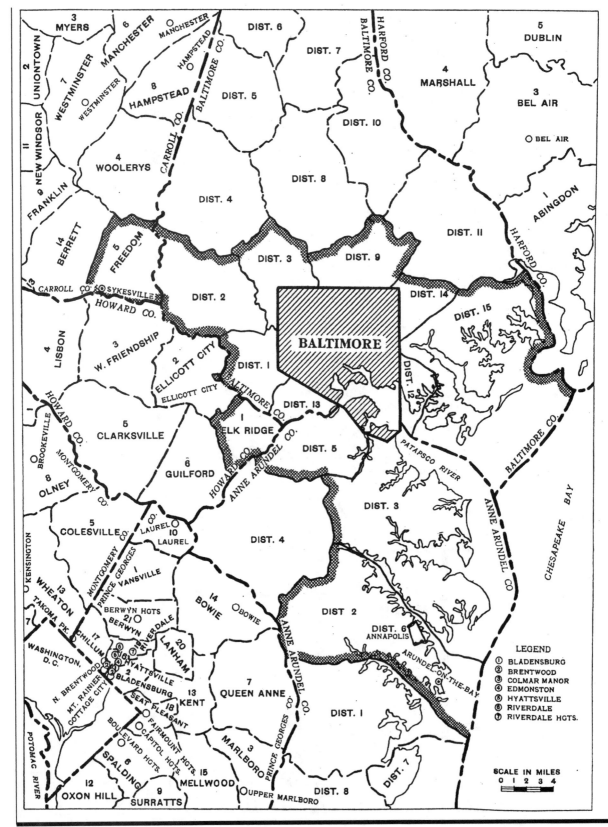

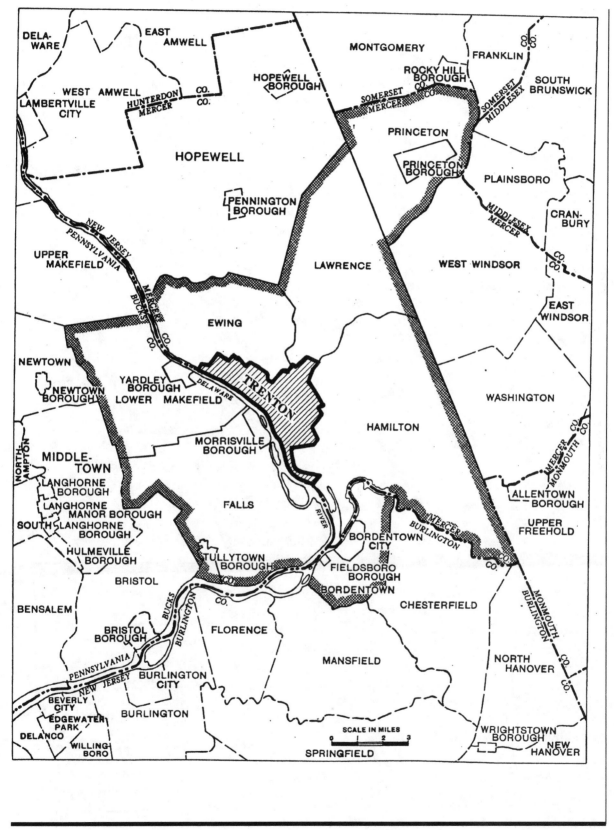

New York – Albany - Schenectady - Troy

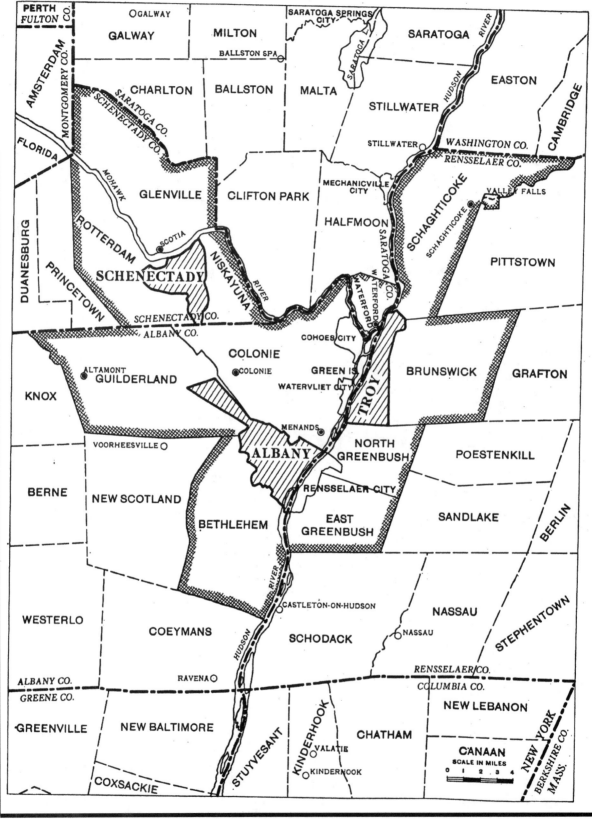

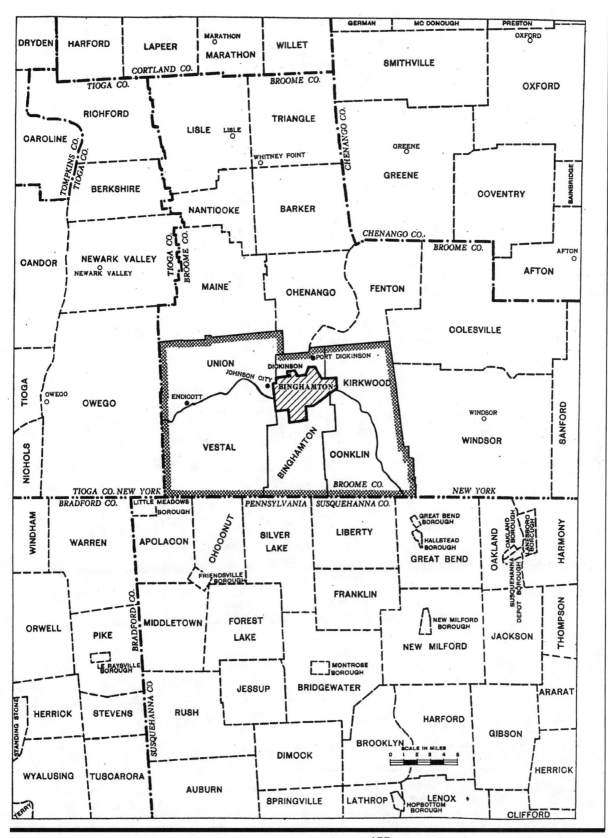

New York – Buffalo - Niagra

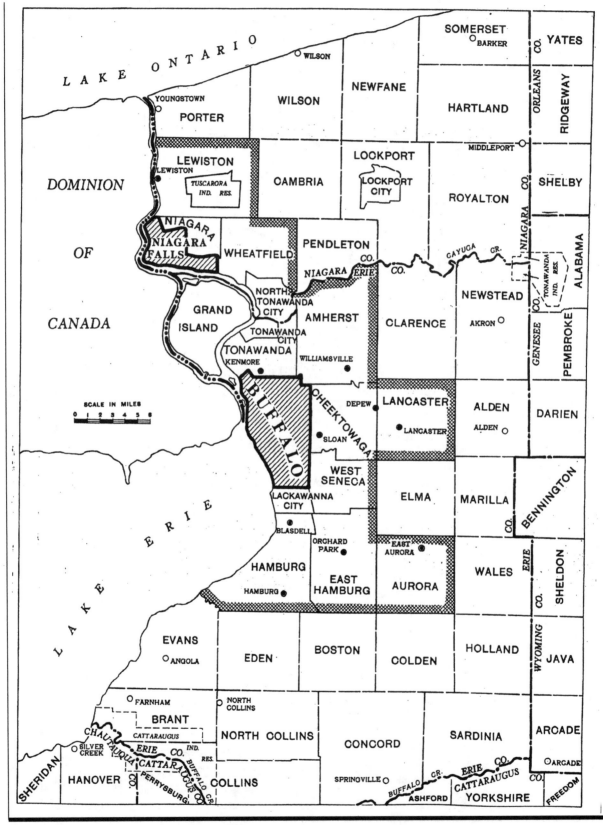

New York – New York City - Northeast New Jersey

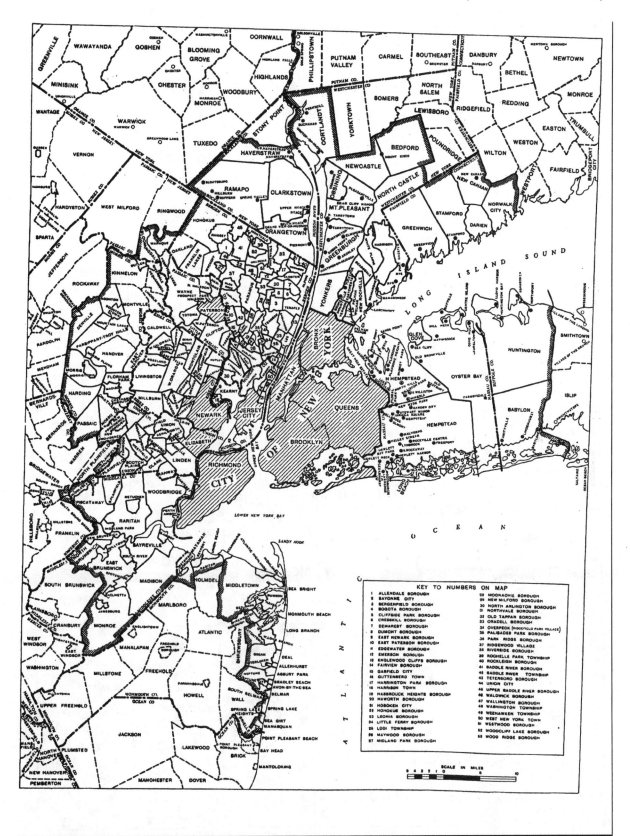

New York – Rochester

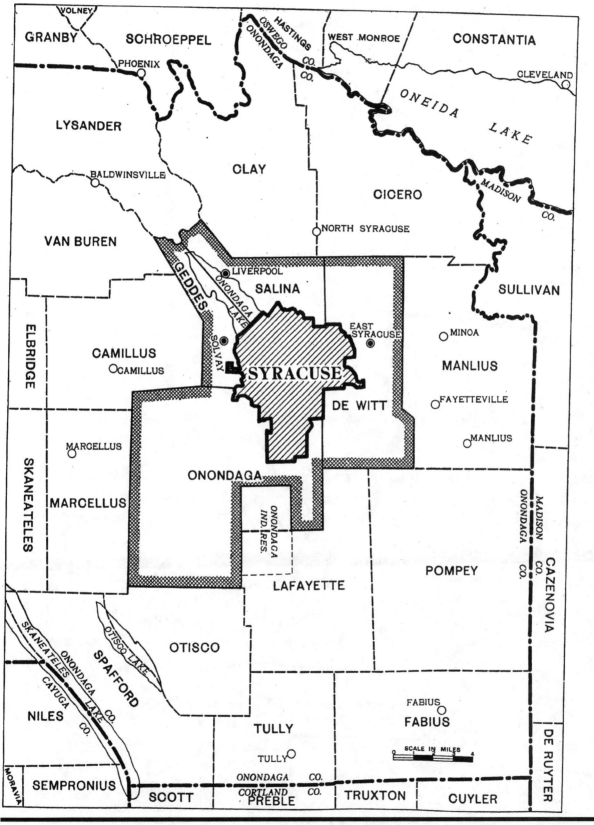

New York – Utica

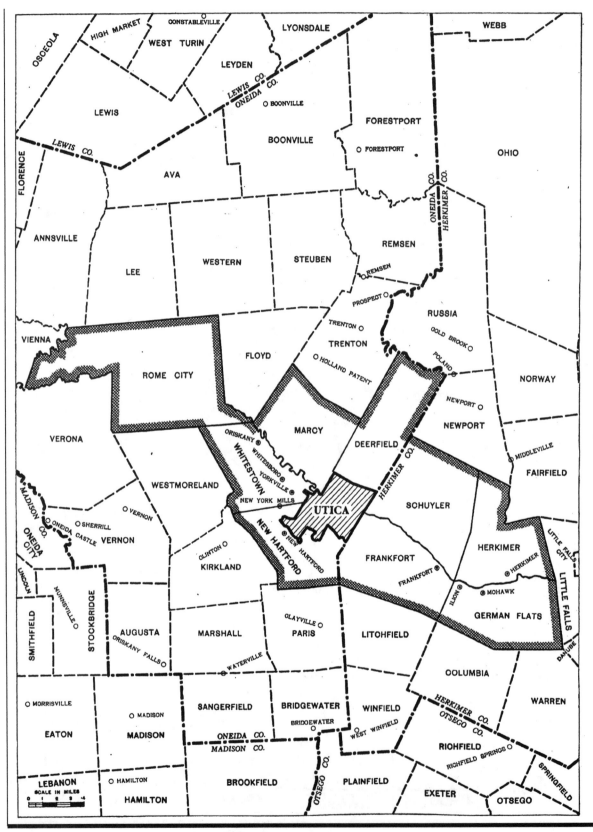

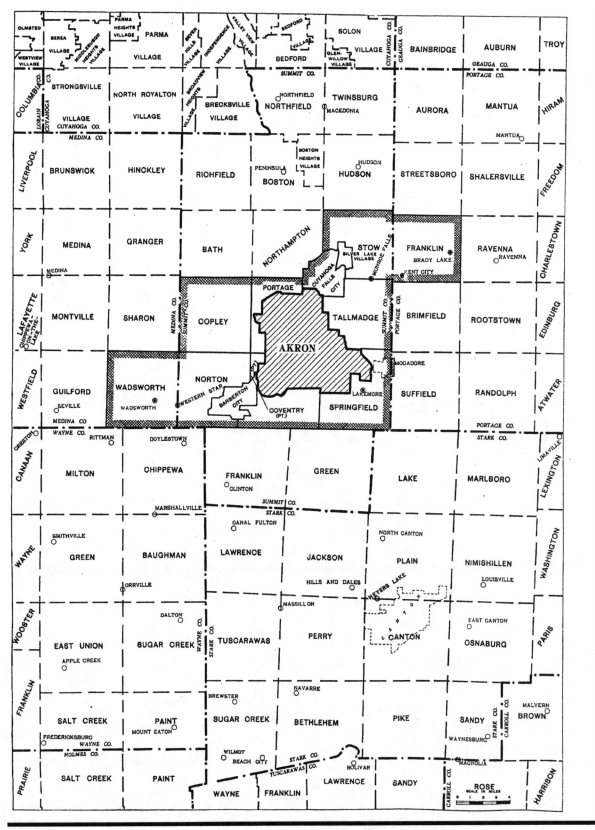

Ohio – Canton

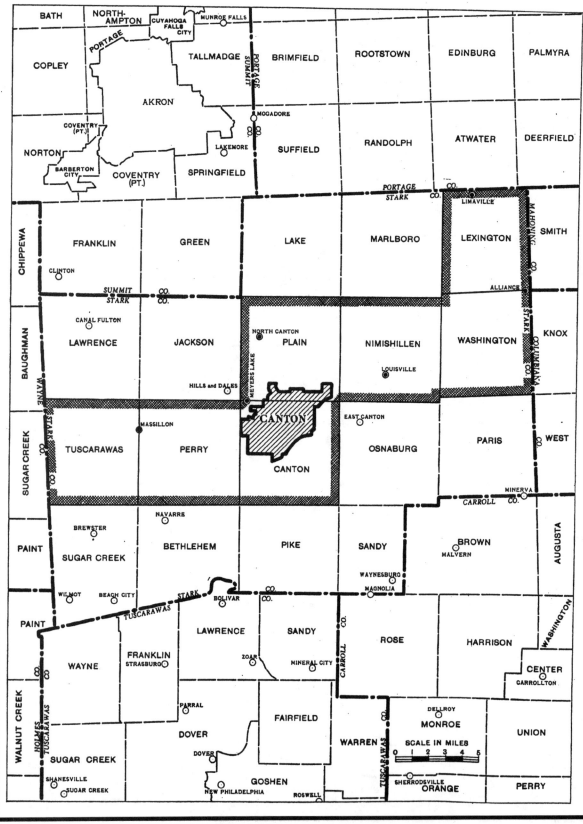

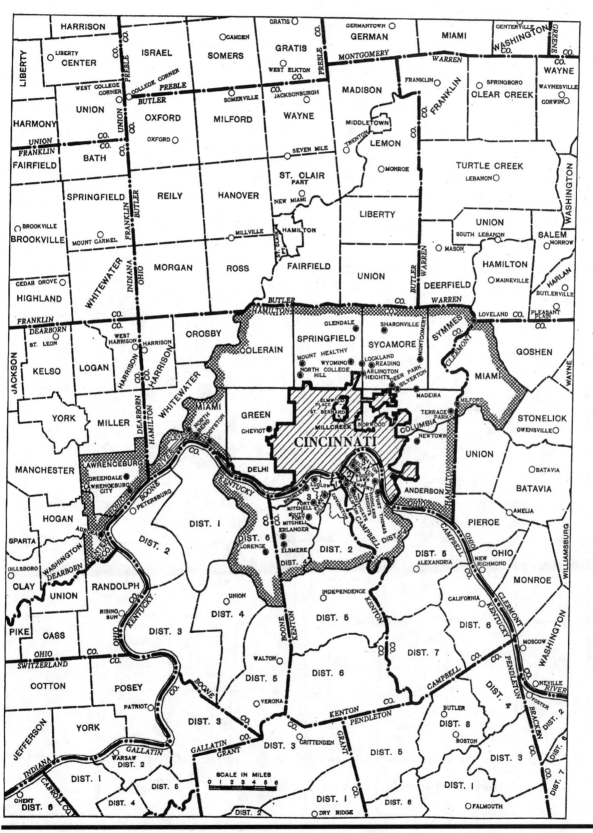

Ohio – Cleveland

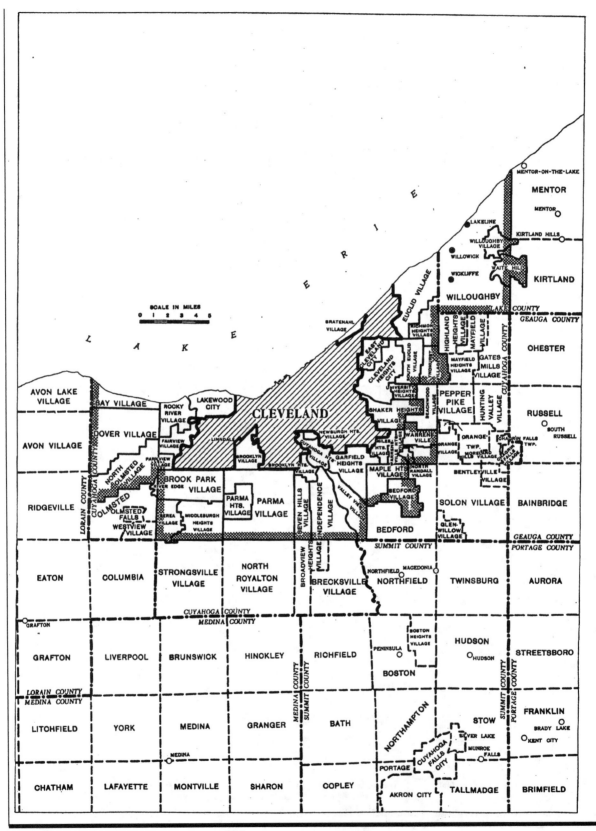

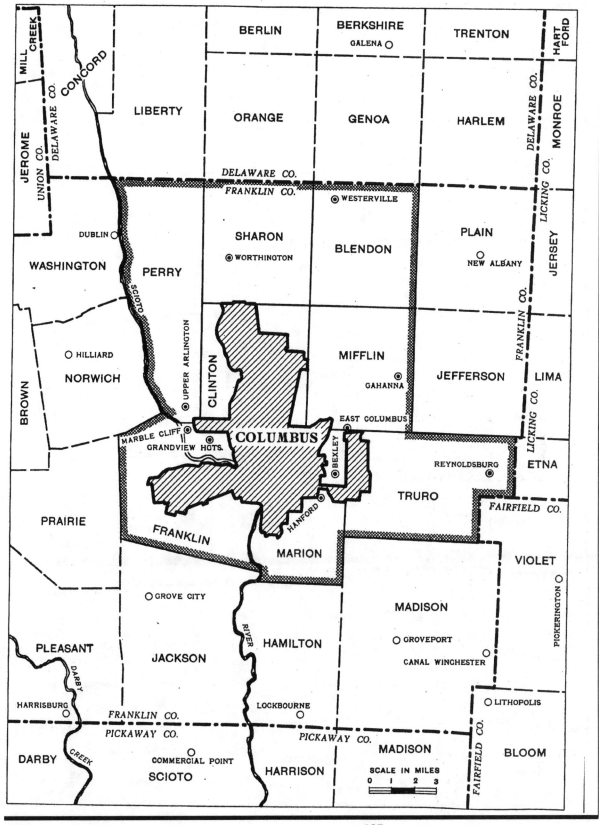

Ohio – Dayton

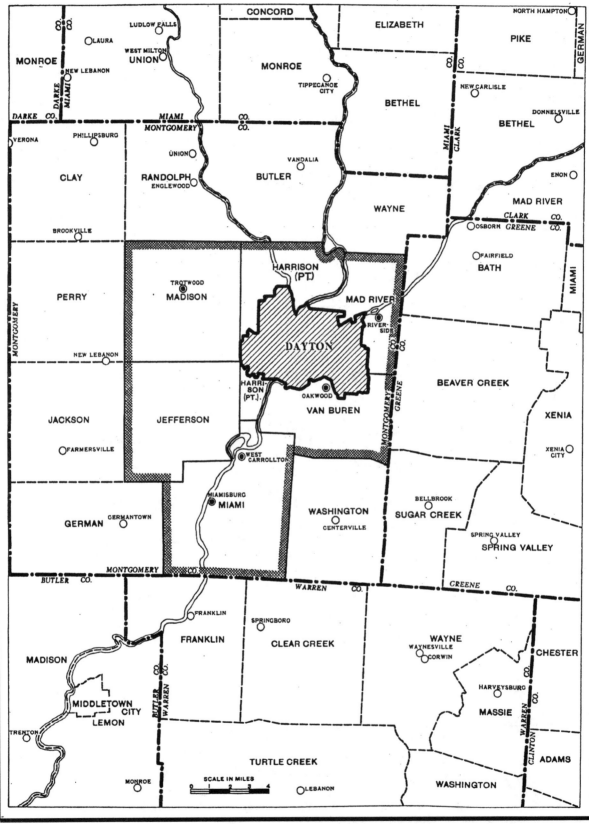

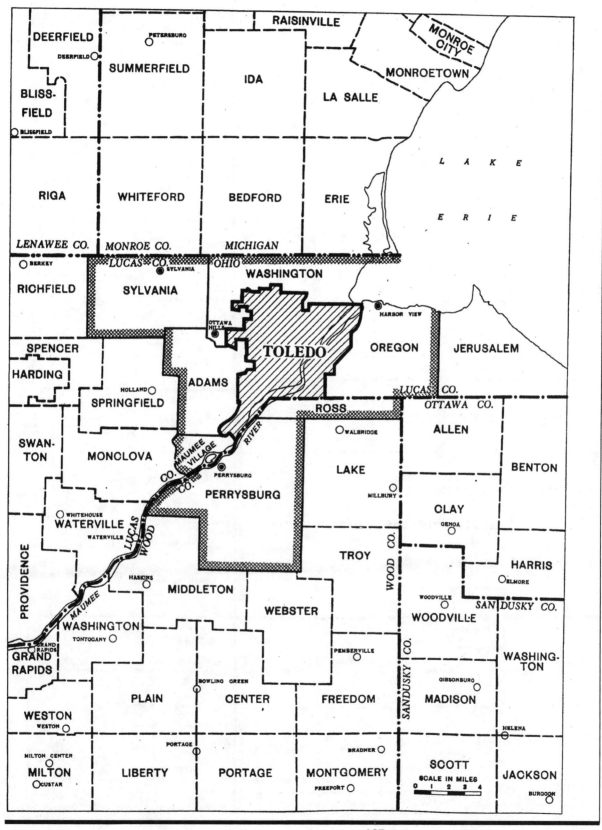

Ohio – Youngstown

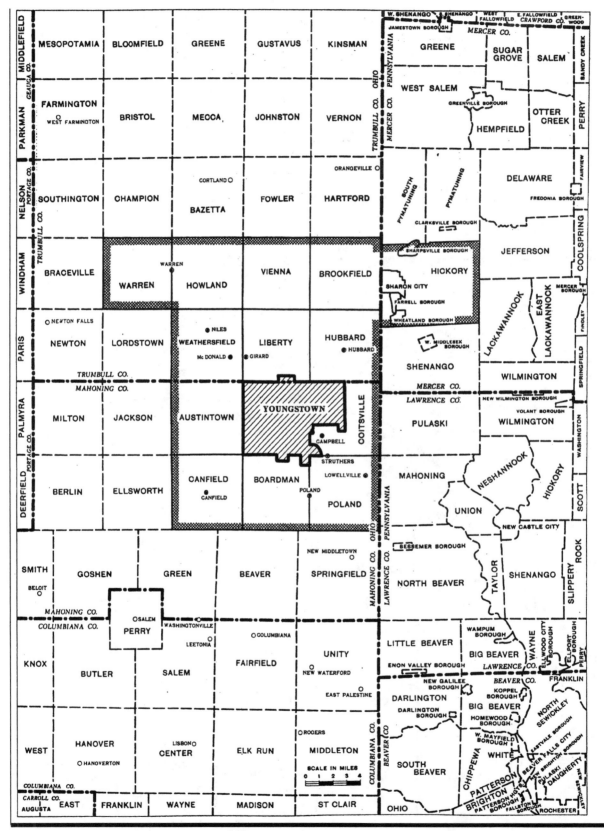

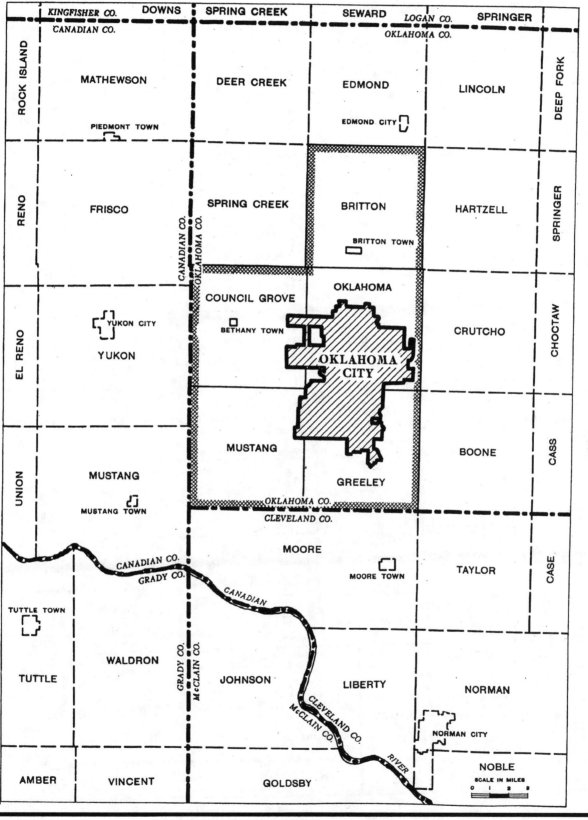

Oklahoma – Tulsa

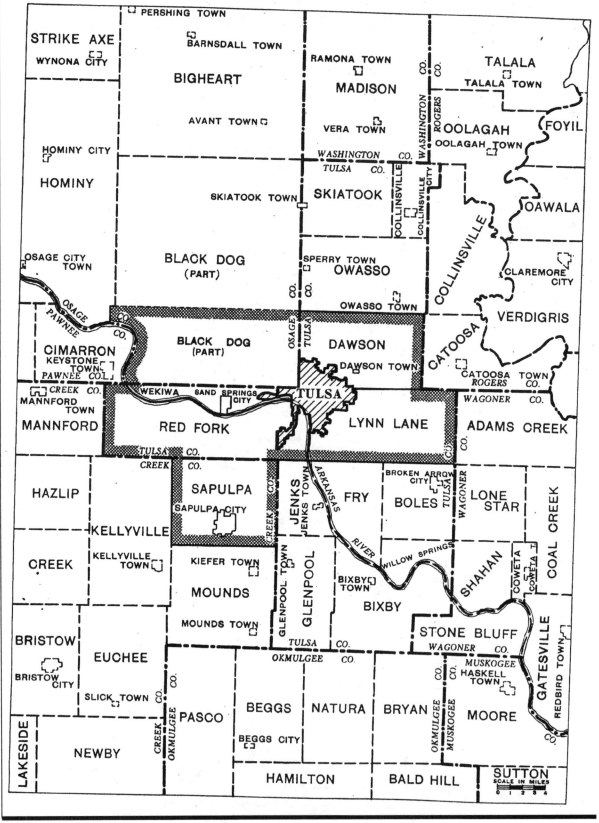

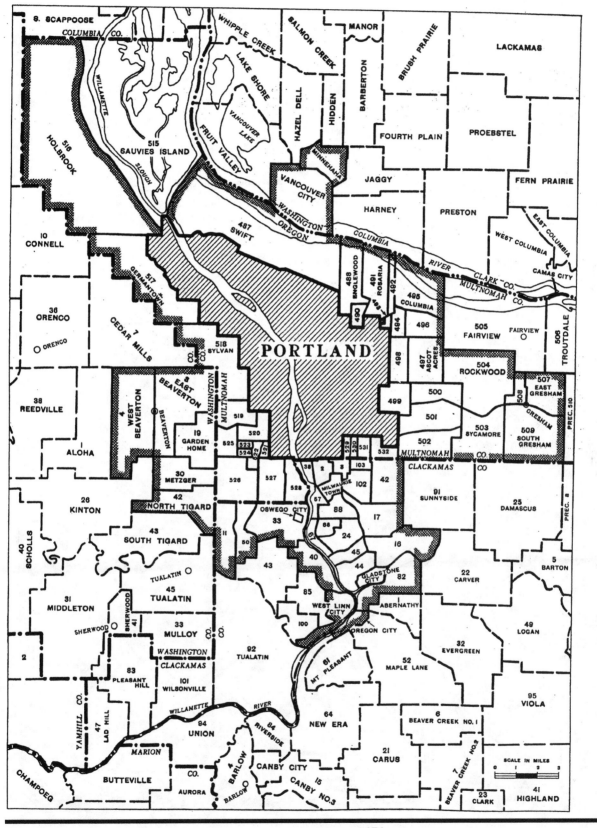

Pennsylvania – Allentown - Bethlehem - Easton

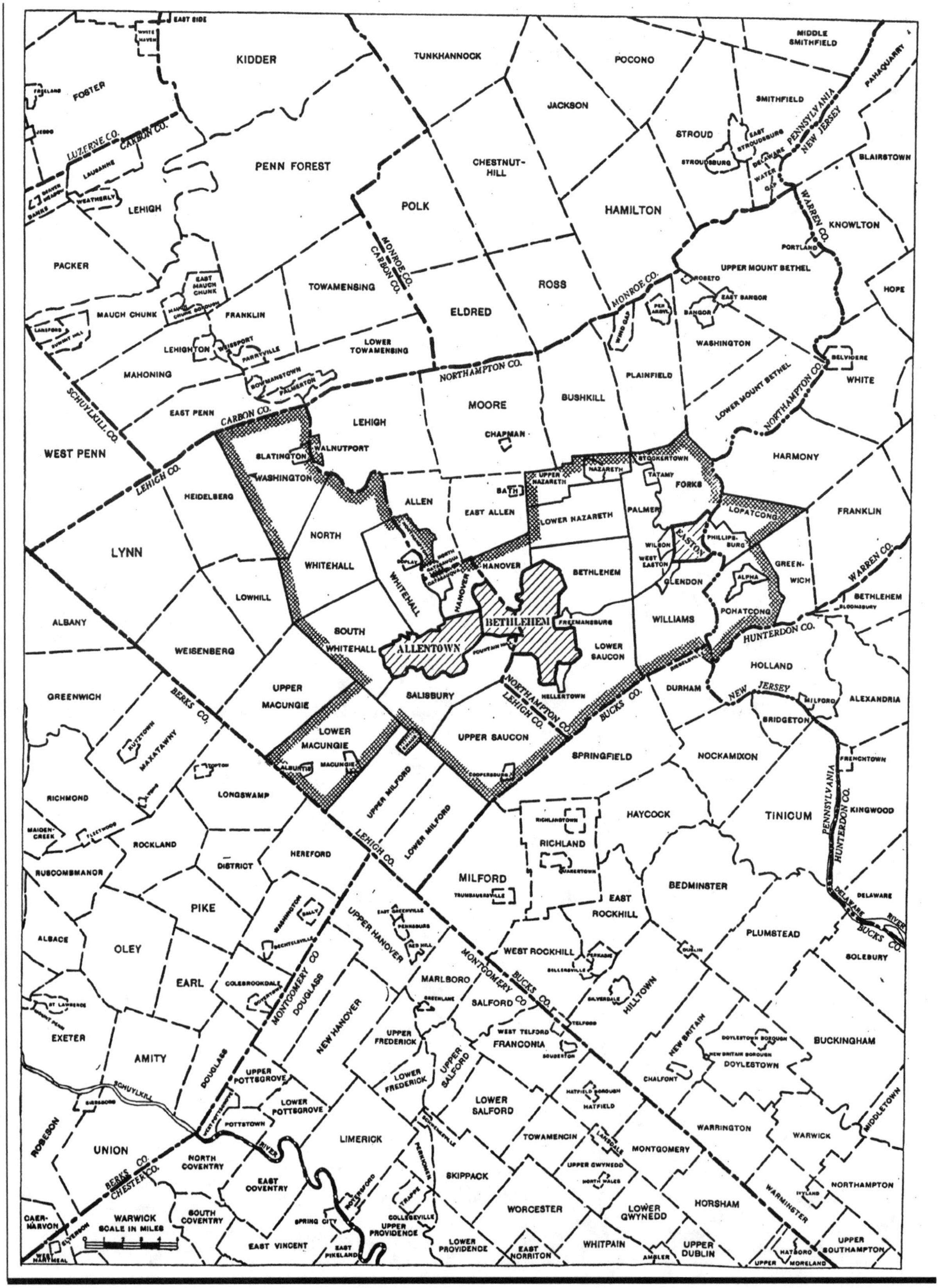

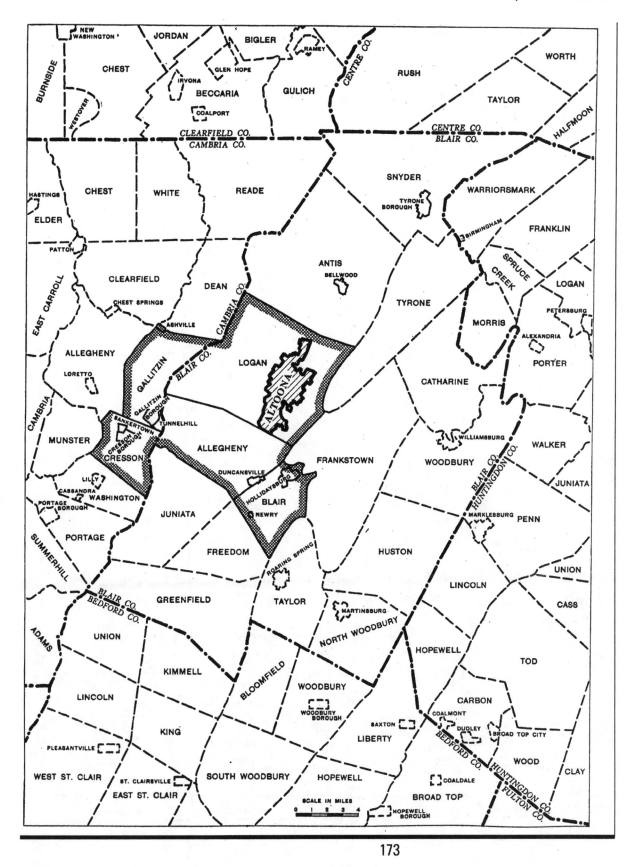

Pennsylvania – Erie

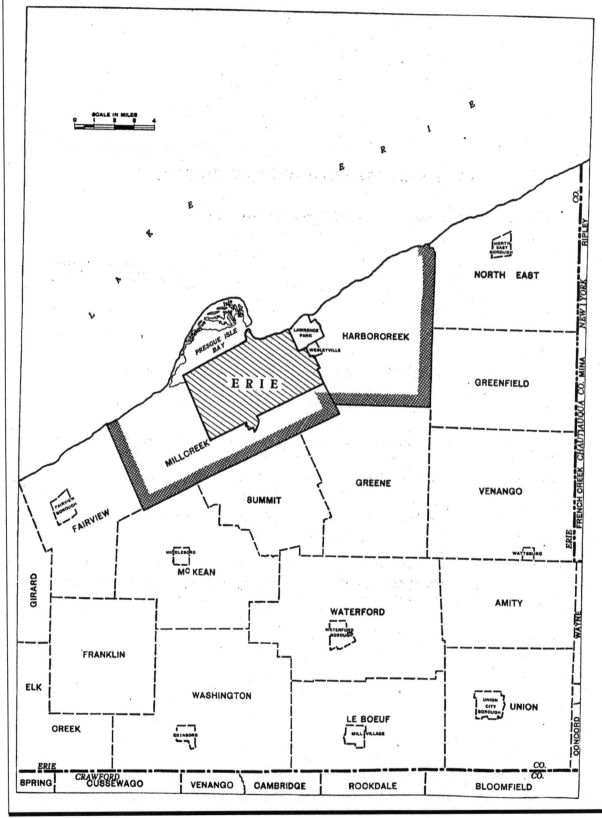

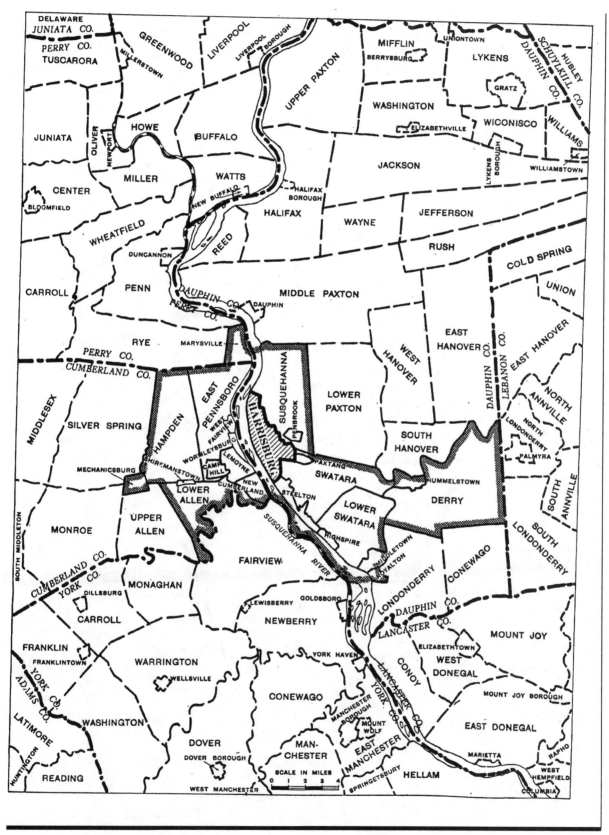

Pennsylvania – Johnstown

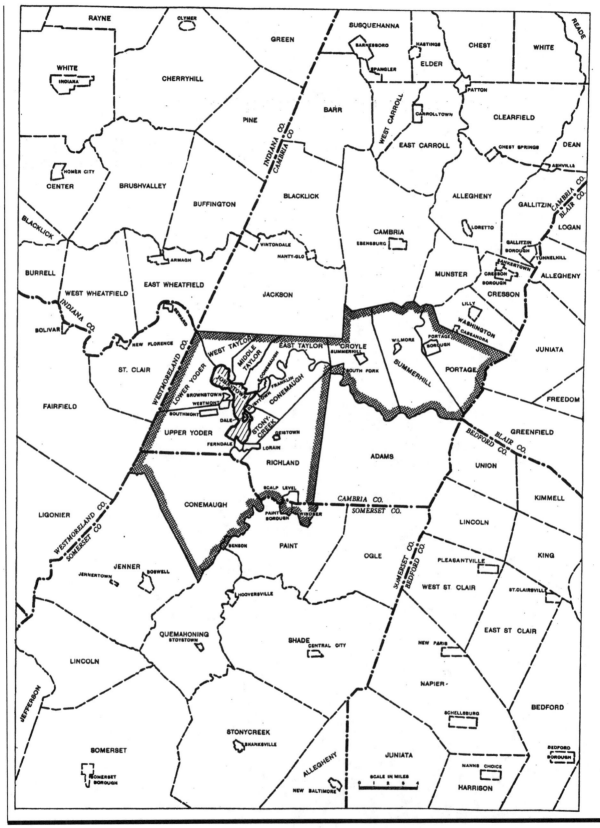

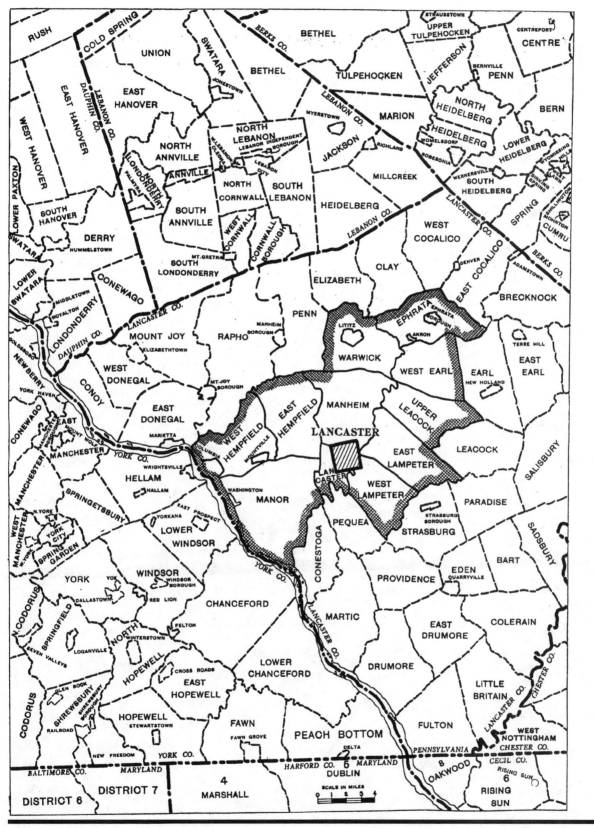

Pennsylvania – Philadelphia

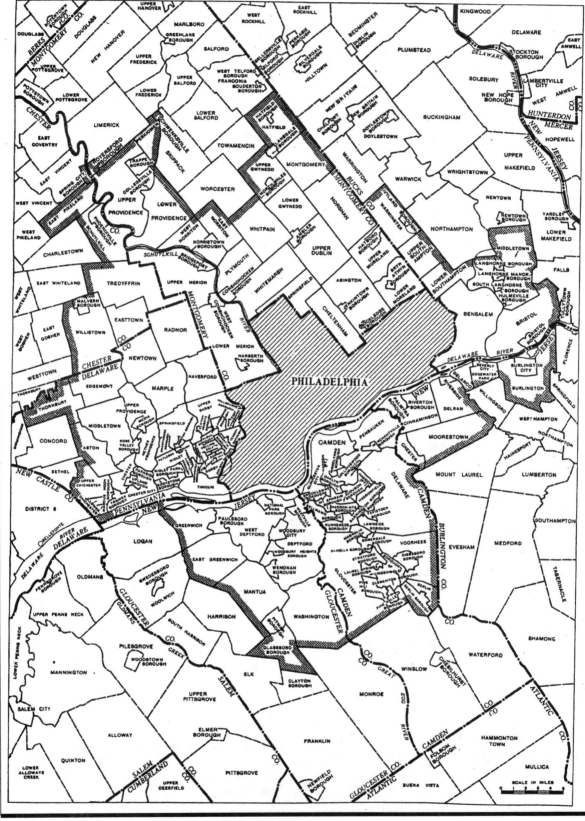

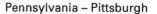

Pennsylvania – Pittsburgh

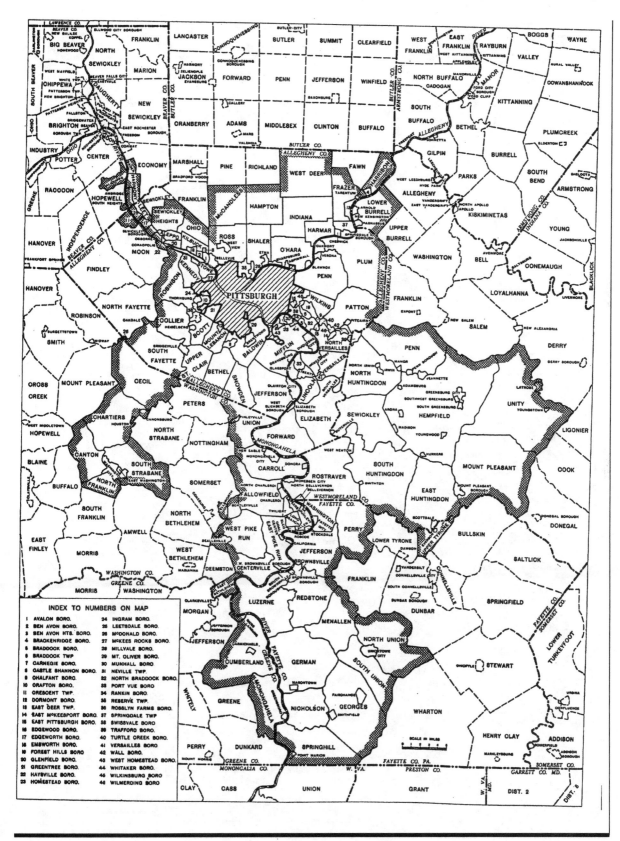

INDEX TO NUMBERS ON MAP

1 AVALON BORO.	24 INGRAM BORO.
2 BEN AVON BORO.	25 LEETSDALE BORO.
3 BEN AVON HTS. BORO.	26 McDONALD BORO.
4 BRACKENRIDGE BORO.	27 McKEES ROCKS BORO.
5 BRADDOCK BORO.	28 MILLVALE BORO.
6 BRADDOCK TWP.	29 MT. OLIVER BORO.
7 CARNEGIE BORO.	30 MUNHALL BORO.
8 CASTLE SHANNON BORO.	31 NEVILLE TWP.
9 CHALFANT BORO.	32 NORTH BRADDOCK BORO.
10 CRAFTON BORO.	33 PORT VUE BORO
11 CRESCENT TWP.	34 RANKIN BORO.
12 DORMONT BORO.	35 RESERVE TWP.
13 EAST DEER TWP.	36 ROSSLYN FARMS BORO.
14 EAST McKEESPORT BORO.	37 SPRINGDALE TWP
15 EAST PITTSBURGH BORO.	38 SWISSVALE BORO
16 EDGEWOOD BORO.	39 TRAFFORD BORO.
17 EDGEWORTH BORO.	40 TURTLE CREEK BORO.
18 EMSWORTH BORO.	41 VERSAILLES BORO
19 FOREST HILLS BORO	42 WALL BORO.
20 GLENFIELD BORO.	43 WEST HOMESTEAD BORO.
21 GREENTREE BORO.	44 WHITAKER BORO.
22 HAYSVILLE BORO.	45 WILKINSBURG BORO.
23 HOMESTEAD BORO.	46 WILMERDING BORO

Pennsylvania – Reading

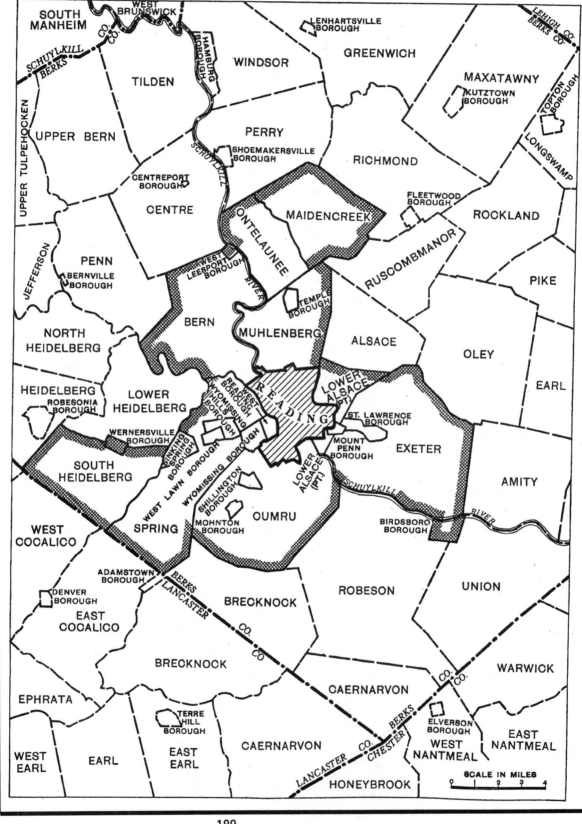

Pennsylvania – Scranton - Wilkes Barre

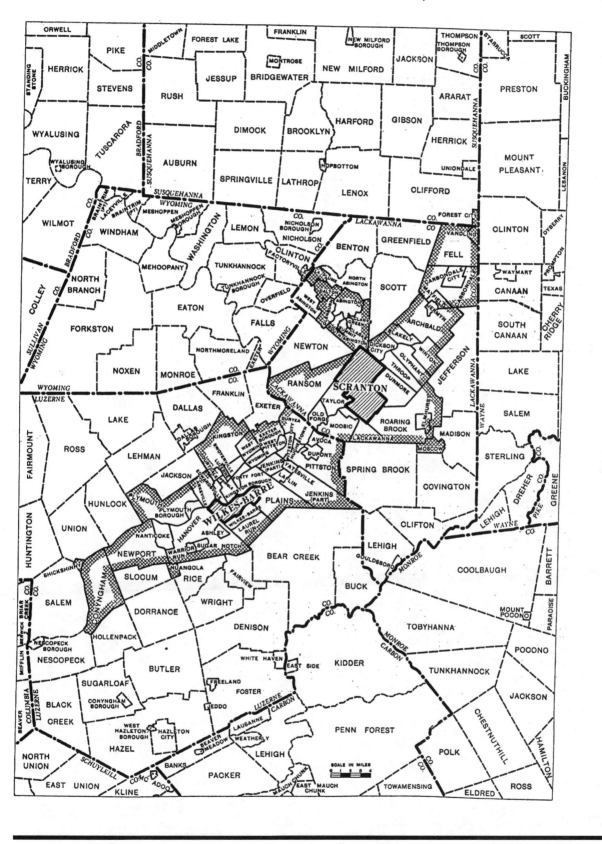

Rhode Island – Providence, RI - Fall River, MA - New Bedford, MA

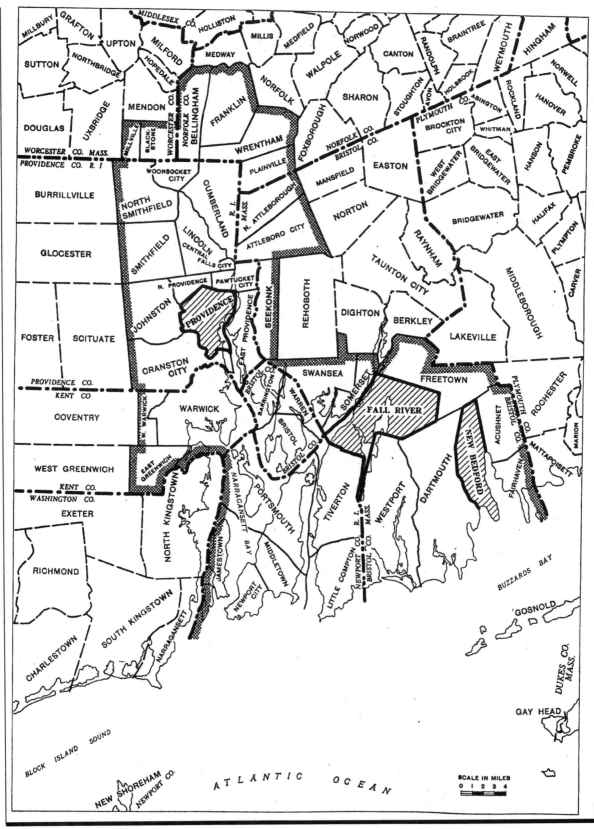

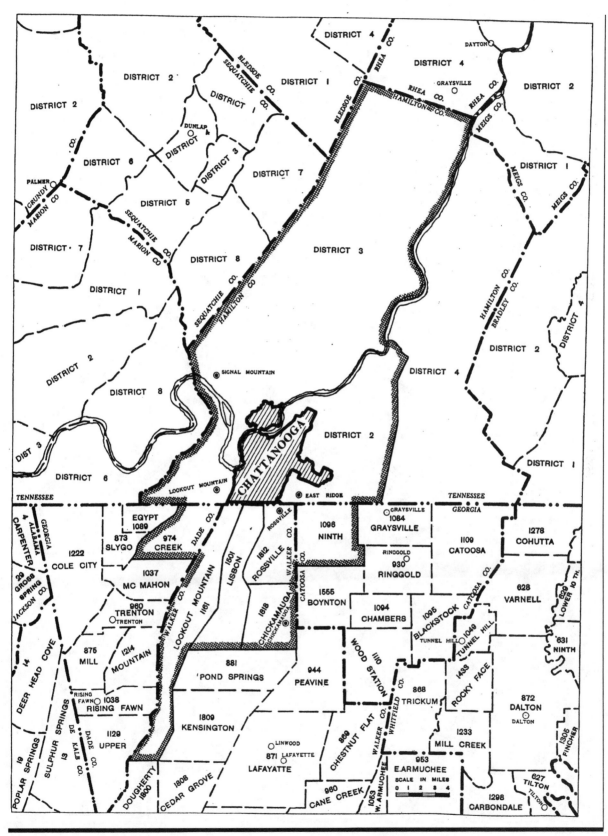

Tennessee – Knoxville

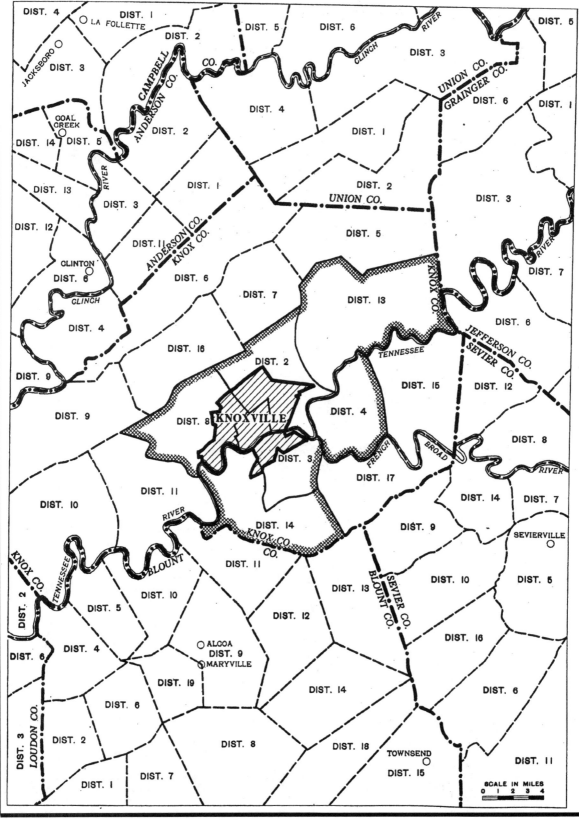

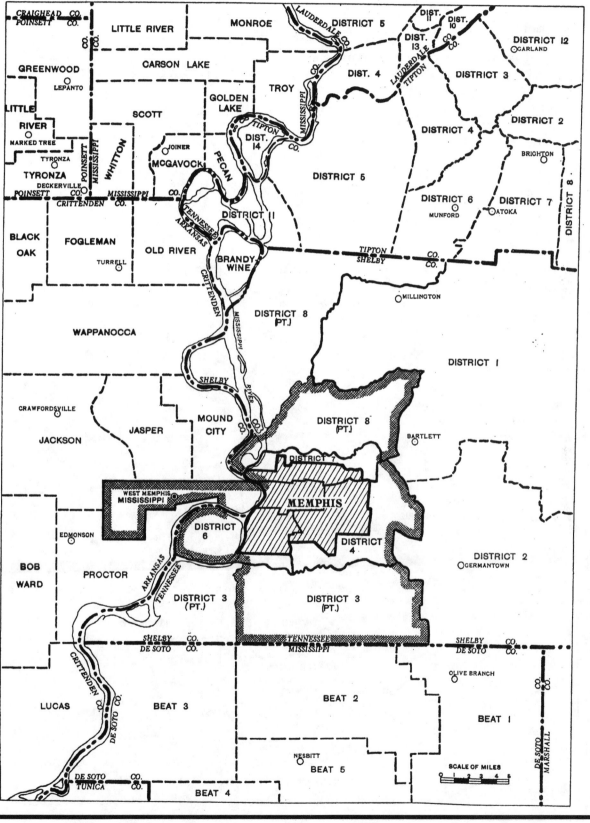

Tennessee – Nashville

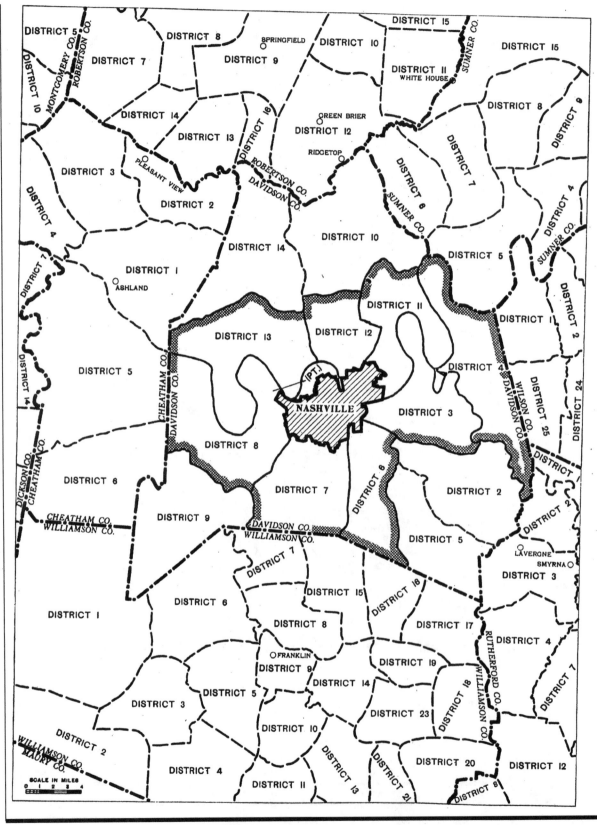

Texas – Dallas

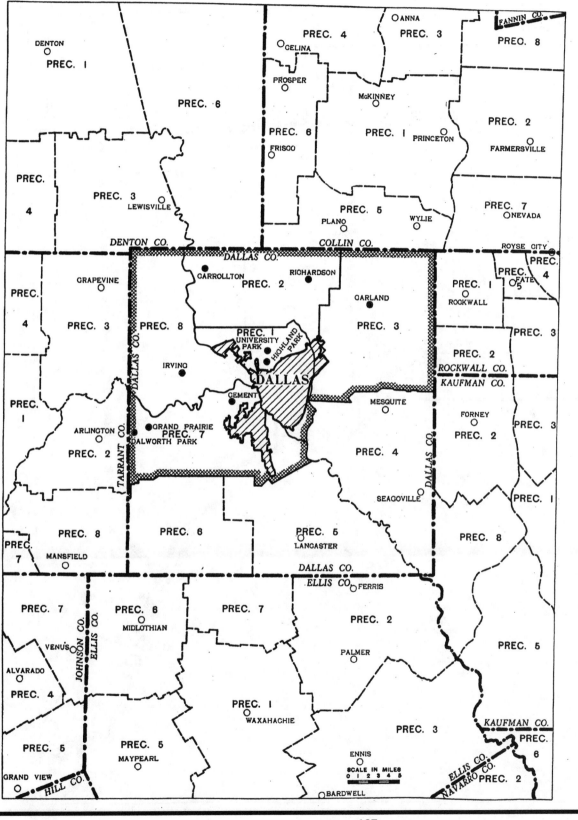

Texas – El Paso

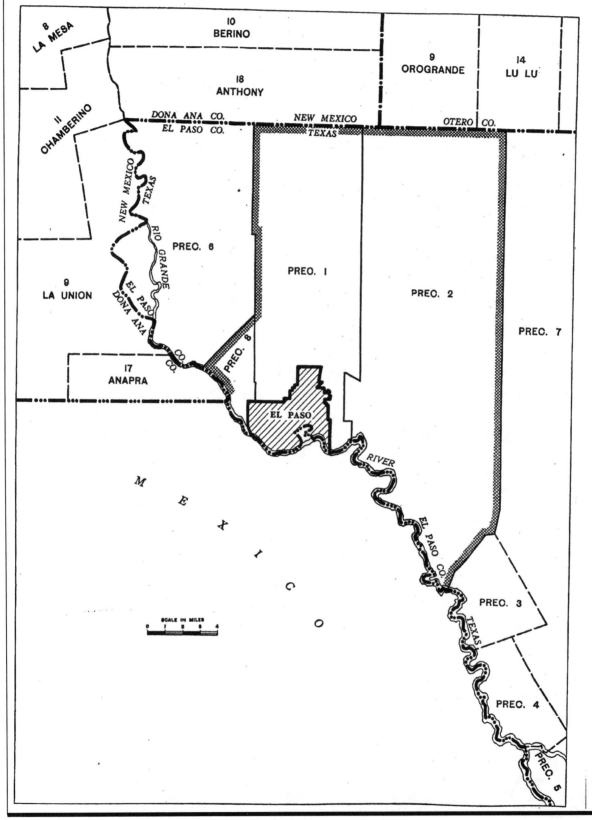

Texas – Fort Worth

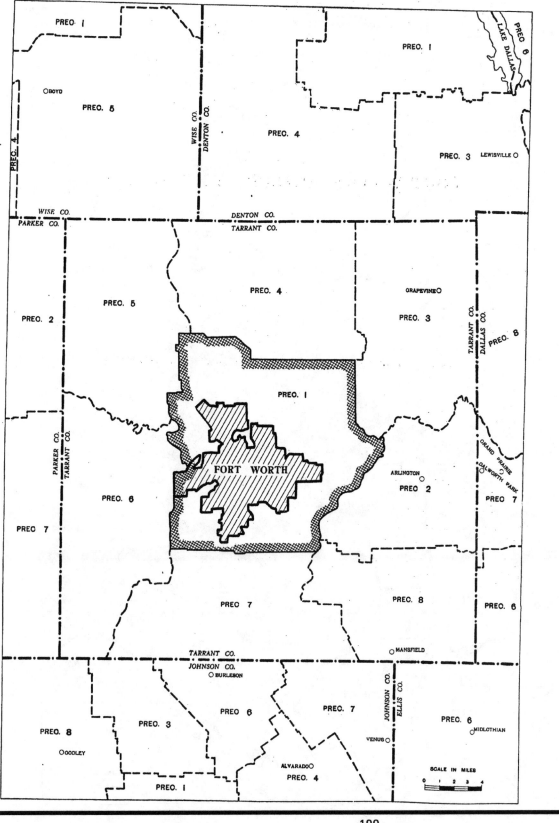

189

Texas – Houston

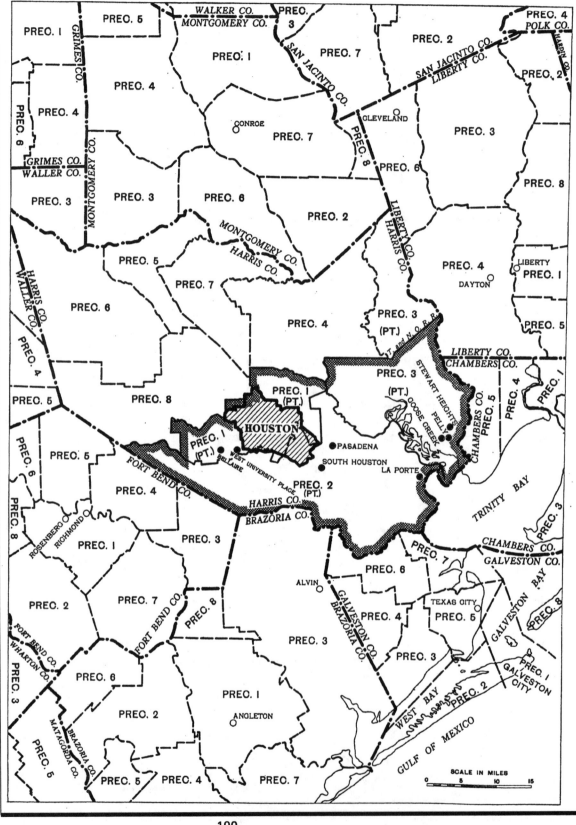

Texas – San Antonio

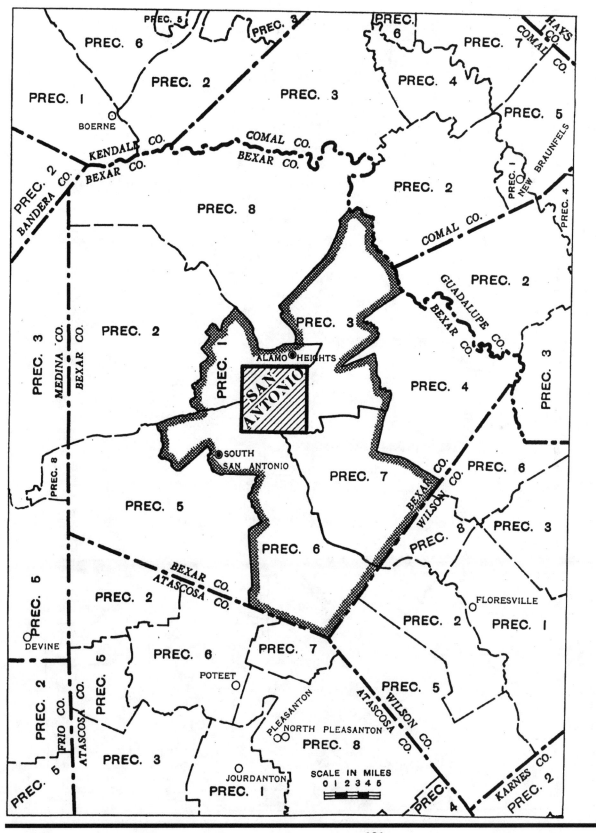

Utah – Salt Lake City

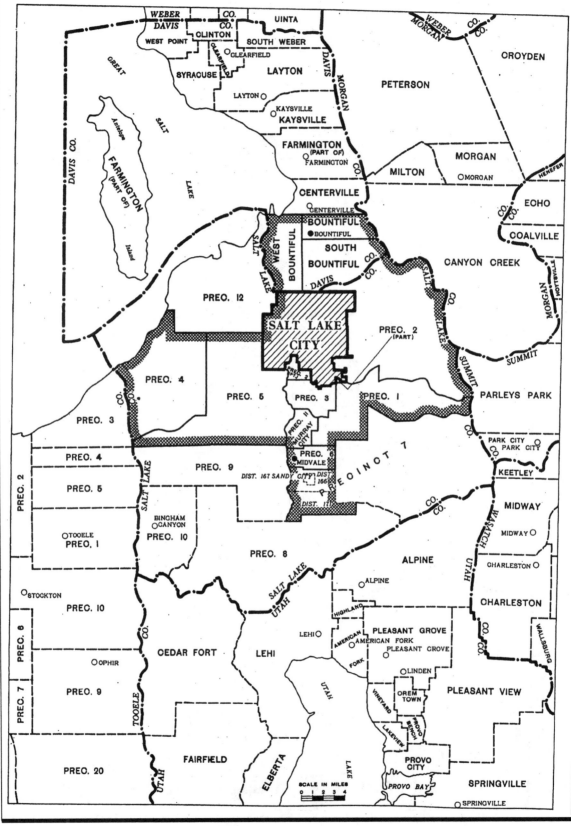

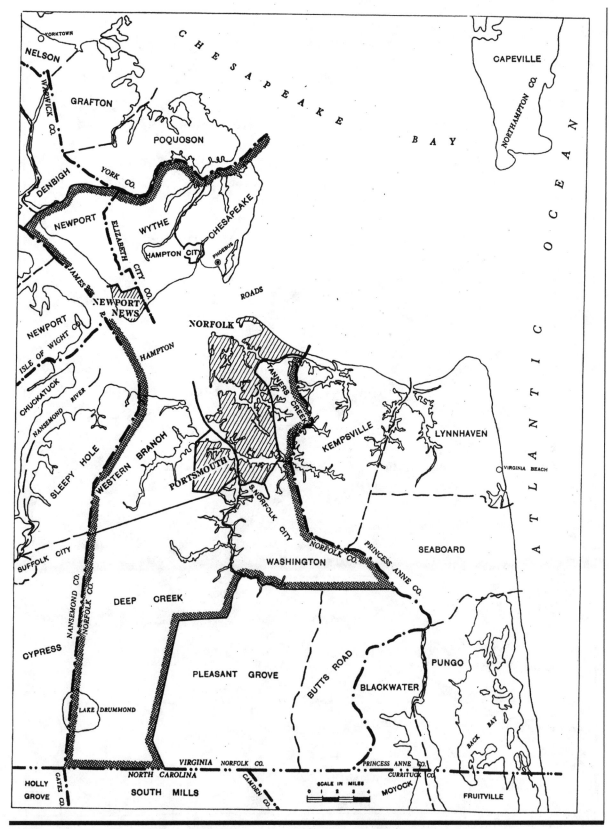

Virginia – Richmond

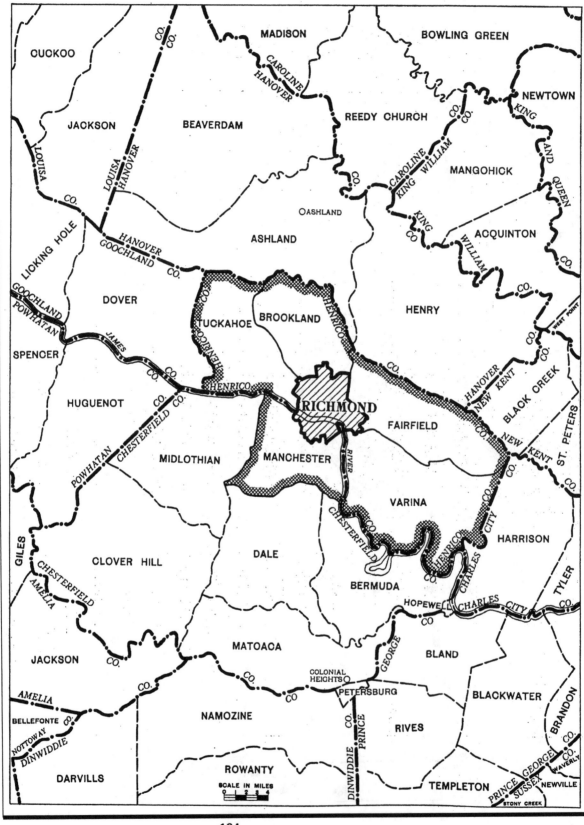

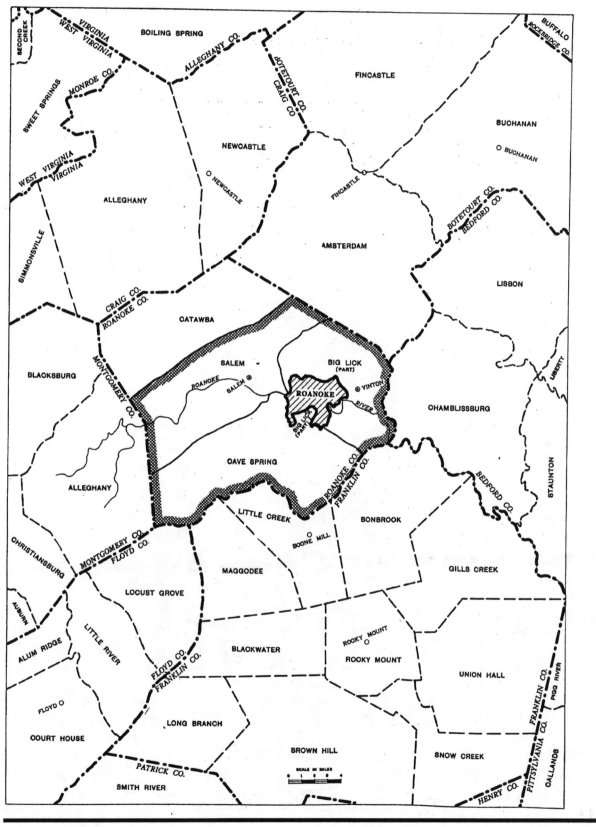

Washington – Seattle

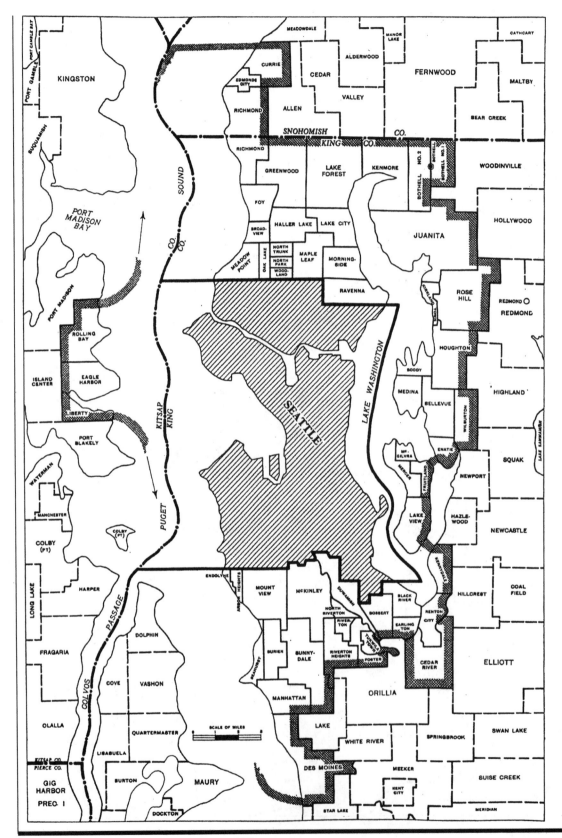

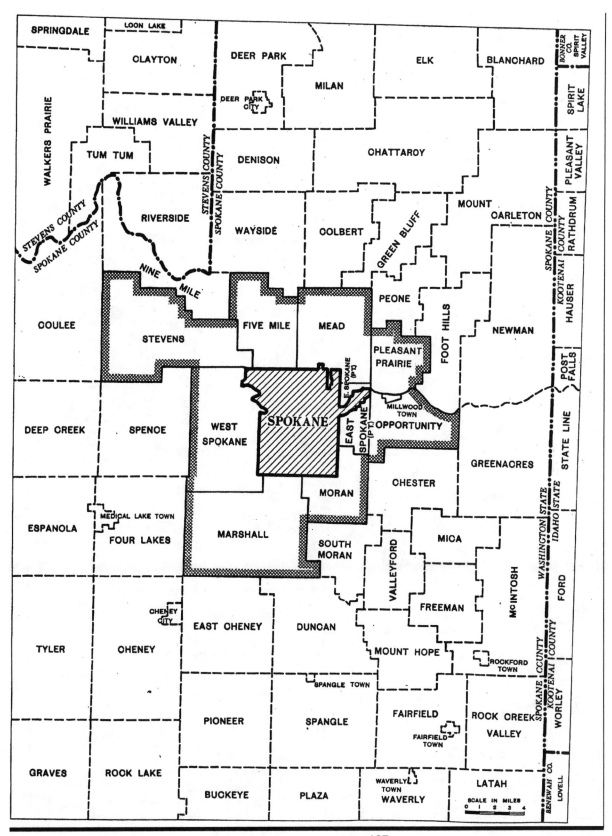

Washington – Tacoma

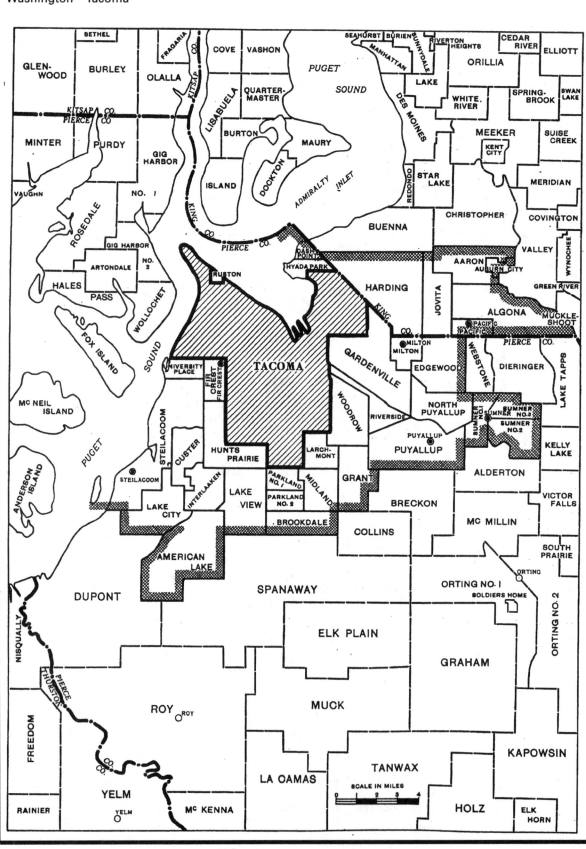

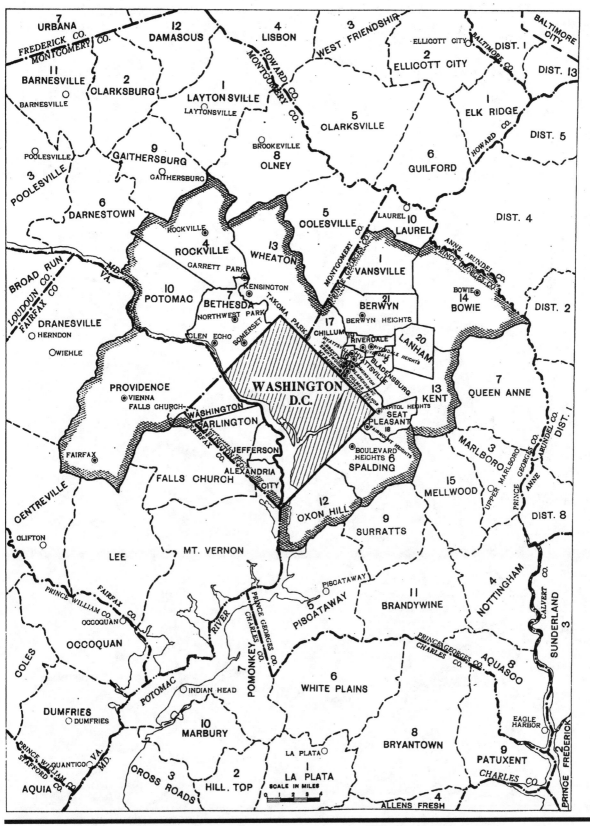

West Virginia – Charleston

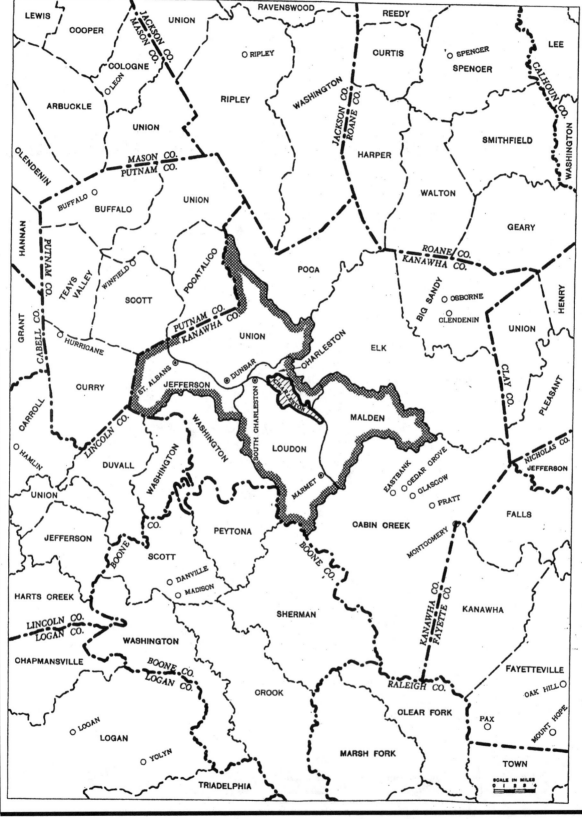

West Virginia – Huntington - Ashland, KY

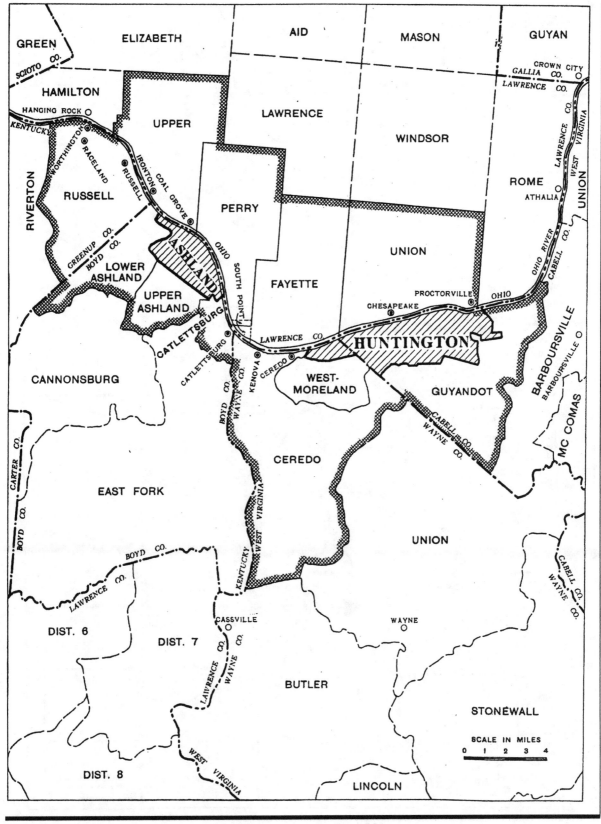

West Virginia – Wheeling

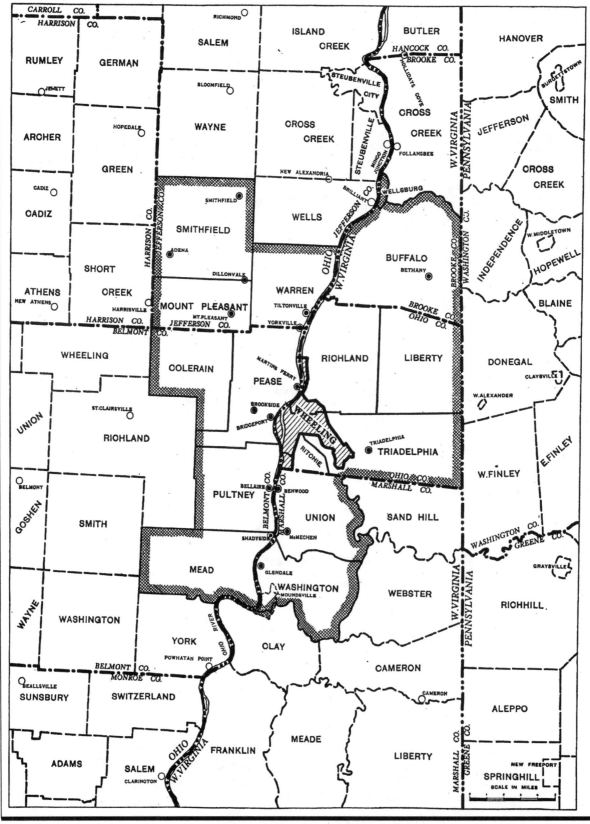

Wisconsin – Milwaukee

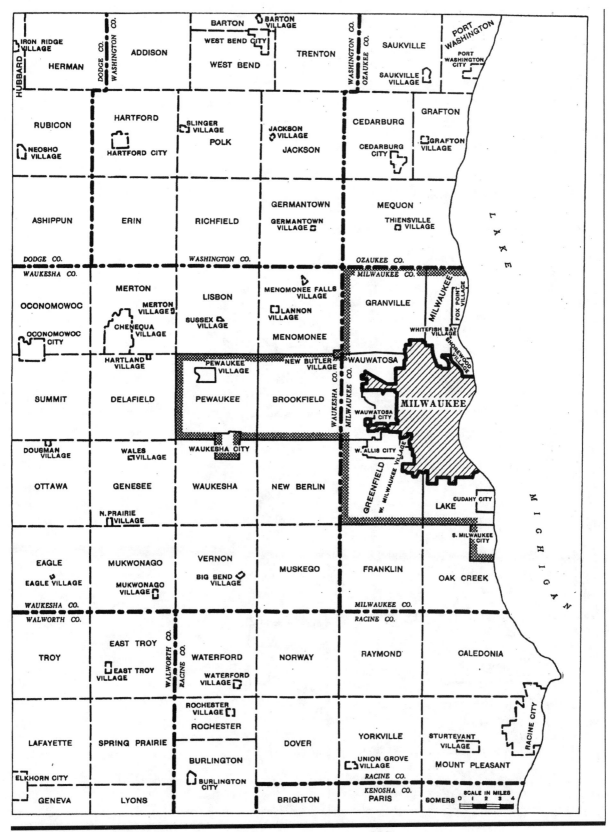

Wisconsin – Racine - Kenosha

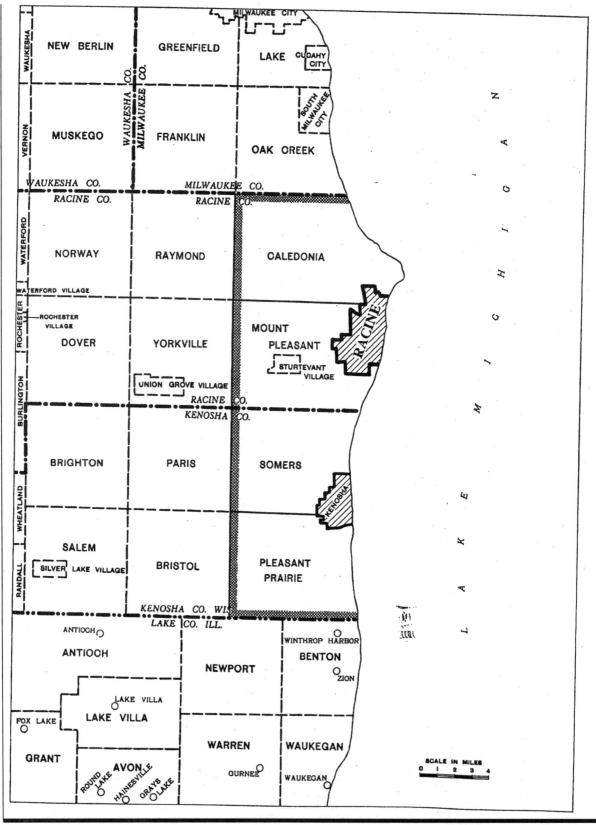

— APPENDIX D —

Instructions to Enumerators

GENERAL INSTRUCTIONS

1. Responsibility of enumerator to supervisor. All of your duties as a census enumerator are to be performed under the direction of the supervisor.

2. Rules and instructions. You must read carefully and observe the rules and instructions which follow. If questions or difficulties arise which are not covered by these instructions, you should apply to your supervisor for further instructions.

3. Receipt of supplies. The supervisor of your district has furnished you with the necessary schedules, blank forms, and other supplies for your work. You should promptly acknowledge the receipt of these supplies upon the card which is inclosed with them, checking off the several items in accordance with the directions printed on the card.

4. Schedules. The schedules to be used by census enumerators include the following:
Population:
    Population Schedule (Form 15-6).
    Unemployment Schedule (Form 15-93).
    Schedule for the Blind and for Deaf-mutes (Form 15-103).
Agriculture:
    Farm Schedule (Form 15-90).
    Schedule for Incidental Agricultural Production and Livestock Not on Farms
    (Form 15-91 or 15-210).

5. Certain other schedules will be used in limited areas. Enumerators in these areas will be given special instructions with regard to the additional schedules.

6. Examples. Illustrative examples of complete population, unemployment, and farm schedules are supplied to show exactly how the entries should be made. (See Forms 15-3b, 15-95, and 15-152.)

7. Extra copies of schedules. If you need additional copies of any schedule or other blank form, notify your supervisor at once, stating the number of copies required.

8. Use of portfolio. The portfolio furnished you is to be used in your daily canvass. It will not be necessary for you to carry in it, on any one day, any more schedules than will be required in that day's work.

9. Care of schedules. Blank schedules not in use and schedules already filled out must be put away in a safe place where they will not be accessible to unauthorized persons. The schedules may be doubled over as they are carried in your portfolio, but they should not be sharply folded or creased, and when not in the portfolio they should be kept flat.

10. Certificate of appointment. Your certificate of appointment is evidence of your authority to ask the questions required by the census act. This certificate is to be signed by you as indicated and should be exhibited whenever its use will aid you in obtaining the information you seek. It must not leave your possession until after you have finished the enumeration of the district which it covers, when it is to be returned to the supervisor with your completed schedules.

11. Assignment of territory. In a majority of cases each enumerator will be assigned one enumeration district (E.D.) and will receive one portfolio, which will contain all the material he will need in his work. Some enumerators, however, will be assigned a group of two or more smaller districts and will receive a separate appointment and portfolio for each.

12. When two or more districts are assigned to an enumerator, he should ordinarily complete all work on the first district before beginning the second, and so on.

13. Enumeration district. The limits of the district (or of each district) within which you are to take the census are stated on the inside of the portfolio. For most districts a map of the district is pasted on the inside of the back cover of the portfolio. Outside of your district (or districts), as thus described, you have no authority and will have no census duties to perform unless otherwise instructed.

14. If you find in the course of your work that the map furnished you is incorrect in any detail, you should report the fact to your supervisor and indicate the necessary corrections, which he will transmit to the Census Bureau in Washington.

15. Complete canvass required. It is your duty *personally* to visit every family and farm within your territory; to obtain the information required with reference to them; and to enter the same on the census schedules.

16. Enumerator's rights. Your rights as an enumerator are clearly indicated in the census act. (See section 9, first paragraph.) You have the right of admission to every dwelling (including institutions) within your territory for the purpose of obtaining information required by the Bureau of the Census. You have the right to ask every question contained in the census schedules and to obtain answers to each and all of them. You are cautioned, however, not to mention or emphasize the compulsory feature of the enumeration unless it is necessary.

17. Refusals to answer. In case your authority is disputed, show your appointment certificate, which you must carry with you. But it is of the utmost importance that your manner should, under all circumstances, be courteous and conciliatory. In no instance should you lose your temper or indulge in disputes or threats. Much can be done by tact and persuasion. Many persons will give information after a night's reflection which they refuse to give when first visited.

18. Should any person object to answering any question on the schedules, you should explain that the *information is strictly confidential*, that it will not be communicated to any person whatever, and that no use will be made of it which can in any way injuriously affect the interests of individuals. After all other means have failed, call the attention of the person refusing to give information to the penalty provided in section 9 of the census act for refusal to give information requested. Should the person still refuse to give the information, enter in your record book the name and address and the words "Refused to answer," and report the facts to your supervisor.

19. Untruthful replies. You have a right not only to an answer, but to a truthful answer. Do not accept any statement which you believe to be false. Where you know that the answer given is incorrect, enter upon the schedule the correct answer as nearly as you can ascertain it.

20. Obligation to secrecy. You are forbidden to communicate to any person any information obtained by you in the discharge of your official duties. By so doing you will render yourself liable, upon conviction, to a fine not exceeding $1,000, or to imprisonment not exceeding two years, or to both fine and imprisonment. (See sec. 8 of the census act.) Be particularly careful, when enumerating a family, that no member thereof is reading the entries you are making or the entries you have made for other families. You are not permitted to show anyone the schedules which you have filled out or to retain copies of the schedules or of any parts of them.

21. If, at the close of the enumeration, you are asked what is the population of your district or of any smaller area, reply that you are forbidden by law to answer. All such requests, whether from newspapers, local officials, or individuals, are to be referred to your supervisor, who will make a preliminary announcement of the population of each political subdivision of the county soon after the enumeration is completed (except that in a few large cities these announcements will be made from Washington).

22. Falsification of returns. You have not the right to omit any dwelling, farm, or resident in your district. You are also forbidden to enter upon the schedule the name of any fictitious person, or of any person not entitled to be enumerated in your district, or to make any fictitious or untruthful statement concerning any person or farm enumerated. The penalty for willful falsification of the returns is a fine not exceeding $2,000 or imprisonment not exceeding five years, or both. (See section 8 of the census act.)

23. What constitutes a day's work. Enumerators are expected to devote at least eight hours every day, beginning April 2, to the diligent canvassing of their districts.

24. Where you can best obtain the required information in the evening, you are at liberty to do so.

25. Canvassing or soliciting not permitted. You will not be allowed to combine with your work as enumerator any occupation, such as canvassing for directory publishers, soliciting subscriptions to newspapers or magazines, or the sale or advertisement of any article whatever.

26. Delegation of authority forbidden. You must not delegate your authority to any other person, or employ or permit anyone to do for you any of the work of enumerating your district.

27. Not to be accompanied or assisted by unauthorized persons. You must not permit anyone to accompany or assist you in the performance of your duties, except duly appointed officers or employees of the Bureau of the Census to whom the oath of office has been duly administered. This does not prevent you, however, from receiving the unpaid assistance of individuals, when necessary, in securing information concerning persons speaking languages other than English or concerning absent members of a family, as provided in paragraphs 44 and 56.

28. Daily report cards. Report cards (Form 15-127) are furnished in sufficient number to cover the period of enumeration in your district. These cards are addressed to your supervisor, and one card is to be mailed each day under ordinary conditions. Where your work is remote from the post office, however, you need not make a special trip for the sake of mailing the cards, but may let them accumulate and mail the cards for two or more days at the first convenient opportunity. A card for each day's work must be filled out at the close of the day, even though it is not mailed until later.

29. The daily report card provides space for reporting ten items. Some of these items refer to inquiries which the enumerator will handle only when he is assigned the work under special instructions. Enumerators who have received no such special instructions will leave these items blank on the report card. The more important items which will be reported by a majority of the enumerators are the following:

1. Number of persons on Population Schedule.
2. Number of persons on Unemployment Schedule.
3. Number of places reported on schedule for Incidental Agricultural Production and Livestock Not on Farms.
4. Number of Farm Schedules filled out...

10. Number of hours worked this day.

30. These items should also be entered day by day on the consolidated time report (Form 15-106). The totals for the items representing work done as they will appear on this consolidated time report will constitute your own record of service rendered and you should keep a copy of these figures for use when you are asked to certify to your voucher upon the completion of your work.

31. Diligence in enumeration necessary. Be prompt and expeditious in doing your work. Do not lose time or loiter by the way. On entering a house state your business in a few words, ask the necessary questions, make the proper entries, and then leave the premises.

32. Time allowed for enumeration. In any city or other incorporated place having 2,500 inhabitants or more under the census of 1920 the enumeration must be completed within two weeks from the commencement of the work, and in all other districts within 30 days. If you find it is going to be difficult or not possible to complete the enumeration of the district or districts assigned to you within these limits, you should notify your supervisor at once.

33. Completion of enumeration. As soon as the work in any enumeration district is finished you are required:

a. To fill out and mail the certificate of the completion of the enumeration (Form 15-128).

b. To complete the consolidated time report (Form 15-106) and place it with the record book (Form 15-111) and the certificate of appointment for the district in the portfolio with your completed schedules.

c. To pack your portfolio and schedules and return them to your supervisor.

34. If possible, you should deliver the portfolio with your completed work and the other material to your supervisor in person. Where you can not do this, return the portfolio by mail in the large manila envelope in which it was received. One of the labels (Form 15-107) bearing the printed address of the supervisor is to be pasted over your address on the envelope, and the gummed label bearing the seal of the Department of Commerce is to be placed over the metal fastener, in order to close the package securely.

35. If you receive the Agricultural Schedules in a separate package, they must be returned in the same way. These schedules should be placed between two pieces of cardboard, carefully wrapped, and securely tied, to prevent damage in transmission through the mail. Another of the labels (Form 15-107) bearing your supervisor's name and address is to be pasted upon the outside of the package. These packages when properly packed, as directed, are to be mailed at your local post office but need not be registered.

36. It is very important that your completed work be returned to the supervisor as directed in paragraphs 33, 34, and 35. No payment can be made for your services until this has been done.

37. In the case of a very small district (one having a population of less than 500), you may hold the completed schedules until another district is completed, so as to make the returns to your supervisor for two districts together, in case this will save you a material amount of time and effort.

38. Payment for services. The rates of compensation to be allowed you for your services as enumerator are stated in the letter notifying you of your appointment. A voucher corresponding to these rates, made out in duplicate on the basis of the schedules you have turned in, will be sent to you by your supervisor for your signature. After you return the voucher to the supervisor and he has announced the population of the area enumerated by you, he will add his certification to your voucher and will forward it to Washington or to a local disbursing office of the Census Bureau, and the amount due will be sent you by mail, in the form of a United States Treasury draft.

39. Expenses. In fixing the rates of compensation it has been assumed that these rates would constitute the enumerator's entire payment for services and for incidental expenses, including transportation. With this end in view, the rates have been made materially higher in thinly settled districts and in other areas where the enumerator is likely to have to incur considerable expenses. It will not be possible, therefore, to make any allowance to the enumerator for expenses or to reimburse him for expenditures which he may make for transportation, for telephone calls, for telegraph messages, or for any other incidental matters.

40. Use of mails. All mail matter of whatever class or weight, relating to the census and addressed to any census official, if indorsed "Official Business, Bureau of the Census," is to be transmitted free of postage (see section 14 of the census act), and an order covering this point has recently been issued by the Postmaster General, a copy of which (Form 15-179) is inclosed in your portfolio. This provision is contained in section 869 of the Postal Laws and Regulations. If a postmaster refuses to receive such mail matter, when properly indorsed, show him your copy of the order of the Postmaster General and ask him to look up section 869 of the Postal Laws and Regulations; in case of further difficulty, report the facts to your supervisor.

41. Use of telegraph and telephone. In communicating with the supervisor of your district, the mails will be found sufficient for all ordinary purposes; but should any emergency arise in which you need immediate counsel or instruction, use the telegraph or telephone. The telegraph companies will accept telegrams signed by you if marked "Official business, charge Bureau of the Census, Washington, D. C., at Government rates," without requiring payment in advance. You must, however, show your appointment certificate to the receiving operator as evidence of your right to avail yourself of this privilege. In case of emergency you may telephone to your supervisor, provided the telephone company will collect the charges from the supervisor; any other telephoning must be at your own expense.

42. Where enumerator has telephone. If you have a telephone in your residence, with unlimited service, or have access otherwise to telephone service, it will be to your advantage to make free use of it for communication with your supervisor. You should by all means make sure that he has your telephone number, so that he may be able to deliver any message to you in this way without delay.

43. Interpreters. The law does not contemplate that interpreters shall be employed to assist enumerators except in extreme cases. If the services of an interpreter seem absolutely necessary for the proper enumeration of a considerable number of families in your district who do not speak English or any language which you can speak, you should report the fact to your supervisor, stating the character and extent of the services of interpreters which you need. In most cases you should know before the
enumeration begins whether the services of an interpreter will be required and should make the necessary arrangements with your supervisor in advance.

44. In the case of an occasional family that does not speak English or any language which you speak, you can usually get along without the aid of a paid interpreter. If you can not make the head of the family understand what is wanted, call upon some other member of the family; and if none of the family can understand, then, if possible, obtain the unpaid assistance of some neighbor of the same nationality.

45. The supervisor for your district, if he is satisfied that it is necessary, will employ an interpreter and will arrange with you as to the most convenient time for his work in your district. The law stipulates that it shall be the duty of an interpreter to accompany the enumerator and faithfully translate his inquiries and the replies thereto, but that an interpreter shall not in any case perform the duties of an enumerator. The interpreter will be paid directly through the supervisor and not by the enumerator, and you will have nothing to do with his employment except as arranged through your supervisor.

46. General method of filling out schedules. Use *black* ink. Take pains to write legibly and to keep your schedules neat and clean. Do not hurry; be sure that you know the proper entry and where it should be made, before making it, so as to avoid erasing and interlining. Write each name on one of the numbered lines of the schedule and *never* crowd an additional name in between the lines, or at the bottom of the sheet, as this makes it difficult to count the names accurately. Never use ditto marks or any other mark to show repetition, except as authorized in the instructions for entering names (see #130).

47. Sign every schedule, wherever a space is left for your signature, as a certificate that the work upon it has been done wholly by you.

48. Copying schedules. Try to make the entries on the schedule with such care that copying will not be required. If schedules are copied, great pains must be taken to see that the copy is exactly like the original. In copying the population schedule, copy line by line and not by columns. Use a ruler to keep the place, and take great pains to see that the ruler is not displaced. Otherwise you are likely to copy entries on the wrong lines.

POPULATON SCHEDULE

49. Entries on the schedule. The illustrative example (Form 15-3b, printed on pink paper) shows the manner in which the entries upon the schedule should be made. These entries should be made at the time of the enumeration, and the recopying of schedules should be avoided so far as possible.

50. Definite answers. Try to get a definite answer to each inquiry according to the instructions herein given. But, if after every effort has been made, you can not obtain the desired information write "Un" (for unknown). For questions like that on age or year of immigration, however, enter an approximate figure, if one can be obtained, rather than "Un." For example, if your informant says that she does not know how old a person is but that he is about 45, enter "45" rather than "Un."

51. The census day. All returns on the population schedule (except in column 28) should relate to the census day, April 1, 1930. Thus persons dying after April 1 should be enumerated, but persons born after April 1 should not be enumerated.

52. Persons who move into your district after April 1, for permanent residence, however, should be enumerated by you, unless you find that they have already been enumerated in the district from which they came.

WHO ARE TO BE ENUMERATED IN YOUR DISTRICT

53. This is the most important and difficult matter you will have to determine. Therefore study with special care the following rules and instructions.

54. Usual place of abode. In general, all persons are to be enumerated at their *usual place of abode* on April 1, 1930. This means, usually, the place which they would name in reply to the question "Where do you live?" or the place which they regard as their *home*. When a young person has left his parents' home and obtained employment elsewhere, the place where he usually stays while engaged in such employment should be considered his usual place of abode, even though he may still think of his parents' residence as "home."

55. As a rule, the usual place of abode is the place where a person usually sleeps. Note, however, that where a man happens to sleep at the time of the enumeration may not be the place where he usually sleeps, as more fully explained below.

56. Residents absent on census day. There will be a certain number of persons having their usual place of abode in your district who are absent at the time of the enumeration. These you must include and enumerate, obtaining the facts regarding them from their families, relatives, acquaintances, or other persons able to give this information. A son or daughter permanently located elsewhere, however, or regularly employed elsewhere and not sleeping at home, should not be included with the family. Persons to be counted as members of the family include the following:

a. Members of the family temporarily absent on the census day, either in foreign countries or elsewhere in the United States on business or visiting.

b. Members of the family attending schools or colleges located in other districts, except cadets at Annapolis and West Point. (But a student nurse who receives even a nominal salary should be enumerated where she is in training.)

c. Members of the family who are ill in hospitals or sanitariums.

d. Servants, laborers, or other employees who live with the family, sleeping on the premises.

e. Boarders or lodgers who sleep in the house.

57. In the great majority of cases it is more than likely that the names of absent members of the family will not be given you by the person furnishing the information, unless particular attention is called to them. Before finishing the enumeration of a family you should in all cases, therefore, *specifically ask the question as to whether there are any absent members,* as described above, who should be enumerated with the family.

58. Designation for absent persons. After you have entered the name of such absent member of the family, write after the name in column 5, well toward the right-hand side of the column, the designation, "Ab," thus, "Smith, Robert B.—Ab."

59. Classes not to be enumerated in our district. There will be, on the other hand, a certain number of persons present and perhaps lodging and sleeping in your district at the time of the enumeration who do not have their usual place of abode there. These you should not enumerate unless it is likely that they will not be enumerated anywhere else (see #61). As a rule, therefore, you should not enumerate, or include with the members of the family you are enumerating, any of the following classes:

a. Persons visiting with this family;

b. Transient boarders or lodgers who have some other usual or permanent place of abode where they are likely to be enumerated;

c. Persons from abroad temporarily visiting or traveling in the United States. (Persons from abroad who are *employed* here should be enumerated, even though they do not expect to remain here permanently.)

d. Students or children living or boarding with this family in order to attend some school, college, or other educational institution in the locality, but not regarding the place as their home;

e. Persons who take their meals with this family, but lodge or sleep elsewhere;

f. Servants, apprentices, or other persons employed by this family and working in the house or on the premises, but *not sleeping* there; or

g. Any person who was formerly in this family, but has since become an inmate of an asylum, almshouse, home for the aged, reformatory, prison, or any other institution in which the inmates may remain for long periods of time (see #71).

60. Such persons will, with occasional exceptions, be enumerated elsewhere, at their homes or usual places of abode, which in some cases may be in your district, but more often will be in other localities.

61. When to make exceptions. In deciding whether to make an exception to the rule and enumerate in your district a person who is present there but whose usual place of abode is elsewhere, the question to be considered is whether or not that person is represented at his or her home or usual place of abode by a husband, wife, father, mother, son, daughter, or other relative, or by a housekeeper, servant, or landlady, or by anybody else who will probably give the name to the enumerator of that district when he calls. If not so represented, and, therefore, likely to be omitted at his usual place of abode, he should be enumerated by you.

62. When you find a whole family temporarily in your district, and the head or other representative states that they are not represented by anyone at their usual place of abode, you should ordinarily enumerate them in the regular way.

62a. If, however, you find a family that objects to being enumerated in the population of your district, claiming that their usual place of abode is elsewhere, you should report the fact to your supervisor, using the report card for nonresident family (Form 15-233) for that purpose and stating that the family wish to be enumerated as a part of the population of the place there designated as their usual place of abode. The supervisor will supply you with a special schedule on which to enumerate such family, in accordance with the instructions given on the report card.

63. Servants. Servants, laborers, or other employees who live with the family and sleep in the same house or on the premises should be enumerated with the family.

64. Boarders and lodgers. Boarders (that is, persons eating and sleeping at the same place) or lodgers should be enumerated at the place where they are rooming or lodging, if they are there permanently or for reasons of a permanent nature—for instance, if that is their usual place of abode while carrying on their regular occupation or business.

65. Transient boarders or lodgers, on the other hand, should not be enumerated at their temporary rooming or lodging place unless it is likely that they will not be enumerated elsewhere. This refers to persons rooming or lodging for a short time at a hotel or a boarding or lodging house, or with a private family, while temporarily absent from their usual places of abode.

66. But transient boarders or lodgers *who have no permanent home* or usual place of abode should be enumerated where they happen to be stopping at the time of the census. This applies in particular to the lodgers in cheap one-night lodging houses who, for the most part, represent a floating population, having no permanent homes.

67. Construction camps. Persons in railroad, road, or other construction camps, lumber camps, convict camps, state farms worked by convicts, or other places which have shifting populations composed of persons with no fixed places of abode, should be enumerated where found, except in so far as certain individuals in such camps may have some other usual place of abode where they are likely to be reported.

68. Students at school or college. If there is a school, college, or other educational institution in your district which has students from outside of your district, you should enumerate only those students who have their regular places of abode in your district. This will include students who live with their parents, permanently and regularly, in your district, together with certain others who have no homes elsewhere. Especially in a university or professional school, there will usually be a considerable number of the older students who are not members of any family located elsewhere and who will be omitted from the census unless you enumerate them. You should make every effort to find and enumerate all such persons.

69. School-teachers. Teachers in a school or college should be enumerated at the place where they live while engaged in teaching, even though they may spend the summer vacation at their parents' home or elsewhere.

70. Inmates of medical or surgical hospitals. Most inmates of medical and surgical hospitals are there only for temporary treatment and have other regular places of abode. Therefore, you should not enumerate as a resident of the hospital any patient unless it appears that he has no other usual place of abode from which he is likely to be reported. A list of persons having no permanent homes can usually be obtained from the hospital records.

71. Inmates of prisons, asylums, and institutions other than hospitals. If there is within your district a prison, reformatory, or jail, an almshouse, an asylum or hospital for the insane, a home for orphans, or for the blind, deaf, or incurable, an institution for the feeble-minded, a soldiers' home, a home for the aged, or any similar institution in which inmates usually remain for long periods of time, *all* the inmates of such an institution should be enumerated as of your district. It is to be specially noted that in the case of jails the prisoners should be there enumerated, however, short the term of sentence.

72. Persons engaged in railway services or traveling. Railroad men, canal men, expressmen, railway mail clerks, traveling salesmen, and the like, usually have homes to which they return at intervals and which constitute their usual place of abode within the meaning of the census act. Therefore, any such persons who may be in your district temporarily on April 1, 1930, are not to be enumerated by you unless they claim to have no other regular place of abode within the United States. But if any such persons have their homes in your district, they should be enumerated there, even though absent on April 1, 1930 (see #56).

73. Soldiers, sailors, marines, and civilian employees of the United States. Soldiers, sailors, and marines belonging to the Army or Navy of the United states, and civilian employees of the United States, are treated as residents at their posts of duty or places where they are regularly employed. If, therefore, any family in your district reports that one of its members is a soldier, sailor, marine, or civilian employee of the United States with a post of duty or station elsewhere, *you should not report him as a member of that family*. Cadets at Annapolis and West Point are enumerated at those places.

74. If, however, any civilian employee of the United States is regularly employed in your district and has his usual place of abode there, or has his headquarters there, you should report him as a resident of your district and a member of the family with which he has his usual place of abode, even though he may be temporarily absent on an official or other trip.

75. Sailors on merchant vessels. The officers of merchant vessels under the United States flag should be enumerated at their homes on land, where they will be reported by some member of the family.

76. Special provision is made for the enumeration of the crews of vessels in foreign or intercoastal trade and on the Great Lakes and of the crews of sea-going private vessels of all kinds, except yachts, under the American flag, even though these crews have homes on shore. You should omit such men from your enumeration, therefore, when they are returned as "absent members" by their families. You are to include, however, and report in the regular way, men employed on boats running on the *inland waters* (rivers, canals, etc.) of the United States, other than the Great Lakes.

77. You are also to enumerate, where found, all persons usually employed on board ship who are *out of employment* on the census date. Crews of *foreign* vessels are not to be enumerated.

78. Citizens abroad at time of enumeration. Any citizen of the United States who is a member of a family living in your district, but abroad temporarily at the time of the enumeration, should be enumerated as of your district. It does not matter how long the absence abroad is continued, provided the person intends to return to the United States. These instructions apply only to *citizens* of the United States and not to aliens who have left this country.

NECESSITY OF A THOROUGH CANVASS

79. All buildings to be visited. Be careful to include in your canvass every occupied building or other place of abode in your district. Before leaving any building make sure that you have included all persons living in that building.

80. If any dwelling house or apartment is closed on the day of your visit, do not take it for granted that the place is unoccupied. Find out whether anyone is living there. In an apartment house you should obtain from the manager or the person in charge a list of the tenants, in order to make sure that you omit no one.

81. If a building appears to be used for business purposes only, do not take it for granted that no one lives in it. Make inquiries. Keep in mind also the fact that many clubhouses have at least a few resident members.

82. Individuals out of families. Be careful not to overlook persons living entirely alone, such as a person occupying a room or rooms in a public building, store, warehouse, factory, shop, or garage, and having no other usual place of abode; or a person living alone in a cabin, hut, or tent; or a person sleeping on a river boat, canal boat, or barge, and having no other place of abode (see #126).

83. Method of canvassing a city block. If your district is in a city or town having a system of house numbers, canvass one block or square at a time. Do not go back and forth across the street. Begin each block at one corner, keep to the right, turn the corner, and go in and out of any court, alley, or passageway that may be included in it until you reach the point of starting. Be sure you have gone around and through the entire block before you leave it.

84. The arrows in the following diagram [not reproduced in this book] indicate the manner in which a block containing an interior court or place is to be canvassed:

(Note that block marked "A" is to be fully canvassed before work is undertaken in block "B.")

85. Enumerator's record book. A record book (Form 15-111) has been provided, in which you are to record each case where you find a family not at home on your first call or where you are not able to secure the required information for all persons of the family. You should also make a record in this book of all buildings in your district in which you find that there are no persons to enumerate. This record book you must send to your supervisor with your completed work.

86. Vacant block certificate. For use in certain cities where the descriptions of the enumeration districts show the individual blocks making up each district, there is provided a vacant block certificate (Form 15-183) to be used as a record of those blocks, if any, in which there is no population.

87. Individual census slip. The individual census slip (Form 15-12) is a blank form provided with spaces for entering all of the census information with regard to one person. It is to be used in securing information for persons who are absent at the time of your call and for whom the required facts can not be supplied by anyone else, especially for boarders and lodgers. It is to be left with the landlady, or with some member of the family, to be given to the person for whom the information is needed, with the request that it be filled out by him, placed in the envelope provided and sealed, and left until you call for it at a later date. (Instructions for filling it out are printed on the slip.) Before leaving an individual census slip for any person, you should make the proper entries in the heading of the slip (items 1 to 5). As you receive these slips, completed, you are to transfer the information to the census schedules just as if you had obtained the information in the regular way.

88. Families out on first visit. In case a family is out at the first visit, or in case the only persons at home are young children, servants, or other persons not able to supply the required information about the members of the family, you must return later to enumerate this family. If you have reliable information as to the number of persons in the family, including possible boarders or lodgers, you may leave space for the entries.

89. Make an entry in your record book, so that there may be no possibility of your overlooking the need for a return call to secure the information for this family. Include as a part of this entry the number of the sheet and of the line on which the first member of the family would normally have been reported, as "Sheet 7, line 17."

90. If you have left space for a family, the entries will of course be made in the regular place on the schedule, as if the family had been enumerated on the first call. If you have not left space, the entries for such a family should be made on the last sheet of the schedules for the district in which the family lives, or, in case the district is subdivided into blocks or otherwise, on the last sheet of the schedules for the proper subdivision. In making the entry for a family which is thus placed out of its proper order on the schedules, be careful to enter clearly under *Place of abode* (columns 1 to 4) the street, the house number, if any, and the visitation numbers of the dwelling and the family. Enter also, in the margin of the schedule, a reference to the place where the family ought to have been entered, thus: "See Sheet 7, line 17."

91. If the family enumerated out of order occupies a dwelling house containing more than one family, some of which were enumerated in regular order at the time of the first visit, enter in column 3 the same visitation number for the dwelling as was given to it when the other family or families were enumerated, so as to insure a correct return of the number of persons and families living in that dwelling house.

92. Individuals out on first visit. In case a family has a boarder, lodger, or other person belonging to it for whom complete information can not be obtained at the time of your first visit, you should enter the name, if it can be ascertained, with the rest of the family, and leave an individual census slip (Form 15-12) requesting that the slip be given to the person for whom information can not be furnished and stating that you will call for it later. It is important that the names of absent persons should be entered at the time of your first visit, wherever possible, or that a blank line be left for each such person, in order that all the members of the family may be listed in one place. If you find later that you have not left enough blank lines, enter the information secured for any additional persons on the last sheet of the schedules for the district or subdivision, as directed in #90 above.

93. Usually you will find the individual census slip ready for you on your second call, with the information required to complete your report for the family; if not, you must either make another attempt to have the slip filled out or arrange to get the information in some other way.

94. Be sure to make a note in your record book (Form 15-111) for every person for whom an individual census slip is left, in order that you may not forget to make a return call for the slip. Include in this note the serial number of the family to which such person belongs, as entered in column 4 of the schedule, as well as the number of the sheet on which the other members of the family are recorded, as "Family 167, Sheet 8."

95. When the entry that you finally make for such an individual has to be placed on the last schedule for the district or subdivision, make a dash in column 3 (number of dwelling), enter the *original* family number in column 4, and make a note in the margin referring to the sheet on which the other members of the family are recorded, thus "See Sheet 8," (An individual living alone, and thus constituting a *family* for census purposes, should be handled as directed in #'s 90 and 91.)

96. Absent families. When you find a dwelling in your district which is usually occupied by a family which is temporarily absent, you should first try to get the required information for this family from some neighbor or other person, in case you find any such person from whom you feel confident that you can obtain accurate information. If you are unable to obtain reliable information with regard to this absent family, you should find out the family's present address and report the same at once to your supervisor, using the report card for *House or apartment closed* (Form 15-221).

97. The supervisor will send to every such family an Absent Family Schedule, asking that the census information be entered on this schedule and returned directly to him. If you are unable to find out where the family is, you should nevertheless report to your supervisor the fact that a family usually living at such a street address is absent, giving whatever information you have been able to secure.

98. Hotel list. The hotel list (Form 15-123) is to be used by the enumerator in obtaining a list of all guests—boarders and lodgers—at each hotel in his district. An individual census slip (Form 15-12) is to be left for each person on the list and called for by the enumerator at a later visit. After the slips have been collected by the enumerator, he is to check them to the hotel list to see if he has a slip for every person on the list. The individual census slip has space in the heading for the *usual place of abode* of the person who is temporarily at the hotel. For temporary residents (or transients) who state (in reply to inquiry 9) that there is someone at their usual place of abode who will report for them to the census enumerator there, the information on the individual census slip should not be transferred to the enumerator's schedules; but all such slips should be turned in to the supervisor, who will forward them to Washington.

SUBDIVISIONS OF DISTRICT

99. Separate enumeration of subdivisions of district. While most enumeration districts are to be handled each as a complete unit, there are cases in which the returns must show separately two or more different parts or subdivisions, such as:

a. The several blocks making up an enumeration district in some of the larger cities; these blocks are to be considered distinct subdivisions of the enumeration district when they are shown separately in the description pasted in the front of the portfolio.

b. Unincorporated towns or villages having 500 inhabitants or more; many of these places will be mentioned in the description of the district, but other similar places, not mentioned, are also to be considered subdivisions of the district.

100. In all cases where there are subdivisions of the district, you should try to complete the enumeration of one such subdivision before beginning another. You should *begin the entries* for each subdivision *at the top of a new sheet* of the population schedule, and at the end of the entries for that subdivision you should write, "Here ends the enumeration of block ____," (giving the number of the block) or "Here ends the enumeration of _____, which is unincorporated," as the case may be, and leave the remainder of the lines on that sheet blank.

101. Boundaries of unincorporated places. Since incorporated villages or towns will ordinarily have no legally or definitely established boundaries, you must determine as best you can what families ought to be included in the village and what in the territory outside. In general, you should include as a part of the village population all families which are locally considered to live in the village. Usually the opinion of the family itself, as to whether it is in the village or outside, may be accepted.

102. Incorporated cities, towns, villages, or boroughs. All incorporated places have been made separate enumeration districts.

THE HEADING OF THE SCHEDULE

103. Fill out the spaces at the top of each page above the heavy black line in accordance with the following explanations. Do this on *each page* before entering any names.

104. Numbering sheets. Number the sheets of the population schedules in the exact order in which you fill them out, as you progress with the enumeration. Each sheet must be numbered the same on the "A" side and the "B" side, thus: 1A and 1B, 2A and 2B, etc.

105. Enumeration district. Enter at the head of each sheet, and on both sides, the number of the enumeration district and the number of the supervisor's district in which it is located.

106. State and county. Enter at the head of each sheet, and on both sides, the name of the State and of the county (or parish in Louisiana).

107. Township or other division of county. Write not only the name or number by which the division of the county is known, but also the name of the class (as township, town, precinct, district, ward, beat, etc.) to which it belongs. For example: "Center township" ("Center" alone is not enough); "Washington town"; "Austin precinct"; "Precinct 10"; etc. In this matter you should, in general, follow the description of your enumeration district as given on the inside cover of the portfolio.

108. In case, however, you are enumerating an incorporated city, town, village, or borough which is not included in or is not a part of any township or other division of a county, write no name in this space, but make an "X" in it to indicate that the omission of the name is not accidental (see #110).

109. Name of incorporated place. Give both the proper name of the incorporated place and, in addition, state whether it is a city, town, village, or borough. For example: "Mount Pleasant city," "Newton borough," etc.

110. Relation of incorporated place to township in which located. If any incorporated place forms a part of the township in which it is located, the name of the township as well as that of the incorporated place must be entered on the head of the sheet, each in the space indicated for it. If, on the other hand, the incorporated place is independent of the township, precinct, or other division of a county, that fact should be indicated by inserting an "X" in the space for the name of the township or other division of the county, as explained in #108.

110a. Name of unincorporated place. Where an unincorporated place is to be enumerated separately (see #99), enter the name of the place in the space provided therefore in the heading of the schedule. The name of the township in which the unincorporated place is located should also be entered in every case.

111. Ward of city, etc. If the city, or other incorporated place, is divided into wards, enter the number or name of the ward in the space provided at the head of each sheet. In the case of a block city, enter also the block number.

112. Name of institution. If you are enumerating the population of an institution, such as a prison, jail, almshouse, or asylum, enter the full name of the institution in the place indicated at the head of the schedule. In case only a portion of the total number of persons enumerated on that sheet of the schedule are in the institution, indicate the lines on which the names of the inmates of the institution appear, as "Jefferson County Almshouse, lines 25 to 69, inclusive."

113. Date. If a page of the schedule is not completely filled at the end of a day's work, do not leave it blank but draw a line in the left-hand margin of the schedule just under the number of the line for the last person enumerated on that day, and on the following day enter the date in the margin under this line and opposite the name of the first person you enumerate. For instance, if at the close of April 7 you had enumerated 40 persons on a schedule, draw a heavy line in the left-hand margin just under the line number 40, and on the next morning write "April 8" in the margin opposite 41, showing that you began work at that number.

PLACE OF ABODE

114. Column 1. Street, avenue, road, etc. This column applies to cities and all other localities where the streets or roads are known by names or numbers or letters. Write the name of the street, avenue, court, place, alley, or road lengthwise, as shown in the illustrative example.

115. The places at which you begin and end work on any street are to be marked by heavy lines in ink across the first and second columns.

116. Column 2. House number. Write the house number, if there is one, opposite the name of the first person enumerated in the house. If a house is in the rear of another one fronting on a street and has no number of its own, give it the same number as the front house and add the word "rear."

117. Column 3. Number of dwelling house in order of visitation. In this column the first dwelling house you visit should be numbered as "1," the second as "2," and so on until the enumeration of your district is completed. The number should always be entered *opposite the name of the first person enumerated in each dwelling house*, and should not be repeated for other persons or other families living in the same house.

118. Dwelling house defined. A dwelling house, for census purposes, is a place in which, at the time of the census, one or more persons regularly sleep. It need not be a house in the usual sense of the word, but may be a room in a factory, store, or office building, a loft over a garage, a boat, a tent, a freight car, or the like. A building like a tenement or apartment house counts as only one dwelling house, no matter how many persons or families live in it. A building with a solid partition wall through it and a front door for each of the two parts, however, counts as two dwelling houses, as does each house in a block or row of row-houses. But a 2-apartment house with one apartment over the other and a separate front door for each apartment counts as only one dwelling house.

119. Column 4. Number of family in order of visitation. In this column number the families in your district in the order in which they are enumerated, entering the number *opposite the name of the head of each family*, as shown on the illustrative example. Thus, the first family you visit should be numbered as "1," the second as "2," and so on, until the enumeration of your district is completed.

120. Family defined. The word *family*, for census purposes, has a somewhat different application from what it has in popular usage. It means a *group of persons living together in the same dwelling place.* The persons constituting this group may or may not be related by ties of kinship, but if they live together forming one household they should be considered as one family. Thus a servant who sleeps in the house or on the premises should be included with the members of the family for which he or she works. Again, a boarder or lodger should be included with the members of the family with which he lodges; but a person who boards in one place and lodges or rooms at another should be returned as a member of the family at the place where he lodges or rooms.

121. It should be noted, however, that two or more families may occupy the same dwelling house *without living together*. If they occupy separate portions of the dwelling house and their housekeeping is entirely separate, they should be returned as separate families.

122. Families in apartment houses. In an apartment or tenement house, there will be as many families as there are separate occupied apartments or tenements, even though use may be made of a common cafe or restaurant.

123. Boarding-house families. All the occupants and employees of a boarding house or lodging house, if that is their usual place of abode, make up, for census purposes, a single family.

124. Families in hotels. All of the persons returned from a hotel should likewise be counted as a single "family," *except* that where a family of two or more members (as a husband and wife, or a mother and daughter) occupies permanent quarters in a hotel (or an apartment hotel), it should be returned separately, leaving the "hotel family" made up principally of individuals having no other family relations. The distinction between an apartment house and an apartment hotel, and in turn between an apartment hotel and a hotel devoted mainly to transients, will often be difficult to establish.

125. Institutional families. The officials and inmates of an institution who live in the institution building or buildings form one family. But any officers or employees who sleep in detached houses or separate dwellings containing no inmates should be returned as separate families.

126. Persons living alone. The census family may likewise consist of a single person. Thus, an employee in a store who regular sleeps there is to be returned as a family and the store as his dwelling place (see #82).

NAME AND RELATION

127. Column 5. Name of each person enumerated. Enter the name of every person whose usual place of abode on April 1, 1930, was with the family or in the dwelling place for which the enumeration is being made.

128. Order of entering names. Enter the members of each family in the following order: *(1)* The head of the family; *(2)* his wife; *(3)* the children (whether sons or daughters) in the order of their ages, beginning with oldest; and *(4)* all other persons living with the family, whether relatives, boarders, lodgers, or servants.

129. How names are to be written. Enter first the last name or surname, then the given name in full, and the initial of the middle name, if any, except that where a person usually writes his first initial and his middle name, as "J. Henry Brown," you should write "Brown, J. Henry," rather than "Brown, John H."

130. Where the surname is the same as that of the person on the preceding line do not repeat the name, but draw a horizontal line (———) under the name above.

131. Column 6. Relationship to head of family. Designate the *head* of the family, whether husband or father, widow, or unmarried person of either sex, by the word "head"; for other members of a family write *wife, father, mother, son, daughter, grandson, daughter-in-law, uncle, aunt, nephew, niece, boarder, lodger, servant*, etc., according to the particular relationship which the person bears to the head of the family.

132. Home-maker. Column 6 is to be used also to indicate which member of the family is the *home-maker*, that is, which one is responsible for the care of the home and family. After the word "wife," "mother," or other term showing the relationship of such person to the head of the family, add the letter "H," thus: *Wife—H*. Only one person in each family should receive this designation.

133. Occupants of an institution or school, living under a common roof, should be designated as *officer, inmate, pupil, patient, prisoner*, etc.; and in the case of the *chief* officer his title should be used, as *warden, principal, superintendent*, etc., instead of the word "head." Pupils who live at the school only during the school term are not usually to be enumerated at the school (see #68).

134. If two or more persons share a common abode as partners, write "head" for one and "partner" for the other or others.

135. In the case of a hotel or boarding or lodging house family (see #'s 123 and 124), the *head* of the family is usually the manager or the person who keeps the hotel or boarding or lodging house.

HOME DATA

136. Column 7. Home owned or rented. This question is to be answered only opposite the name of the *head* of each family, and relates to the home or dwelling in which they are living on the date of the enumeration. If the home is *owned*, write "O"; if the home is *rented*, write "R." Make no entries in this column for the other members of the family.

137. If a dwelling is occupied by more than one family it is the home of each of them, and the question should be answered with reference to each family in the dwelling. The whole dwelling may be owned by one family and a part rented by the other family, or both may rent.

138. Owned homes. A home is to be classed as "owned" if it is owned wholly or in part by the head of the family living in the home or by the wife of the head, or by a son, or a daughter, or other *relative* living in the same house with the head of the family. It is not necessary that full payment for the property should have been made or that the family should be the sole owner.

139. Rented homes. Every home not owned, either wholly or in part, by the family living in it should be returned as "rented," whether rent is actually paid or not.

140. Where the owner of a house occupies a room or floor, but rents out the major portion of the house, including the first floor, the person hiring the house is to be entered as "head," the home as "rented," and the owner as a "lodger"; or if the owner's living arrangements are entirely separate, he (or she) should be reported as a separate family with "owned" home.

141. Column 8. Value of home, if owned, or monthly rental, if rented. If the house or apartment is *owned*, as indicated by the entry "O" in column 7, give in column 8, on the line for the head of the family, the current market value of the home as nearly as it can be ascertained. Unless the house has been recently purchased it will be necessary to estimate its value. The estimate should represent the amount for which the home, including such land as belongs to it, would sell under normal conditions—not at forced sale. The assessor's value, on which taxation is based, is not generally a safe guide, being usually below the market value. Make it clear to your informant that the values returned on the census schedule are not to be used in any way in connection with taxation and are not open to public inspection.

142. If the home is *rented*, as indicated by the entry "R" in column 7, give in column 8 the amount paid *each month* as rent, or one-twelfth of the annual rental, in case payment is not made monthly.

143. If no actual rental is paid, as where a workman receives the use of a house as a part of his wages, give in column 8 the estimated monthly rental value of the house. This estimate may be based on the amount of rent paid for similar houses in the neighborhood.

144. For a farm family (indicated by the entry "Yes" in column 10) make no entry in column 8. The value of the farm home is given on the farm schedule.

145. Column 9. Radio set. If the family, or any member of the family, has a radio set, write "R" opposite the name of the head of the family. If the family has no radio set, leave this column blank.

146. Column 10. Does this family live on a farm? This question is to be answered, "Yes" or "No," for every family, except that in a thickly settled city district a statement may be made on the first schedule to the effect that there are no farms in the district, and the column may then be left blank.

147. If the family lives on a farm, that is, a place for which a Farm Schedule is made out *and which is also locally regarded as a farm,* the answer should be "Yes," even though no member of the family works on the farm. It is a question here of residence, not of occupation.

148. Occasionally there will be a place for which a Farm Schedule is required, but which is not commonly regarded as a farm. A greenhouse establishment located in a city or village and having little land attached would be an example. For such a place the entry in column 10 should be "No." Likewise for a one-time farm on which no farming is now being done, the place being occupied as a residence only, the entry in column 10 should be "No," even though the place is still called a farm. Where the farmer and his family do not live on the farm, the entry should, of course, be "No."

149. Column 11. Sex. Write "M" for male and "F" for female, as indicated in the notes at the bottom of the schedule.

150. Column 12. Color or race. Write "W" for white; "Neg" for Negro; "Mex" for Mexican; "In" for Indian; "Ch" for Chinese; "Jp" for Japanese; "Fil" for Filipino; "Hin" for Hindu; and "Kor" for Korean. For a person of any other race, write the race in full.

151. Negroes. A person of mixed white and Negro blood should be returned as a Negro, no matter how small the percentage of Negro blood. Both black and mulatto persons are to be returned as Negroes, without distinction. A person of mixed Indian and Negro blood should be returned a Negro, unless the Indian blood predominates and the status as an Indian is generally accepted in the community.

152. Indians. A person of mixed white and Indian blood should be returned as Indian, except where the percentage of Indian blood is very small, or where he is regarded as a white person by those in the community where he lives (see #151 for mixed Indian and Negro).

153. For a person reported as Indian in column 12, report is to be made in column 19 as to whether "full blood" or "mixed blood," and in column 20 the name of the tribe is to be reported. For Indians, columns 19 and 20 are thus to be used to indicate the degree of Indian blood and the tribe, instead of the birthplace of father and mother.

154. Mexicans. Practically all Mexican laborers are of a racial mixture difficult to classify, though usually well recognized in the localities where they are found. In order to obtain separate figures for this racial group, it has been decided that all persons born in Mexico, or having parents born in Mexico, who are definitely white, Negro, Indian, Chinese, or Japanese, should be returned as Mexican ("Mex").

155. Other mixed races. Any mixture of white and nonwhite should be reported according to the nonwhite parent. Mixtures of colored races should be reported according to the race of the father, except Negro-Indian (see #151).

156. Column 13. Age at last birthday. This question calls for the age in completed years at last birthday. Remember, however, that the age question, like all other questions on the schedule, relates to April 1, 1930. Thus a person whose exact age on April 1, the census day, is 17 years, 11 months, and 25 days should be returned simply as 17, because that is his age at his last birthday prior to April 1, even though at the time of your visit he may have completed 18 years.

157. Age in round numbers. In many cases persons will report the age in round numbers, like 30 or 45, or "about 30" or "about 45," when that is not the exact age. Therefore, when an age ending in "0" or "5" is reported, you should inquire whether it is the exact age. If, however, it is impossible to get the exact age, enter the approximate age rather than return the age as unknown.

158. Ages of children. Take particular pains to get the exact ages of children. In the case of a child less than 5 years old, the age should be given in completed months, expressed as twelfths of a year. Thus the age of a child 3 months old should be entered as 3/12, a child 7 months old as 7/12, a child 1 year and 3 months old as 1-3/12, a child exactly 3 years old as 3-0/12, a child 3 years and 1 month old as 3-1/12, etc. If a child is not yet a month old, enter the age as 0/12. But note again that this question should be answered with reference to April 1.

For instance, a child who is just a year old on the 5th of April, 1930, should nevertheless be returned as 11/12, because that is its age in completed months on April 1.

159. Enumerators must make a special effort to obtain returns for all infants and young children. Children under 1 year of age, in particular, have frequently been omitted from the enumeration in past censuses.

160. Column 14. Marital condition. Write "S" for a single or unmarried person of whatever age, "M" for a married person, "Wd" for widowed (man or woman), and "D" for divorced.

161. Column 15. Age at first marriage. This question applies only to married persons; that is, those for whom the entry in column 14 is "M." Where the marriage is evidently a first marriage, it may be good policy to ask for "age at marriage," rather than "age at first marriage," or to ask the question in this form and then make certain that the parties have not been married before.

EDUCATION

162. Column 16. Attended school or college any time since September 1, 1929. Write "Yes" for a person who attended school, college, or any educational institution at any time since September 1, 1929, and "No" for any person who has not attended school since that date. Include attendance at night school.

163. Column 17. Whether able to read and write. Write "Yes" for a person 10 years of age or over who can read and write in any language, whether English or some other, and "No" for such person who can not both read and write in some language. Do not return any person as able to read and write simply because he can write his own name. For persons under 10 years of age, leave the column blank.

164. For a blind person, write "Yes" if he could read and write in any language before becoming blind or, if, being born blind, he has been taught to read and write in any language.

PLACE OF BIRTH

165. Column 18. Place of birth of person. If the person was born in the United States, give the State or Territory in which born. The words "United States" are not sufficiently definite. A person born in what is now North Dakota, South Dakota, or Oklahoma should be so reported, although at the time of his birth the particular region may have had a different name. For a person born in Washington, D. C., write District of Columbia. Do not abbreviate the names of States or Territories.

166. If the person was born in a foreign country, enter the name of the country only, as

Belgium, Czechoslovakia, France, Italy, Yugoslavia, Norway, Poland, China, etc., as the case may be, *except as noted in the following paragraphs.*

167. Since it is essential that each foreign-born person be credited to the country in which his birthplace is now located, special attention must be given to the six countries which lost a part of their territory in the readjustments following the World War. These six countries are as follows:

> Austria, which lost territory to Czechoslovakia, Italy, Yugoslavia, Poland, and Rumania.

> Hungary, which lost territory to Austria, Czechoslovakia, Italy, Poland, Rumania, and Yugoslavia.

> Bulgaria, which lost territory to Greece and Yugoslavia.

> Germany, which lost territory to Belgium, Czechoslovakia, Danzig, Denmark, France, Lithuania, and Poland.

> Russia, which lost territory to Estonia, Finland, Latvia, Lithuania, Poland, and Turkey.

> Turkey, which lost territory to Greece and Italy, and from which the following areas became independent: Iraq (Mesopotamia), Palestine (including Transjordan), Syria (including Lebanon), and various states and kingdoms in Arabia (Asir, Hejaz, and Yemen).

168. If the person reports one of these six countries as his place of birth or that of his parents, ask specifically whether the birthplace is located within the present area of the country; and if not, find out to what country it has been transferred. If a person was born in the Province of Bohemia, for example, which was formerly in Austria but is now a part of Czechoslovakia, the proper return for country of birth is "Czechoslovakia." If you can not ascertain with certainty the present location of the birthplace, where this group of countries is involved, enter *in addition to the name of the country*, the name of the province or state in which the person was born, as *Alsace-Lorraine, Bohemia, Croatia, Galicia, Moravia, Slovakia*, etc., or the city, as *Warsaw, Prague, Strasbourg*, etc.

169. Do not return a person as born in Great Britain but indicate the particular country, as *England, Scotland, Wales*, etc. Distinction must be made between *Northern Ireland* and *Irish Free State*. It is not sufficient to report that a person was born in Ireland.

170. French Canadians should be distinguished from other Canadians. For a French-speaking person born in Canada, enter "Canada-French"; for all other persons born in Canada, enter "Canada-English" (even though they may not actually speak English).

171. If a person was born in Cuba or Puerto Rico, so state, and do *not* write West Indies.

172. If a person was born abroad, but of American parents, write in column 18 both the birthplace and "Am. cit."—that is, American citizen. For a person born at sea, write "At sea."

173. Spell out the names of countries, provinces, etc., and *do not abbreviate* in any case.

174. **Columns 19 and 20. Place of birth of parents.** Enter in columns 19 and 20, respectively, the state or country in which were born the father and the mother of the person whose own birthplace was entered in column 18. In designating the birthplace of the parents, follow the same instructions as for the person himself (see # 165-173). In case, however, a person does not know the state or territory of birth of his father (or mother), but knows that he (or she) was born in the United States, write "United States" rather than *unknown*.

174a. For the Indian population, which is practically all of native parentage, these columns are to be used for a different purpose. In column 19 is to be entered, in place of the country of birth of the father, the degree of Indian blood, as, "full blood" or "mixed blood." In column 20 is to be entered, in place of the country of birth of the mother, the tribe to which the Indian belongs.

MOTHER TONGUE

175. Column 21. Mother tongue of foreign born. The question, "What is (his or her) mother tongue or native language?" is to be asked with regard to every person who was born in any foreign country. By *mother tongue* is meant the language usually spoken in the home before the person came to the United States. Where persons have come to the United States by way of some other country, what is wanted is the native language of the person, or the language that he spoke in his native country. Do *not* abbreviate the language, and do not ask for the mother tongue of persons born in the United States.

176. Do *not* neglect to report the mother tongue simply because it is the same as the language of the country in which the person was born. Thus if a person reports that he was born in "France" and that his mother tongue is "French," it is quite essential to enter the mother tongue as well as the country of birth. On the other hand, do not assume that the mother tongue is the same as the country of birth. For instance, do not report persons born in Austria as of Austrian mother tongue, or persons born in Hungary as of Hungarian mother tongue, especially since Austrian and Hungarian are not languages. The principal language of present-day *Austria* is "German," and of *Hungary*, "Magyar." Therefore make specific inquiry as to the language spoken. Do not accept *Scandinavian* as a mother tongue but specify whether "Danish," "Norwegian," or "Swedish"; similarly, do not report *Slavic* but specify whether "Croatian," "Serbian," "Slovak," "Slovenian," etc.

177. Principal foreign languages. Following is a list of the principal languages, which are likely to be reported as the mother tongue or native language of foreign-born persons:

Albanian	Flemish	Korean	Ruthenian
Arabic	French	Kurdish	Scotch
Armenian	Frisian	Lappish	Serbian
Basque	Friulian	Lettish	Slovak
Breton	Gaelic	Lithuanian	Slovenian
Bulgarian	Georgian	Little Russian	Spanish
Czech	German	Macedonian	Swedish
Chinese	Great Russian	Magyar	Syrian
Croatian	Greek	Montenegrin	Turkish
Dalmation	Gypsy	Norwegian	Ukrainian
Danish	Hebrew	Persian	Walloon
Dutch	Hindu	Polish	Welsh
Egyptian	Icelandic	Portuguese	Wendish
English	Irish	Romansh	White Russian
Estonian	Italian	Rumanian	Yiddish
Finnish	Japanese	Russian	

CITIZENSHIP, ETC.

178. Column 22. Year of immigration to the United States. This question applies to all foreign-born persons, male and female, of whatever age. It should be answered, therefore, for every person whose birthplace was in a foreign country. Enter the year in which the person came to the United States. If he has come into the United States more than once, give the year of his first arrival.

179. Column 23. Naturalization. This question applies to all foreign-born persons, male and female, of whatever age. Prior to September 22, 1922, a foreign-born woman became a citizen when her husband was naturalized. Since that date, she must take out papers in her own name, and if she does not do this she remains an alien even though her husband becomes naturalized. The question should be answered, therefore, for every person whose birthplace was in a foreign country, as follows:

180. For a foreign-born male 21 years of age and over, write "Na" (for *naturalized*) if he has either *(1)* taken out second or final naturalization papers, or *(2)* become naturalized while under the age of 21 by the naturalization of either parent.

181. For a foreign-born female 21 years of age and over write "Na" if she has either *(1)* taken out final papers, or *(2)* become naturalized through the naturalization of either parent while she was under the age of 21, or *(3)* if she became naturalized prior to 1922 by the naturalization of her husband (see # 179).

182. For a foreign-born person under 21 years of age write "Na" if either parent has been naturalized. This applies to infants and young children as well as to older persons under 21.

183. For all foreign-born persons who have not been naturalized but have taken out first papers write "Pa" (for *papers*). Note that a person must be at least 18 years of age in order to take out first papers. Minor children should *not* be returned "Pa" merely because their parents have taken out first papers.

184. For all foreign-born persons neither naturalized nor having first papers, write "Al" (for *alien*).

185. Column 24. Whether able to speak English. Write "Yes" for a person 10 years of age and over who can speak English, and "No" for such a person who can *not* speak English. For persons under 10 years of age leave the column blank.

OCCUPATION AND INDUSTRY

186. Column 25. Occupation. An entry should be made in this column for every person enumerated. The entry should be either *(1)* the *gainful occupation* pursued—that is, the word or words which most accurately indicate the particular kind of gainful work done, as *physician, carpenter, dressmaker, salesman, newsboy*; or *(2)* "none" (that is, no gainful occupation). The entry "none" should be made in the case of persons who follow no gainful occupation. A *gainful occupation* in census usage is an occupation by which the person who pursues it earns money or a money equivalent, or in which he assists in the production of marketable goods. The term *gainful worker*, as interpreted for census purposes, does not include women doing housework in their own homes, without wages, and having no other employment (see # 194), nor children working at home, merely on general household work, on chores, or at odd times on other work.

187. Occasionally there will be doubt as to whether an occupation should be returned for a person who works only a small part of the time at the occupation. In such cases the rule may generally be followed that, unless the person spends at least the equivalent of one day per week at the occupation, he or she should *not* be returned as a gainful worker—that is, the entry in column 25 should be "none."

188. Persons retired or incapacitated. Care should be taken in making the return for persons who on account of old age, permanent invalidism, or other reasons are no longer following any occupation. Such persons may desire to return the occupations formerly followed, which would be incorrect. If living on their own income, or if they are supported by other persons or institutions, or if they work only occasionally or only a short time each day, the return should be "none."

189. Occupation of persons unemployed. On the other hand, persons out of employment when visited by the enumerator may state that they have no occupation, when the fact is that they usually have an occupation but happen to be idle or unemployed at the time of the visit. In such cases the return should be the occupation followed when the person is employed or the occupation in which last regularly employed, and the fact that the person was not at work should be recorded in column 28 (see # 225).

190. Persons having two occupations. If a person has two occupations, return only the more important one; that is, the one from which he gets the more money. If you cannot learn that, return the one at which he spends the more time. For example: Return a man as a "farmer" if he gets more of his income from farming, although he may also follow the occupation of a clergyman or preacher; but return him as a "clergyman" if he gets more of his income from that occupation.

191. Column 26. Industry. Make an entry in this column in all cases where an occupation is reported in column 25. But when the entry in column 25 is "none," leave column 26 blank. The entry in column 26, when made, should be the name of the industry, or the business, or the place in which this person works, as *cotton mill, coal mine, dry-goods store, insurance office, bank*, etc.

192. Never use the word "Company" in column 26. An oil company, for example, may operate *oil wells*, a *pipeline*, an *oil refinery*, or a *cottonseed oil mill*, or it may be engaged in *selling oil*. Never enter in column 26 such indefinite terms as "factory," "mill," "shop," or "store," without stating the kind of factory, etc., as *soap factory, cotton mill, blacksmith shop, grocery store*. Likewise, never enter a firm name in column 26, as "Jones & Co.," but state the industry or business in which the person works, as *coal mine, real estate*, etc. Avoid entering the word "Contractor" in column 26. Enter, instead, the name of the industry in which the person works, as *building construction, street construction*, etc.

193. The purpose of columns 25 and 26 is to bring out the specific occupation or work performed and the industry, business, or place in which such work is performed. In rare cases, especially with professions, you may use in column 26 the expression "general practice" or "independent," or, for some laborers, "odd jobs." The supervisor has been instructed *not to certify your vouchers for payment* if he does not find an entry in *both* of these columns for every person gainfully employed.

194. Women doing housework. In the case of a woman doing housework in her own home and having no other employment, the entry in column 25 should be "none." But a woman doing housework for wages should be returned in column 25 as *housekeeper, servant, cook,* or *chambermaid*, as the case may be; and the entry in column 26 should state the kind of place where she works, as *private family, hotel,* or *boarding house*.

195. Where a woman not only looks after her own home but also has employment outside or does work at home for which she receives payment, the outside work or gainful employment should ordinarily be reported as her occupation, unless this takes only a very small fraction of the woman's time. For instance, a woman who regularly takes in washing should be reported as *laundress* or *washerwoman*, followed in column 26 by "at home."

196. Farm workers. Return a person in charge of a farm as a "farmer," whether he owns it or operates it as a tenant, renter, or cropper; but a person who manages a farm for some one else for wages or a salary should be reported as a "farm manager." A man who directs farm labor under the supervision of the owner or of a manager should be reported as a "farm foreman" or a "farm overseer"; and a person who works on a farm for some one else, but not as a manager or foreman should be reported as a "farm laborer."

197. Women doing farm work. A woman who works only occasionally, or only a short time each day at outdoor farm or garden work, or in the dairy, or in caring for livestock or poultry should not be returned as a farm laborer; but for a woman who works regularly and most of the time at such work, the return in column 25 should be "farm laborer." Of course, a woman who herself operates or runs a farm or plantation should be reported as a "farmer" and not as a "farm laborer."

198. Unusual occupations for women. There are many occupations, such as carpenter and blacksmith, which women usually do not follow. Therefore, if you are told that a woman follows an occupation which is very peculiar or unusual for a woman, verify the statement.

199. Children on farms. In the case of children who work *regularly* for their own parents on a farm, in an orchard, on a truck farm, etc., the entry in column 25 should be *farm laborer, orchard laborer,* or *garden laborer*, as the case may be.

200. Children working for parents. Children who work for their parents at home merely on general household work, at chores, or at odd times on other work, should be reported as having no occupation. Those, however, who somewhat regularly assist their parents in the performance of work other than household work or chores should be reported as having the occupation represented by this work.

201. Unusual occupations for children. It is very unusual for a child to be a farmer or other proprietor of any kind; to be an official, a manager, or a foreman; to follow a professional pursuit; or to pursue any of the skilled trades, such as blacksmith, carpenter, machinist, etc. Therefore, whenever you are told that a child is following an occupation usually followed only by adults, ask whether the child is not merely a "helper" or an "apprentice" in the occupation, and make the entry accordingly.

202. Keeping boarders. Keeping boarders or lodgers should be returned as an occupation if the person engaged in it relied upon it as his (or her) principal means of support or principal source of income. In that case the return should be "boarding-house keeper" or "lodging-house keeper." If, however, a family keeps a few boarders or roomers merely as a means of supplementing the earnings or income obtained from other occupations or from other sources, no one in the family should be returned as a boarding or lodging house keeper.

203. Officers, employees, and inmates of institutions or homes. For an *officer* or *regular employee* of an institution or home, such as an asylum, penitentiary, jail, reform school, or convict camp, return the occupation followed in the institution. For an *inmate* of such institution, if regularly employed, return the occupation pursued in the institution, whether the employment be at productive labor or at other duties, such as "cooking," "scrubbing," "laundry work," etc.; but *if an inmate* is not regularly employed—that is, has no specific duties or work to perform—write "none" in column 25. *Do not* return the occupation pursued prior to commitment to the institution.

204. Do not report any inmates of institutions on the Unemployment Schedule. Where the entry "No" has been made in column 28 for such an inmate, write in column 29 "Inst" to indicate the reason for not making the usual entries on the Unemployment Schedule.

205. Builders and contractors. Only persons engaged principally in securing and supervising the carrying out of building or other construction contracts should be returned as "builders" or "contractors." Craftsmen who usually work with their tools should be returned as "carpenters," "plasterers," etc., and *not as contractors.*

206. Doctors or physicians. In the case of a doctor or physician, enter in column 26 the class to which he belongs, as "medical," "osteopathic," "chiropractic," etc.

207. Engineers. Distinguish carefully the different kinds of engineers by stating the full descriptive titles, as *civil engineer, electrical engineer, locomotive engineer, mechanical engineer, mining engineer, stationary engineer,* etc.

208. Nurses. In the case of a nurse, always specify whether she is a *trained nurse,* a *practical nurse,* or a *child's nurse.*

209. Cooks and general houseworkers. Distinguish carefully between cooks and general houseworkers. Return a person who does general housework as a *servant* and not as a *cook.*

210. Workers attending school. In the case of a person who is at work and also attends a school or college, enter the occupation followed in columns 25 and 26, and indicate the fact of school or college attendance in column 16.

211. Avoid general or indefinite terms. Give the occupation and industry precisely. For example, return a worker in a coal mine as a *foreman—coal mine; laborer—coal mine; driller—coal mine,* etc., as the case may be.

212. The term "laborer" should be avoided if any more precise statement of the occupation can be secured. Employees in factories and mills, for example, usually have some definite designation, as *weaver, roller, puddler,* etc. Where the term "laborer" is used, be careful to state accurately the industry or business in column 26.

213. Avoid the use of the word "mechanic" whenever a more specific occupation can be given, such as *carpenter, painter, electrician*, etc.

214. Distinguish carefully the different kinds of "agents" by stating in column 26 the line of business followed, as *real estate, insurance*, etc.

215. Distinguish carefully between retail and wholesale merchants, as *retail merchant—dry goods; wholesale merchant—dry-goods*.

216. Avoid the use of the word "clerk" wherever a more definite occupation can be named. Thus, an employee in a store who is wholly or principally engaged in selling goods should be called a *salesman* and not a clerk. A *typist, accountant, bookkeeper*, or *cashier*, etc., should be reported as such, and not as a clerk. Do not return a stenographer as a "secretary."

217. Distinguish a traveling salesman from a salesman in a store; the former should be reported as a *commercial traveler*.

218. You need not give a person's occupation just as he expresses it. Always find out exactly the *kind of work* he does and the *industry, business,* or *place* in which he works, and so state it. For instance, if a person says that he is "in business," find out what branch of business, and what kind of work he does or what position he holds.

219. Columns 25 and 26. Illustrations of occupation returns and industry or business. The following illustrations will indicate the method of returning some of the common occupations and industries. They will also suggest to you distinctions that you should make in other cases:

Farm laborer	Farm	Commercial traveler	Dry goods
Clergyman	Baptist church	Salesman	Department store
Laborer	Shipyard	Bookkeeper	Department store
Laborer	Street construction	Assembler	Automobile factory
Laborer	Garden	Cashier	Department store
Laborer	Odd jobs	Cashier	Bank
Laborer	Steam railroad	Conductor	Steam railroad
Brakeman	Steam railroad	Conductor	Street car
Weaver	Cotton mill	Farmer	General farm
Laborer	Cotton mill	Author	Independent
Doffer	Cotton mill	Gardener	Private estate
Locomotive engineer	Steam railroad	Manager	General farm
Lawyer	General practice	Overseer	Truck farm
Stationary engineer	Lumber mill	President	Life-insurance co.
Fireman	Lumber mill	President	Bank
Fireman	Fire department	Superintendent	Steel works
Civil engineer	General practice	Florist	Flower shop
Electrical engineer	Street railway	Florist	Flower garden
Carpenter	Car factory	Foreman	Cotton mill
Carpenter	Shipyard	Newsboy	Street
Carpenter	House	Newsdealer	News stand
Teacher	Public school	Deliveryman	Grocery store
Machinist	Steel mill	Teamster	Express co.
Agent	Real estate	Chauffeur	Taxicab co.
Agent	Insurance	Chauffeur	Private family
Cook	Hotel	Miner	Coal mine
Servant	Private family	Laborer	Coal mine
Retail merchant	Groceries	Quarryman	Marble
Wholesale merchant	Leather	Trained nurse	Hospital
Janitor	Apartment house		

220. Column 27. Class of worker. For an employer—that is, one who employs helpers other than domestic servants in transacting his *own* business—write in column 27 "E"; for a wage or salary worker write "W"; for a person working on his own account write "O"; for an unpaid family worker—that is, a member of the family employed without pay on work which contributes to the family income—write "NP." For all persons returned as having no gainful occupation, leave column 27 blank.

221. Employer ("E"). An employer is one who employs helpers, other than domestic servants, in transacting his *own* business. The term *employer* does not include the superintendent, agent, manager, or other person *employed* to manage an establishment or business; and it does not include the foreman of a room, the boss of a gang, or the coal miner who hires his helper. All such should be returned as wage or salary workers, for, while any one of these may employ persons, none of them does so in transacting his *own* business. In short, no person who himself works for wages or a salary is to be returned as an employer.

222. Wage or salary worker ("W"). Any person who works for wages or salary, at piece rates, or on commission, and is subject to the control and direction of an employer, is to be considered a wage or salary worker. This classification will include the president of the bank or the manager of the factory as well as the clerks and the laborers who may be also employed by the bank or the factory.

223. Working on own account ("O"). A person who has a gainful occupation and is neither an employer, nor a wage or salary worker, nor an unpaid family worker, is considered to be working on his own account; such persons are the independent workers. They neither pay nor receive salaries or regular wages. Examples of this class are: Farmers and the owners of small establishments who do not employ helpers; professional men who work for *fees* and employ no helpers; and, generally speaking, hucksters, peddlers, newsboys, bootblacks, etc.

224. Unpaid family worker ("NP"). A wife, son, daughter, or other relative of the head of the family who works regularly and without wages or salary on the family's farm, in a shop or store from which the family obtains its support, or on other work that contributes to the family's income (*not including housework or incidental chores*) is to be returned as an unpaid family worker. Examples are: A son working regularly and without wages on his father's farm; a wife working regularly without salary in her husband's store or office; a girl assisting her mother regularly without wages on sewing done in the home for a clothing factory.

EMPLOYMENT

225. Column 28. Whether actually at work yesterday ("Yes" or "No"). This question is to be asked with regard to all persons for whom an occupation has been entered in column 25. It will ordinarily refer to the day preceding the enumerator's call, and can be asked in the simple form "Was he at work yesterday?" In case "yesterday" was a holiday or the worker's "day off" or "rest day," the question should apply to his last regular working-day.

226. In certain occupations the employees have "rest days" in rotation. Some street car men, for example, begin their week's work on Tuesday and finish on Sunday, having a "rest day" on Monday. If you are enumerating such a man on Tuesday, you should find out whether or not he was at work Sunday, which would be his last regular working-day. Railway men may make runs on alternate days, working Monday, Wednesday, and Friday, for example, and "resting" on the intervening days. In every such case the question "Whether actually at work," must apply to the last regular working-day of the person enumerated.

227. Some men, such as longshoremen, coal miners, and laborers, have very irregular hours of work. In a case of this kind find out whether the man actually worked on the last working-day on which he might have been occupied. This will usually be literally "yesterday," unless "yesterday" was Sunday or a holiday.

228. Persons at work. Write "Yes" if the person enumerated worked any part of the day to which the question applies. In the case of wage earners the question will offer no difficulty. In the case of men who run a business of their own it may not always be easy to determine whether the man is actually at work. In general, such men should be returned as "at work" if the business operates continuously under their orders, even though they may have been temporarily absent on the last regular working-day. The same return should be made for the professional or business man who is the active manager of an office, store, or factory, although he may be absent or not occupied with matters for which he receives pay on the day in question. For example, a man operating a cobbler's shop or an automobile repair and service station should be returned as at work on a given day if he spends any part of that day at the shop, even though he may not make any sales or do any work for which he receives payment. Similarly doctors, lawyers, dentists, and other professional men, and proprietors and managers of retail stores, who put in time at their place of business should be returned as "at work."

229. Farmers and farm laborers, including the members of the farmer's family who usually work on the farm, are to be considered at work if they are doing anything whatever in connection with the farm or with any farming activities or supplemental occupations.

230. Teachers in schools and college professors and instructors, if they hold positions, will be regarded as "at work," even though the enumeration date falls within the Easter or spring vacation. Highly skilled workmen, salesmen, foremen, superintendents, and managers whose pay is on a monthly or annual basis are to be returned as "at work" if they receive full pay and their working time is definitely engaged, even though they have days of partial or complete idleness now and then.

231. Persons who normally work only part time and who do not wish a full time job are to be returned as "at work," unless such part-time employment itself fails. For example, the waitress who works three hours daily during the lunch period is to be returned as at work if she was employed for this period "yesterday"; and the seamstress or laundress who regularly works one or more days a week, either at her own home or elsewhere, is to be returned as at work if she worked on her last regular working-day preceding the enumerator's visit.

232. **Persons not at work.** Write "No" in case the person enumerated worked no part of the last regular working day. Men and women temporarily absent because of sickness, accidents, voluntary lay-offs, and all personal reasons are to be regarded as not at work, even though they continue to hold their positions.

233. Men locked out or on strike are "not at work," although in receipt of trade-union strike benefits or occupied in the conduct of the strike. Men who customarily work "by the job" are not at work if they have no job in process, even though actively seeking new contracts. Retail dealers are not at work if their last business has been permanently closed, although they may be planning a new enterprise. You will find, every now and then, a man who has been operating a small grocery or other retail store which has failed and who is, at the time of the enumeration, doing nothing at all which yields an income, but spending his time seeking new opportunities. Return such a man as not at work.

234. A woman reported as regularly pursuing some gainful occupation, in her own home or outside, in addition to doing her own housework, is to be returned as "not at work" if, for any reason, this gainful occupation fails, although she may continue to perform her household duties. Thus a woman who usually works as a laundress two days a week, in addition to her housework, is to be returned as "not at work" when the work as a laundress fails, even though she is quite fully occupied at home. Similarly the saleswoman in a store working daily in the rush hours, or on days of special sales, or on week-ends, is to be returned as not at work when this employment fails, although she may be busy at home duties.

235. Men who busy themselves with repair jobs, gardening, and home duties in the intervals of their regular occupation are to be returned as "not at work." Coal miners and longshoremen are to be returned as "not at work" if they are idle on the day to which the question applies, even though they get in as much time weekly as is usual at the mines or wharves where they are accustomed to labor. In general the list of those "not at work" should include all who did not labor at their gainful occupation on their last regular working day preceding the enumerator's visit.

236. Column 29. Line number on unemployment schedule. Every gainful worker for whom the answer "No" is entered in column 28 is to be reported on the Unemployment Schedule. Enter in column 29 the number of the line on that schedule where this report appears. If you use more than one sheet of the Unemployment Schedule in a given enumeration district, enter in this column for the second and subsequent sheets both the sheet number and the line number, as "2-17" or "3-46."

VETERANS

237. Column 30. Veterans. Write "Yes" for a man who is an ex-service veteran of the United States forces (Army, Navy, or Marine Corps) mobilized for any war or expedition, and "No" for a man who is not an ex-service veteran. No entry is to be made in this column for males under 21 years of age nor for females of any age whatever.

238. Column 31. What war or expedition. Where the answer in column 30 is "Yes," give the name of the war or expedition in which the man served. The principal military activities in which service will be reported, together with a convenient abbreviation for each which you may use in this column, are listed below:

World War . . . . .WW
Spanish-American War . . . .Sp
Civil War Civ
Philippine insurrection . . . .Phil
Boxer Rebellion . . . . .Box
Mexican Expedition . . . . . . .Mex

239. Those men are to be counted as "veterans" who were in the Army, Navy, or Marine Corps of the United States during the period of any United States war, even though they may not have gotten beyond the training camp. A World War veteran would have been in the service between 1917 and 1921; a Spanish-American War veteran, between 1898 and 1902; a Civil War veteran, between 1861 and 1866.

240. Persons are not veterans of an expedition, however, unless they actually took part in the expedition. For example, veterans of the Mexican expedition must have been in Mexico or Mexican waters at the time of the expedition; veterans of the Boxer rebellion, in China or Chinese waters at the time of the rebellion, etc.

241. Persons in the military or naval service of the United States during peace times *only* are not to be listed as veterans.

FARM SCHEDULE NUMBER

242. Column 32. Number of farm schedule. If the head or any member of the family operates a farm or any other place for which you have filled out a farm schedule, enter in this column the number of the farm schedule filled out for that place. Make this entry opposite the name of the member of the family operating the farm. If the place is one that is not locally regarded as a farm (see pars. 147, 148), write "N" after the schedule number. Thus, if your twenty-fourth farm schedule covers a greenhouse establishment in a city, you should enter the farm schedule number "24-N," the "N" indicating that the family living on this place is not to be counted as a farm family. Likewise if the farm operator *does not live on the farm*, but lives in a near-by village or elsewhere, write "A" after the farm schedule number, thus, "65-A."

UNEMPLOYMENT SCHEDULE

243. Persons to be reported. An entry is to be made on the Unemployment Schedule for every gainful worker who was *not at work* on the day preceding the visit of the enumerator (or on the last previous work day in case that day was not a regular working day for the person enumerated). These are the persons for whom the entry "No" is made in column 28 on the Population Schedule. In other words, whenever you write "No" for any person in reply to the question "Whether actually at work yesterday" on the Population Schedule you must also report that person on the Unemployment Schedule.

244. Method of filling out the schedule. The illustrative example of the Unemployment Schedule (Form 15-95) shows in general how the schedule should be filled out. The entries for a given person should ordinarily be made immediately after you have completed the entries for that person on the population schedule; that is, you should ask the necessary additional questions for the person not at work and make the entries on the Unemployment Schedule before you enumerate the remaining members of the family on the Population Schedule. If it seems better in special cases to complete the entries on the Population Schedule and then come back to the unemployment items, this may be done. Be sure, however, that you do not neglect making the unemployment entries for any person who has the entry "No" in column 28 on the Population Schedule.

245. The heading of the schedule. Fill out the heading of the Unemployment Schedule in exactly the same way as the heading of the Population Schedule for the same district, entering state, county, township, etc., as may be needed.

246. Column 1. Date of enumeration. Enter on line 1 the date of the first entry on the Unemployment Schedule. On each succeeding day enter the date for the first entry on that day.

247. Columns 2 and 3. Sheet and line number on Population Schedule. Enter in column 2 the number of the population sheet on which the person not at work was enumerated, and in column 3 the number of the line on which his name appears.

248. Column 4. Name. Enter the names exactly as on the Population Schedule, except where it may be necessary to spell out a surname represented on that schedule by a dash.

249. Column 5. Does this person usually work at a gainful occupation? Write "Yes" if the person is usually employed at any occupation yielding an income of any amount. This applies to part-time workers even though they work only a few hours a day or only a day or two a week. For example, for a woman employed one day a week as a laundress, in addition to doing her housework at home, the answer should be "Yes"; and a home worker regularly making garments or artificial flowers in the intervals of home or school duties, and getting in the equivalent of a day's work or more each week, should also be recorded as usually working at a gainful occupation. For workers whose occupation is very irregular and uncertain, such as common laborers and longshoremen, the answer should be "Yes," even though they have been idle for a long time and have no immediate prospects of finding a job.

250. Persons will be found who have been long unemployed because of change in industry, the introduction of machines, or the decline of production in certain lines. If able and willing to do work of any kind, these persons should be returned as usually working at a gainful occupation, without regard to the length of the period of idleness, provided they still expect to find employment and resume work.

251. Write "No" for any person who could not say that he "usually" worked, including young persons who have not yet begun to work, old persons who have retired from active service, persons living on their incomes or on accumulated funds, and those who for any reason decline to work or choose not to work. For housewives not usually employed outside the home, but accepting small jobs to be done at home or occasionally accepting a temporary position; for school boys and girls and for college students who may accept jobs if, and when, the pay is especially tempting, the answer should be "No." For the aged, or those unable to work except occasionally because of sickness, the answer should be "No." In all cases where "No" is entered, no further answers should be given on the Unemployment Schedule. Further, you should at once turn back and cancel the occupation returns in columns 25-29 on the Population Schedule, since a person who does not usually work at a gainful occupation, as defined above, should have no occupation returned, but rather the entry "None" in column 25.

252. Column 6. Does this person have a job of any kind? Write "Yes" if the person found idle expects to return to his former job. It is not necessary that there be a contract, written or oral. Thus, building-trades workers, carpenters, bricklayers, plasterers, etc., who are regularly attached to certain employers or contractors are to be returned as possessed of jobs if their customary employer has work in sight. And men temporarily laid off at a factory, mill, or mine, are to be so returned if they expect to be taken on again in their former places. Difficulties will arise because of the length of the period of idleness. Endeavor to ascertain whether there is reason to expect the closed plant to reopen, and if so, return the individual as possessed of a job.

253. Write "No" in column 6 when the person has no job nor any promise or understanding that he will be employed. Workers who have no reasonable expectation of returning to their former jobs; those actively seeking new employment in their old occupations; those found idle who are planning to change their occupation; and those formerly attached to plants so long closed that it is improbable that they will reopen, should be reported as not having a job.

If this person has a job:

254. Column 7. How many weeks since he has worked on that job? In answering this question, write "0" for periods less than the individual worker's regular full-time week and omit all fractions of a week. For example, if the worker has been idle two weeks and four days, write "2." For men and women found idle but definitely engaged to begin work in new engagements, the proper entry in column 7 is "0."

255. Column 8. Why was he not at work yesterday? Enter the exact reason for absence from work. Make every effort to discover the correct reason. Avoid general statements and be specific. Thus, in case the individual is detained from work because of illness, you should differentiate between the sickness of the person enumerated and that of members of the family, other relatives, or friends. Write "Ill" or "Sick" if the person enumerated is idle because he is sick; write "Sickness in family," in case the person is not at work because of aiding others who are ill.

256. Distinguish carefully between voluntary and involuntary lay-offs. Write "Vol. lay-off" in case the individual has taken days off on his or her own accord or for personal reasons. In the case of workers laid off at the orders of the employers, discover and enter wherever possible the cause of the lay-off, as "Plant burned," "Mine closed," "Job completed," etc.

257. Be similarly explicit in other cases. Do not confuse accidents which injure the wage earner with those which force the closing of plants or stoppage of some workmen. Write "Injured by accident" for the former and "Machinery broke down," "Wreck," or some similar expression for the latter.

258. Other causes will include lack of materials, supplies, equipment, or cars; weather conditions; and strikes or lockouts. (Make clear whether the worker enumerated is himself on strike or is idle because of strike by other workmen.) You will find many workers idle because the winter occupations are slackening and the summer occupations are not yet in full force. This will be true of bituminous coal mining and the clothing factories. Write "Off season" in such cases, but remember that certain types of men may use this statement as an excuse for idleness.

259. Avoid general expressions such as "slack work"; "no work"; etc.

260. Column 9. Does he lose a day's pay by not being at work? Write "Yes" in all cases where the enumerated person fails to receive the day's pay from his employer. Disregard supplementary income from tips, overtime, or bonus payments, which may be lost even though the regular wages or the basic salary may be paid for the time in question. And write "Yes" even though the loss is made up in whole or in part by income from workmen's compensation, from insurance, from trade union benefit funds, or from mutual benefit funds. When the worker does not know whether he will receive his pay or not, write "Yes."

261. Write "No" for those who report that they will not lose any pay. This group will be made up mainly of workers on monthly or annual contracts and of those who have somewhat irregular working days and are allowed to take some time off on account of extra work rendered at other times.

262. Column 10. How many days did he work last week? Write the number of days (or nights) on which the person actually worked. Include all short-time, makeshift, or supplementary jobs.

263. Column 11. How many days in a full-time week? State the length of the worker's full-time week in days. Count work on a night shift as equivalent to a day although the shift may be shorter. For persons regularly and voluntarily working fewer days that a full-time week, return the number of days usually worked. Thus a woman spending the rest of her time at work in her own home may be employed as a laundress two days a week. The proper entry in such a case is "2." A railroad worker may make a run on alternate days, getting in four days one week and three the next. In such a case the proper entry is "3-1/2." Some workers will be found working short days as well as short weeks. Thus a waitress or sales person may work in the noontime rush hours from Monday to Friday and a longer period on Saturday. For such a case the proper entry is "6."

If this person has no job of any kind:
264. Column 12. Is he able to work? In deciding whether a person is able to work it is necessary to remember that there are many kinds of jobs and that many of them require little physical or mental effort. Write "Yes" if the individual is neither too young nor too old to be capable of some kind of regular employment and has no mental or physical disability which makes it impossible for him to work. It is not necessary that he be capable of heavy labor or that he be able to continue in his regular trade or occupation.

265. Write "No" for those of advanced age, for the mentally weak, for those unable to work because of ill health, and for those temporarily or permanently disabled by accidents.

266. Column 13. Is he looking for a job? Write "Yes" if the person is actively engaged in seeking employment, is listed by a public or private employment agency, is being represented by a trade union, or is being actively aided by parents, relatives, or friends in finding a job.

267. Write "No" for those voluntarily without a job, whether for a short time or indefinitely. Men who are resting at the end of a season's work; men who are living on the income from investments, etc.; men who are constitutionally disinclined to work; and men who have thrown up jobs to go on vacations, to enter school or college, or to undertake a business, should not be counted as seeking employment. For such persons write "No" in column 13.

268. Column 14. For how many weeks has he been without a job? Give the length of time in weeks that the individual has been without regular employment. Disregard short-time, make-shift, pick-up, or odd jobs of less than a day's duration. Unpaid labor at the person's own home or work which merely covers the person's own maintenance, as when a farm laborer (not a member of the family) does chores for his board and lodging, is not to be regarded as "a job" in answering this question.

269. Column 15. Reason for being out of a job. In giving the reason for being unemployed it is desirable to separate those who voluntarily left employment from those discharged or displaced by changes in industry. Endeavor to find out and state the exact reason for being out of a job. Reasons frequently given by those who left of their own accord will include: "Seeking better pay," "desire to enter other industry," "Dissatisfied with work or conditions," "Moved," etc.

270. Reasons frequently given by those discharged or displaced will include: Closing of plants (write "Mine closed," "Factory closed," etc.); completion of jobs; discontinuance of production of certain fabrics, materials, or commodities; introduction of machines; reduction of force because of slack or off seasons (write "Off season"); lockout; worker too old; etc.

271. Signature. The date of completing enumeration of the sheet and your signature should be entered in the proper space after you fill the last line. You should regard your signature as a certification that the work is correct and complete. Sign no sheet until you have made it as nearly perfect as you can.

SCHEDULE FOR THE BLIND AND FOR DEAF-MUTES

272. The purpose of this schedule is to obtain the names and addresses of all persons found by the enumerators to be blind or deaf-mutes, together with certain additional information.

273. When to be used. Upon the completion of the enumeration of each family, be sure to ask before leaving the house whether any one among the persons you have enumerated is either blind or a deaf-mute. If so, enter the name, post-office address, and other facts called for on the Supplemental Schedule, in accordance with the instructions printed on that schedule, provided the person comes within the class of blind or deaf-mutes there defined.

Endnotes

[i] Bureau of the Census. Fifteenth Census of the United States. Form 15-100. Instructions to Enumerators. Population and Agriculture. Revised. (Washington, DC: GPO, 1930). 90p.

1930 Census of Population, Blank Form

(FORM 15-6 FOLDOUT)